STUDENTS WITH OCD:
A HANDBOOK FOR SCHOOL PERSONNEL

Gail B. Adams, Ed.D.

Pherson Creek Press
Campton Hills, Illinois

Publisher's Cataloging-in-Publication (Provided by Quality Books, Inc.)

Adams, Gail B.
    Students with OCD : a handbook for school personnel / Gail B. Adams.
    p. cm.
    Includes bibliographical references and index.
    LCCN 2011924740
    ISBN-13: 978-0-9834364-0-9
    ISBN-10: 0-9834364-0-1

    1. Obsessive-compulsive disorder in children–Patients–Education–Handbooks, manuals, etc.
    2. Obsessive-compulsive disorder in adolescence–Patients–Education–Handbooks, manuals, etc. I. Title.

    RJ506.O25A33 2011   618.92'85227
                       QBI11-600071

ocdhandbook.com

This book is dedicated to...

my beloved family and friends, without whose love, support, and encouragement this book would not have been possible;

the amazing young people who battle OCD so heroically, their devoted families, and the treatment professionals who help them navigate their struggles; and

the dedicated school personnel who toil, day after day, to improve the lives of their students.

ACKNOWLEDGEMENTS

Writing this book was a labor of love. But it also required a huge amount of time, energy, and determination – especially determination. Moreover, it entailed the help, directly or indirectly, of a significant number of people. To them, I offer my deepest gratitude; without their support, I could not have completed this journey. And although I mention many of them by name below, I am grateful to everyone who in any way, shape, or form, was an inspiration for this book.

My heartfelt thanks to...

- Bette Hartley and Maggie Baudhuin at the Madison Institute of Medicine, who faithfully sent out monthly literature updates on OCD and related disorders, which provided the foundation for my research;

- Jeff Szymanski, Executive Director of the International OCD Foundation, for his support and guidance;

- Jared Kant, Leslie Packer, John March, Lisa Merlo, Susan Conners, Aureen Pinto Wagner, Deborah Ledley, and Radhika Pasupuleti – professionals in the field of OCD and Tourette Syndrome who most generously allowed me to use some of their materials, which greatly enhanced the quality of my book (a special thanks to Leslie for pulling me out of a black hole more than once!);

- Tamar Chansky, Kathy Giordano, Karen Cassiday, and Ellen Sawyer, experts in the field who so graciously gave of their time to review various sections/chapters of my book and provided invaluable feedback (a special thanks to Ellen, who believed in me and was one of my biggest cheerleaders);

- Toni VanLaarhoven, Dennis Munk, Lynette Chandler, and Greg Conderman, dear former colleagues at Northern Illinois University who lent their amazing expertise to various segments of this book;

- Matt Cohen and my dear friend Linda Moran, for their legal expertise on various sections of this book;

- Lisa Liace and Sara Bolt, good friends and school psychology professionals who made important contributions to my book: Lisa for her wonderful and greatly-appreciated feedback on conjoint behavioral consultation and Sara for her expertise on the topic of Response to Intervention and other issues;

- Louise Dabkey, dear friend and school psychology professional for her unending patience fielding my questions, reviewing content, and consistent support;

- Nick Brichetto, whose artistic and creative talents were invaluable in my website and book design;

- Eric Storch, to whom I will be forever grateful for reviewing the OCD content in the first three parts of my book; he is a great teacher, researcher, and human being.

Many also sustained me on a daily basis throughout the sometimes arduous and solitary writing process. In particular, I owe a special debt of gratitude to my friends at my favorite coffee shop whose smiles and special treats for Molly – my dog and beloved companion – warmed my heart each morning: Nilesh, Maulik, Pushpa, Sunny, Rosa, Abel, Rosial, Shayne, Betty, Marlena, and John. And to many other friends – too numerous to name – thank you so much for your ongoing interest in this undertaking.

Needless to say, I owe a huge debt of gratitude to my family for their love, support, and encouragement: my husband, Steve, who patiently listened to my endless ramblings and supported me throughout the entire process (his proof reading is amazing!); my wonderful daughter, Heather, and her husband, Anthony (thank you two, so very much, for making me a grandma!); my terrific son, Aaron; and my loving sisters, Karen and Dawn. I am grateful, too, to many special extended family members for their encouragement: my beloved cousins; Aunt Bonnie; Uncle Al; mother-in-law, Lorraine; and many nephews and nieces. And to my four-legged family members, Molly, Tammy, Charlie, and Persia: your constant companionship was a Godsend.

A special and heartfelt thanks go to my son, Aaron, whose support and enthusiasm sustained me from the beginning of this journey to the end. His hard work, talent, creativity, and undying belief in this project made this book a reality.

Finally, I wish to acknowledge and honor the love and support of those who left this earth too soon: my loving parents, Lucille and Joe; my big brother, cherished friend, and mentor, Richard; my beloved Aunt Stelle; my dearly-loved cousin, Rita; my father-in-law, Paul; and my special boy, Shadow, the cat. You are sorely missed…

We adults know how much our jobs define our identities. Our occupations serve as a yardstick by which we measure our successes and failures. Our self-esteem and self-worth frequently are dependent upon our perceptions of our ability to function within our work-related positions.

School is the job of children. The average school-aged child in the United States spends somewhere in the vicinity of 1,100 hours a year in the school setting. And like adults, children's perceptions of their success and failure, their self-esteem – indeed their very emotional well-being – are largely a function of their experiences in school.

Consider now children and adolescents with OCD, a disorder that has a strong potential for impeding success at school academically, behaviorally, emotionally, and socially. For many of these students, the ability to function in the school context will virtually make or break their ability to function, overall. And so it is critical that we adults – school personnel, parents, mental health professionals, and others – do everything in our power to ensure the most successful school experience possible for these young people. Indeed, unless and until OCD-related issues are addressed at school, treatment for children and adolescents with OCD is incomplete.

There is no doubt but that recognition of OCD has grown by leaps and bounds since it first began receiving considerable attention in the late 1980's and early 1990's. The advent of Judith Rapoport's seminal book, *The Boy Who Couldn't Stop Washing*, as well as research conducted by Dr. Rapoport and her colleagues at the National Institute of Mental Health, ushered in a new era of research on OCD. Although a respectable body of literature on pediatric OCD has developed over the years, scant information has been available regarding the impact of OCD on students and what school personnel can do to facilitate their ability to function in educational settings. Indeed, resources for educators have been very limited over the past two decades.

More recently, several excellent texts on educating students with a variety of different disorders (e.g., AD/HD, Tourette Syndrome, OCD) have emerged, but none has been devoted solely to children and adolescents with OCD. *Students with OCD: A Handbook for School Personnel* was born out of a need to fill that void. Although the major audience for this book is school professionals, parents of children who struggle with OCD, health care providers whose pediatric patients face OCD-related challenges in school, and others, will find this book valuable.

The information in this book is based upon a careful review of the literature on pediatric OCD and school-based practices for helping students with disabilities – especially those with neurobiological disorders. My experiences working closely with students who have disabilities, teaching coursework in special education at Northern Illinois University, serving as a school consultant on behalf of students with OCD, and providing dozens of workshops on OCD for school personnel throughout the country also have contributed significantly to the content of this book.

This book is divided into six parts.

Part I is an introduction to what OCD is and why it is so important for school personnel to know about it.

Part II provides an overview of obsessions and compulsions in young people with OCD, how they frequently manifest in school, and other characteristics of obsessions and compulsions.

Part III focuses on a number of key issues related to childhood OCD, including prevalence, age at onset, gender, causes, disorders/other difficulties that occur regularly with OCD, and clinical assessment and treatment.

Part IV addresses the effects of OCD on school functioning and how school personnel can assist in identifying and referring students with the disorder.

Part V is a comprehensive section on school-based treatment for OCD, covering:

- school-based accommodations and support strategies for students with OCD;
- special issues related to the school-based treatment of OCD;
- laws pertaining to educational services for students with OCD;
- categorizing students with OCD under the Individuals with Disabilities Education Act of 2004 (IDEA 2004);
- IDEA, discipline, and OCD behavior;
- school-based cognitive-behavioral therapy when an outside therapist is involved; and
- school-based interventions when an outside therapist is not involved.

Part VI is the conclusion, which offers some final thoughts about students with OCD.

OCD is considered one of the most common psychiatric illnesses of childhood. Yet it frequently goes unrecognized. It is critical that individuals on the front lines with young people understand what OCD is and know how to help them with this potentially debilitating disorder. It is my sincere hope that this book will help – if even in a small way – to achieve that end.

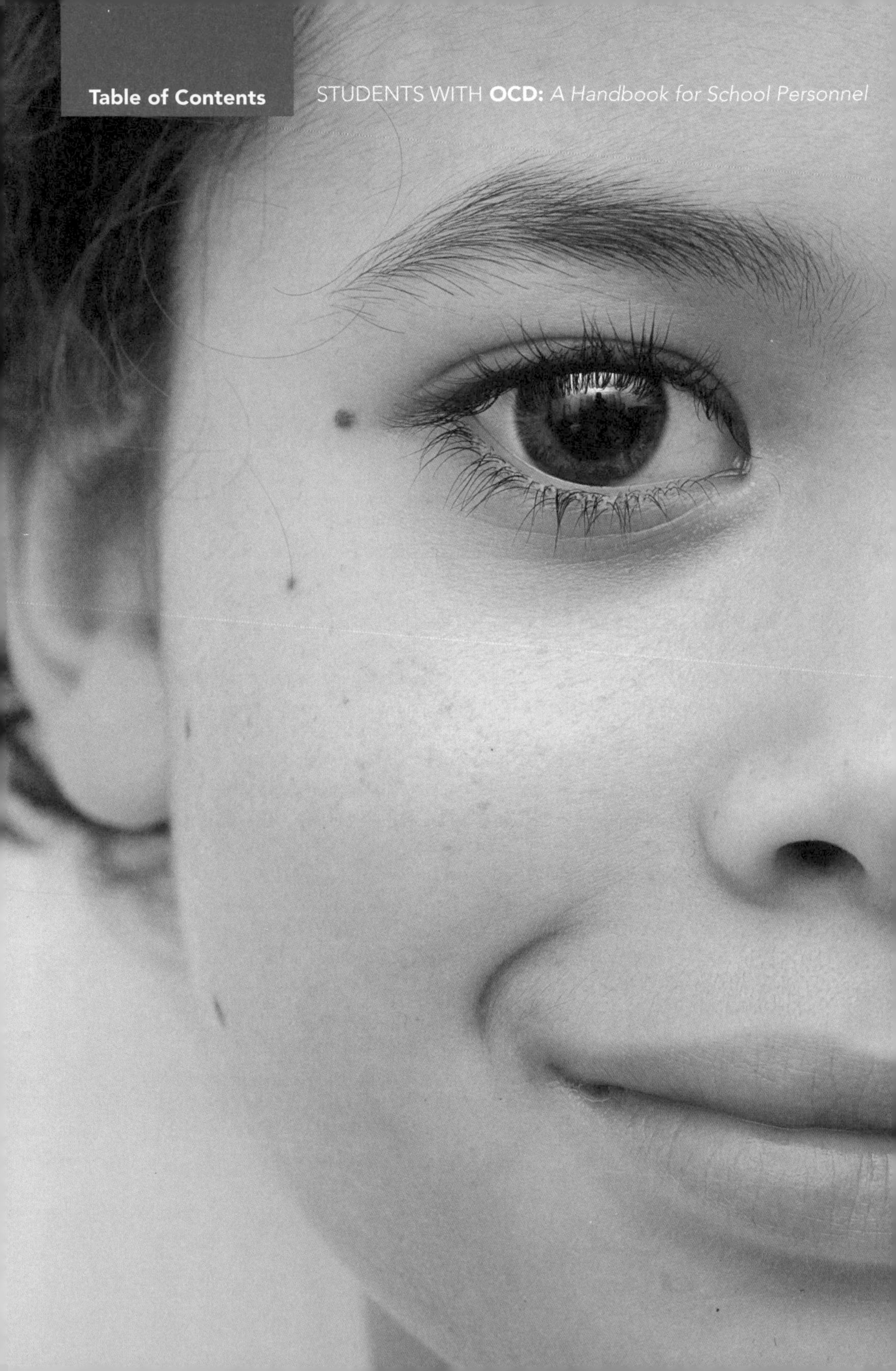

Part I: Introduction

Part II: An Overview of Obsessions and Compulsions in Children and Adolescents with OCD

Part III: Important Issues Related to Childhood OCD

Part IV: What are the Effects of OCD on School Functioning? How Can School Personnel Help?

PART 1: Introduction

Ch:1

INTRODUCTION TO OCD IN CHILDREN AND ADOLESCENTS

Aaron, an extremely bright high school freshman, sits in algebra class, staring into space. He hasn't taken his pencil out of his backpack, because he fears he'll contract lead poisoning if he touches it. Aaron has a pen in his pocket, so he uses that. He can't bring himself to take his algebra book from his backpack, either. If he did, he would have to open and close the cover a certain number of times. Moreover, the book is filled with number patterns that are different from his lucky number patterns. It is stressful for Aaron to look at, or even think about, his algebra book.

The teacher looks at Aaron and asks if he has a pencil. To avoid having to open his backpack, he tells her he doesn't. She offers to loan him a pencil, but asks for one of his shoes as a "deposit." Unbeknown to the teacher, Aaron also has a devastating fear of lawn chemicals – chemicals he believes cover his shoes. As a result, he never touches his shoes; he puts them on without using his hands and never ties the laces. Aaron can't give the teacher his shoe as a deposit. He sits in class, unable to take notes. He tries to memorize the information his teacher presents in class. Obsessions about the chemicals on his shoes and the pencil lead race through his mind, however, making it almost impossible to concentrate. Moreover, he worries that when class is dismissed, he'll have to walk through the halls of the school, endlessly tracing and retracing his steps. To the teacher and outside observers, it appears as though Aaron is inattentive in class...

Aaron suffers from **obsessive-compulsive disorder, or OCD**, an anxiety disorder characterized by the presence of *obsessions* and/or *compulsions*. The vast majority of individuals with OCD have both obsessions and compulsions. Rarely, however, a person may experience only one or the other. Obsessions and compulsions are time-consuming, cause marked distress, and/or interfere with a person's usual routine, occupational or academic functioning, social activities, or relationships with others — *American Psychiatric Association, 2000*.

Obsessions are recurrent and persistent ideas, thoughts, impulses, or images that intrude into a person's thinking. Individuals with OCD usually have insight into the senseless or irrational nature of their obsessions. Depending upon their cognitive and developmental levels, however, some children, particularly young children and/or those with poorer intellectual functioning, may have limited insight. Even when insight is present, obsessions can be associated with high levels of anxiety or other negative emotions, such as disgust, all of which are associated with distress or discomfort. Commonly-reported obsessions include worries about contamination; fears of harm, illness, or death; intrusive thoughts about harming oneself or others (even though there is no intent to do so); excessive religious fears; a compelling need for symmetry or order; and obsessive doubt.

Compulsions, also known as rituals, consist of repetitive, purposeful behaviors or mental acts that individuals perform to relieve, prevent, or undo the anxiety or discomfort created by the obsessions. In some cases, rituals are carried out to prevent some dreaded event or situation from happening. For example, a young boy may place multiple sticky notes inside his father's car, each containing a message imploring his dad to drive carefully, to prevent him from being killed in an automobile accident. These behaviors or mental acts clearly are excessive or not realistically connected with what they are supposed to prevent or neutralize — *American Psychiatric Association, 2000.* Some children, however, especially those who are younger, may not realize their behaviors are excessive or appear unusual to the outside observer. In a similar vein, young children may be unaware of or have difficulty verbalizing their obsessions. When obsessions cannot be identified clearly, rituals may be the more prominent sign of OCD. Common compulsions include excessive washing, cleaning, checking, repeating, reassurance seeking, confessing, counting, and avoidance of objects, substances, or situations that trigger fear or discomfort. It is important to note that covert mental rituals, e.g., mental praying, counting, or repeating words silently, can be every bit as disruptive and distressing as overt rituals.

Compulsions frequently are preceded by an obsessive thought that shapes the nature of the compulsive act. Individuals who struggle with contamination obsessions, for example, may wash excessively. Concerns about bodily harm may lead to compulsive checking. As indicated above, however, obsessions and compulsions sometimes are connected in an unrealistic way – one that defies explanation. For example, a child experiencing an obsession related to the death of his pet may read the same paragraph repeatedly to keep the animal from dying. If questioned as to how reading and rereading the paragraph would avert his pet's death, the child may not be able to provide an explanation but feels he "just has to do it."

Following are the current diagnostic criteria for OCD included in the Diagnostic and Statistical Manual of Mental Disorders, Fourth Edition, Text Revision (DSM-IV-TR) - *American Psychiatric Association, 2000*. The DSM-IV-TR, which provides a common language and standard criteria for the classification of mental disorders, usually is considered the "gold standard" for mental health professionals in the United States.

DSM-IV-TR Criteria for Obsessive-Compulsive Disorder (Code 300.3)

A. *Obsessions as defined by:*

 1. *Recurrent and persistent thoughts, impulses, or images that are experienced, at some time during the disturbance, as intrusive and inappropriate and that cause marked anxiety or distress*

 2. *The thoughts, impulses, or images are not simply excessive worries about real-life problems*

 3. *The person attempts to ignore or suppress such thoughts, impulses or images, or to neutralize them with some other thought or action*

 4. *The person recognizes that the obsessional thoughts, impulses or images are a product of his or her own mind (not imposed from without as in thought insertion)*

B. *Compulsions as defined by:*

 1. *Repetitive behaviors (e.g., hand washing, ordering, checking) or mental acts (e.g., praying, counting, repeating words silently) that the person feels driven to perform in response to an obsession, or according to rules that must be applied rigidly*

 2. *The behaviors or mental acts are aimed at preventing or reducing distress or preventing some dreaded event or situation; however, these behaviors or mental acts either are not connected in a realistic way with what they are designed to neutralize or prevent or are clearly excessive*

C. *At some point during the course of the disorder, the person has recognized that the obsessions or compulsions are excessive or unreasonable. Note: This does not apply to children.*

D. *The obsessions or compulsions cause marked distress, are time consuming (take more than one hour a day) or significantly interfere with the person's normal routine, occupational (or academic) functioning, or usual social activities or relationships.*

E. *If another Axis I disorder is present, the content of the obsessions or compulsions is not restricted to it (e.g., preoccupation with food in the presence of an Eating Disorder; hair pulling in the presence of Trichotillomania; concern with appearance in the presence of Body Dysmorphic Disorder; preoccupation with drugs in the presence of a Substance Use Disorder; preoccupation with having a serious illness in the presence of Hypochondriasis; preoccupation with sexual urges or fantasies in the presence of a Paraphilia; or guilty ruminations in the presence of Major Depressive Disorder).*

F. *The disturbance is not due to the direct physiological effects of a substance (e.g., a drug of abuse, a medication) or a general medical condition.*

Specify if:
With Poor Insight: if, for most of the time during the current episode, the person does not recognize that the obsessions and compulsions are excessive or unreasonable.

Reprinted with permission from the Diagnostic and Statistical Manual of Mental Disorders, Text Revision, Fourth Edition, (Copyright 2000). American Psychiatric Association.

Why Should School Personnel Know about OCD?

Why is it so important that school personnel – including general and special education teachers, school psychologists, social workers, school nurses, counselors, administrators, paraprofessionals, inclusion facilitators, educational diagnosticians, and others – know about OCD? Following are some thoughts from several experts in the field of OCD.

_____

"Obsessive-compulsive disorder is a mental illness that frequently affects children and adolescents. It may be under-recognized by parents, teachers and other caregivers due to the secretive nature of the disorder and its associated shame. Prompt diagnosis of OCD among affected children and adolescents is necessary to limit the suffering directly resulting from OCD, in addition to the distraction from normal childhood development that this illness brings"
— Stewart, 2008.

_____

"Teachers could easily be trained to recognize telltale signs of OCD, such as overerased homework papers – often so erased that there are holes in the paper – or to spot the child who won't give up his paper because he must check it 'just one more time.' If we added rough, chapped hands…teachers would be able to spot some cases that everyone has missed. Their help could save years of grief"
— Rapoport, 1991.

_____

"The main concern with early-onset OCD is its deleterious effect on the child's developmental trajectory. OCD can interfere severely with role functioning, affecting everything from academics to friendships to family relationships. Left untreated, OCD not only tends to persist but is linked to the development of other psychiatric disorders... Thus, in addition to the risk of OCD persisting into adulthood and causing impairment, pediatric OCD can severely divert the course of normal development, leading to long-term deficits across many areas of functioning" — *Moore, Mariaskin, March, & Franklin, 2007.*

Childhood OCD has been associated with serious difficulties related to academic performance, social competence, and family functioning. Moreover, research has indicated that for a large proportion of adults with OCD – possibly as high as 80% – the onset of OCD occurs during childhood or adolescence — *Grados, Labuda, Riddle, & Walkup, 1997.* Therefore, it is essential that individuals who work closely with children and adolescents be aware of OCD and know how to recognize its symptoms. Early intervention during childhood or adolescence can be critical to preventing long-term illness into adulthood, because OCD tends to run a chronic course without appropriate intervention.

School personnel may represent a first line of defense in the identification of childhood OCD for several reasons. First, parents may not always be first to recognize that their child has a problem. Although many parents are aware of their child's difficulties, research has indicated that some parents recognize their child's problems only after months or years have passed since they began — *Lenane, 1989.* In some cases in which parents have missed OCD symptoms, children actually have been known to bring their problems to the attention of their parents and ask for help. Second, research clearly indicates that teachers and other education personnel can effectively identify youth at risk. School professionals frequently have worked with hundreds of students over a period of many years. Thus, they have developed an awareness of and sensitivity to behavior that deviates from the norm. Third, the typical school-aged child spends approximately 1,100 hours per year in the school setting. As a result, school personnel are uniquely positioned to observe and interact with students for extended periods of time on a consistent basis. Therefore, it is essential that educators learn to recognize OCD symptoms in the school setting, assist with assessment and referral, and participate in various facets of treatment.

This book is divided into six parts.

Part I provides an introduction to OCD in children and adolescents.

Part II presents an overview of obsessions and compulsions in young people with OCD, how they frequently manifest in school, and other characteristics of obsessions and compulsions.

Part III focuses on a number of key issues related to childhood OCD, including prevalence, age at onset, gender, causes, disorders/other difficulties that frequently occur with OCD, and clinical assessment and treatment.

Part IV addresses the effects of OCD on school functioning and how school personnel can assist in identifying and referring students with the disorder.

Part V is a comprehensive section on school-based treatment for OCD covering:

    a. accommodations and support strategies for students with OCD;

    b. special issues related to the school-based treatment of OCD;

    c. school-based cognitive-behavioral therapy when an outside therapist is involved;

    d. school-based interventions when an outside therapist is not involved;

    e. laws pertaining to educational services for students with OCD;

    f. categorizing students with OCD under the Individuals with Disabilities Education Act of 2004 (IDEA 2004) – a major federal law governing special education and related services; and

    g. IDEA, discipline, and OCD behavior.

Part VI is the conclusion, which offers some final thoughts about students with OCD.

This book is intended to provide essential information not only to elementary and secondary-level school personnel but also to parents of school-aged children with OCD and mental health professionals who work with this population of young people.

PART II: An Overview of Obsessions and Compulsions in Children and Adolescents with OCD

Ch:2

DEVELOPMENTALLY NORMAL VS. OCD BEHAVIOR

It is extremely important to note that most children and adolescents exhibit habits, routines, and superstitions that are developmentally normal. These behaviors help them gain control and mastery over their environment. A preschool-aged child, for example, may have a specific bedtime ritual that involves reading the same book, singing the same song, and reciting the same prayer each night before she can go to sleep. Such rituals are soothing, provide predictability, and promote mastery of separation anxiety. Or a young boy may insist upon wearing the same red shirt to every baseball game, because it's his "lucky" shirt. Such superstitions help the child respond to an unpredictable world. Even adults find themselves "knocking on wood" or refusing to open an umbrella in the house for fear that bad luck will follow.

As children mature, earlier rituals normally disappear, and new interests frequently develop, such as collecting items or learning all the details about a certain topic or individual. A 10-year-old boy with a sizable comic book collection may have frequent and animated discussions with friends who share his interest. A 13-year-old girl with a "crush" on an adored rock star may know all the words to every song her idol has ever produced. Such hobbies and interests are enjoyable and even help young people gather information about their world.

In a similar vein, children, adolescents, and even adults experience normal fears. At approximately 8 months of age, infants become fearful of being separated from their mothers. As children mature, they develop normal worries about dangers such as car accidents, natural disasters, and death. Likewise, adults may worry about finances, relationships, and families.

There are several characteristics, however, that distinguish normal, developmentally-appropriate fears and rituals from those associated with OCD. First, the content or theme of typical childhood fears and routines usually is commonplace, e.g., fear of thunderstorms, eating the same cereal for breakfast each morning. OCD fears and rituals, however, often are unusual and even may appear bizarre to the outside observer, e.g., the child who constantly checks the electrical outlet in the wall next to his desk at school to make sure it isn't emitting an electrical current that could cause a fire.

Second, normal fears and routines of childhood are age appropriate, whereas OCD fears and rituals are not. It is not uncommon, for instance, for a 5 year-old boy to ask his mother to tuck him into bed several times before she leaves his room each night. It is unusual, however, for a girl in middle school to call home every period of the school day to confirm that her mother is safe.

Third, typical routines and fears neither consume an inordinate amount of time nor interfere with daily functioning. By contrast, obsessions and compulsions are excessive, time consuming, and have a negative impact on an individual's social, academic, and/or occupational functioning. Indeed, OCD often is associated with high levels of impairment – not only for the child but also for the family.

Fourth, developmentally appropriate rituals are associated with enjoyment or satisfaction; the child *wants* to engage in them. And although some children with OCD do not perceive their symptoms as excessive or bizarre (a subset of young people may seem untroubled by their symptoms or actually report that they enjoy engaging in OCD behaviors; — *Merlo & Storch, 2006*), most young people with OCD are distressed – if not overwhelmed – by OCD rituals.

Finally, normal childhood fears and routines usually respond to logic or reason, and the child is able to stop rituals at will. OCD behaviors do not respond to reasoning or common sense, however, and must be carried out dutifully in response to an obsession or feelings of discomfort. The following vignettes provide a distinction between a normal childhood ritual and an OCD ritual.

It is Heather's 7th birthday party. As she opens one of her gifts, she squeals with delight to find the doll she had hoped to receive along with several new outfits. As soon as the last guest has left, she dashes into her bedroom to play with her new toy. She carefully tries each of the outfits on her doll two times, exclaiming that the outfits look better each time she tries them on. After 20 minutes, Heather neatly arranges the doll clothes in a special box, with the longer clothes on the bottom and the shorter clothes on top. She places her new doll on her dresser with the rest of her dolls. It's hard for her to decide the best place for her new toy: she puts the new doll first in front, then in back, and finally in front of the other dolls.

Twelve-year old Tanya has a doll collection on a shelf in her bedroom. Each day after school, Tanya goes upstairs to her room to change her clothes. Upon seeing the dolls, Tanya must gather them up, place them on the floor, and arrange them in order, from tallest to shortest. When she is uncertain whether one doll is really taller than another, she may spend up to an hour arranging and rearranging the dolls. Tanya's mother calls her to come downstairs, but Tanya cannot leave her room. She must continue to arrange the dolls until they are "just right."

ch:3

RECOGNIZING OBSESSIONS IN THE SCHOOL SETTING

Obsessions and compulsions are the hallmark symptoms of OCD, and children and adolescents with OCD frequently experience more than one obsession and/or compulsion at any given time. But because young people can be extremely secretive about their symptoms, signs of OCD may not be obvious to the outside observer. If school personnel are to play an integral role in recognizing OCD in children and adolescents, they must become knowledgeable about these signs. Following is a description of obsessions children and adolescents with OCD frequently experience.

Contamination obsessions

One of the most commonly-reported obsessions in youth with OCD is a fear of contamination. Young people with these obsessions often fear that they or a loved one will be contaminated by germs or toxins which, in turn, will lead to illness or even death. They fear contamination from a whole host of other materials and substances, as well, including dirt, ink, paint, clay, radiation, environmental toxins, excrement, body secretions, blood, chemicals, and cleaning solutions. For some children, particularly younger children, contamination fears may be related more generally to dirty floors, stains or spots on the ground, or things that feel sticky or gummy.

Intriguingly, researchers recently have described a subgroup of individuals with OCD whose contamination concerns are unrelated to fear or anxiety but rather to an overreaction or extreme sensitivity to disgust. For these individuals, the sight of something repulsive – maggot-ridden meat or cockroaches feasting on rotten food – may drive them to wash their hands excessively rather than a fear that something terrible would happen if they didn't wash. Researchers actually have found that threatening, or fearful, images activate different regions of the brain than disgusting images — *Shapira et al., 2003*.

Contamination obsessions may be shaped by world events. Over the past few decades, for example, there has been an increase in AIDS-related obsessions. Similarly, there was a rise in contamination fears related to anthrax after September 11, 2001 and the swine flu after the outbreak of the H1N1 virus in 2009. Societal norms also may shape contamination obsessions. For example, Americans tend to be a germ-phobic society that promotes over-cleaning. During the cold and flu season, bottles of hand sanitizer are placed strategically throughout public places. Sanitizing wipes are available at the entrance to most grocery stores for customers to clean their shopping carts. And purse hangers – little hooks that attach to tables, shelves, and desks to hold one's handbag lest it touch the floor – are becoming ever more popular.

A group of researchers has named a rather unusual obsession that sometimes is connected with fears of contamination a "transformation obsession" — *Volz & Heyman, 2007*. Young people experiencing transformation obsessions have a fear of turning into someone or something else or acquiring unwanted characteristics of that person or thing. Volz and Heyman described numerous cases of individuals with this type of obsession, including:

1. a young adolescent who feared breathing on or touching someone and becoming that person or assuming some negative attribute of that individual, and

2. a 16 year-old male who worried about being contaminated by a "weird" person and turning into him.

Harm, illness, or death obsessions

Young people with OCD commonly fear that they or someone they love will be the victims of harm, illness, or death. As previously noted, worries about harm, illness, or death may be associated with contamination concerns. These fears also may focus on safety issues – a concern for their own safety or the safety of others. Fear of catastrophic events such as tornadoes, hurricanes, and floods may be present. Some children, especially young children, may be unable to verbalize a specific fear but have a vague feeling that "something bad" is going to happen. Moreover, children and adolescents sometimes assume a sense of personal responsibility for protecting others from harm or injury or preventing something bad from happening.

Not uncommonly, children and adolescents are afraid they will inflict, rather than encounter, harm. In some cases, their thoughts are aggressive or violent in nature and include thoughts of killing or injuring oneself or others (e.g., stabbing a family member). They also may fear acting out sexually in a way that violates society's norms (e.g., molesting a child). These fears, sometimes known as morbid or taboo obsessions, can be debilitating for the individuals experiencing them. They

15

frequently believe having these thoughts renders them insane, or crazy, because if they think it, it must be real. And yet people who suffer from these thoughts neither have a history of violence nor act upon their ideas or urges.

Dawn is a teen plagued by thoughts that she will try to run down animals with her car when she drives. She has always loved animals and has two cats and a dog of her own. She tries to tell herself that these thoughts aren't real; she loves animals, so why in the world would she think she'd try to injure them? Dawn wonders what kind of person she must really be for these horrible thoughts to enter her mind. Her fears have become so strong that she avoids driving. In fact, she hasn't driven in over six months. But Dawn's mother is very ill and must get to the doctor today. Dawn's mom can't drive herself, and no one else is home. So she asks Dawn to drive her. Thoughts and images of running down a dog, then a cat, then another dog dart through her mind. Dawn's heart begins to race…

"Just right"/"Perfect" obsessions/sensory phenomena

Some young people engage in ritualistic behavior due to a fear of making mistakes; an action has to be repeated until it is "perfect," or "just right" (e.g., a boy writes and rewrites a word on a page until it is "perfect" for fear that if he makes a mistake, his sister will die). Other children have a compelling need to know everything about a particular topic or remember everything they have read.

Still other children with OCD engage in rituals not in response to a discrete obsession or fear, but rather to various sensory phenomena that precede their rituals — *Prado et al., 2008*. In some cases, visual, auditory, or tactile sensations trigger a need for something to look, sound, or feel "just right." Upon hearing someone's voice, for example, a child may experience a need to hear that voice in a pitch that is "just right." Or seeing an uppercase "A" may trigger the need to have the letter look a certain way, or "just right."

In other cases, external triggers are absent, but the individual has an inner feeling and/or perception of discomfort that causes him or her to repeat a behavior until the feeling is relieved. In other words, when a person has an inner sense of something not being "just right" or "complete," a behavior needs to be repeated until it *feels* "just right" or "complete." In yet other situations, repeating behavior is preceded neither by obsessions nor by sensations of feeling, but rather by a need or urge. Research has indicated that sensory phenomena are more frequent among individuals with OCD and co-occurring Tourette Syndrome than among those with OCD only. In addition, significantly higher frequencies of sensory phenomena have been found among individuals with early-onset OCD (less than 10 years of age), compared with late onset OCD (after 18 years of age) — *Prado et al., 2008* (see section on issues related to age of onset in Chapter 6).

A case report in the OCD research describes a young boy in the United Kingdom who had Tourette Syndrome and a number of obsessive-compulsive behaviors. At one point in his treatment, his tics had worsened, as had his general demeanor. An evaluation of his behavior revealed that obsessive-compulsive behaviors were consuming the majority of his day; a formal diagnosis of OCD therefore was rendered. One of his prominent OCD symptoms was the need to step "correctly" on a particular white mark as he was walking down the road. On one particular day, he forgot to step correctly on that white mark. That day happened to be September 11, 2001. And he was convinced that the day of the atrocities – in particular, the World Trade Center terrorist attack – was, in fact, his fault.

A medication frequently used to treat OCD was added to the boy's medication regimen. In addition, he learned that the USA-UK time difference is such that he had failed to step on the mark in the road "correctly" well after the 9/11 disaster had occurred. This knowledge, along with the medication, resulted in his no longer feeling responsible for the World Trade Center tragedy.

From: Robertson, M. M., & Cavanna, A. E. (2007). The disaster was my fault! *Neurocase*, 13(5) 446-451.

Symmetry or order obsessions/sensory phenomena

Some children and adolescents with OCD experience obsessions or feelings involving a compelling need for order or symmetry. In some cases, obsessions are associated with anxiety, e.g., "If I don't pile my books up in alphabetical order, I'll fail all my tests." In other instances, obsessions are absent, but visual, auditory, or tactile sensations trigger a ritual, e.g., a child has to put his socks on and off until they feel "just right." Or there may be a strong, uncomfortable feeling that something has to be done "just so." For example, a child may have to brush each side of her hair exactly the same number of times and with even pressure on both sides. In yet other situations, there may be a strong urge to have things balanced, symmetrical, or evened up, e.g., a child may feel the need to fix a shoelace until both sides of the lace are perfectly balanced, or "even."

Scrupulosity obsessions

Some children with OCD have serious concerns related to religion. They may fear, for example, they somehow are praying to the devil or will go to hell if they look at a religious statue the wrong way. Some young people fear having blasphemous thoughts or not having enough faith. Such worries about imagined sins and other religious matters have been referred to as *religious* scrupulosity — March, 2007. Other children with OCD have fears of breaking moral rules and experience such concerns as lying, cheating on a test, allowing someone to provide an answer on homework, or failing to say "please" and "thank you" all the time – sometimes referred to as *moral* scrupulosity — March, 2007. In reality, these young people have not violated religious or social norms, yet their anxiety is very real.

Sexual obsessions

Not uncommonly, youth with OCD – particularly adolescents – experience sexual obsessions. The content of these obsessions may include homosexuality (e.g., a heterosexual male adolescent fears that he has become a gay man merely by looking at a male in a magazine), engaging in sexual relationships with family members, having intrusive images of genitals and perverted sexual acts, and other sex-related issues. Although these obsessions, like other obsessions, are irrational and have no personal meaning, they can be extremely distressing; young people experiencing them often carry a heavy burden of shame and guilt. Sexual obsessions frequently are connected to religious concerns and feelings of being sinful.

Number obsessions/sensory phenomena

Some children and adolescents with OCD experience obsessions with numbers. Certain numbers are "good," or "safe," while others are "bad." For instance, a child may believe that odd numbers are good, whereas even numbers are bad and must be avoided. While completing a math worksheet, this child may need to find an odd number on his paper each time he sees an even number to undo the anxiety associated with even numbers. Not infrequently, previously "good" numbers become "bad" numbers, and vice versa. In fact, numbers may change constantly, sometimes by the hour or even minute — *Björgvinsson, Hart, & Heffelfinger, 2007*. Children with OCD also may have "magical" numbers. Thus, if a child's magical number is "8," she may feel compelled to repeat everything 8 times, either to avoid harm or to feel "just right" or complete.

It is 10 a.m. and math period is just beginning. Jeremy is waiting for the teacher to pass out the weekly math test. He gets the test and starts working on the problems. But soon he encounters the numeral "4." For Jeremy, 4 is a bad number – one that makes him feel very anxious. To relieve the anxiety associated with seeing the 4, he must find a "7" – a good number. Jeremy frantically looks for a 7 and finds one. His anxiety subsides. He starts working on another math problem only to encounter a "3" – another bad number. Luckily, the next numeral he sees is a "6" – a safe number. Jeremy struggles to complete his math test, but each time he see a bad number, he has to find a good number to neutralize his anxiety. Suddenly, the teacher announces that time is up and tells the students to pass in their papers. Jeremy has completed 5 of the 20 problems.

Obsessive doubting

In some cases, children and adolescents with OCD are unsure about whether they have completed an action. It is important to mention that doubting is normal and even beneficial. Almost everyone can recall checking to make sure an oven has been turned off or a door locked. *Obsessive* doubting is distinguished from normal doubting by its frequency, intensity, and/or duration. Doubting associated with OCD may be so severe that it literally begins to take over an individual's life, dominating one's thoughts and actions. The French even have referred to OCD as "la folie de doute" – the doubting disease. Although one's senses (e.g., sight, sound, smell) verify that the door *is* locked or the gas stove *is* off, the person mistrusts his or her senses.

In some situations, individuals doubt their memories rather than their senses (e.g., "Did I really lock that door?"). A number of studies suggest that distrust in memory may be associated with repeatedly checking an item. Rather than altering actual memory accuracy, continuous checking may result in recollections of the checking event that become less vivid and detailed. Confidence in memory therefore is undermined — *van den Hout & Kindt, 2003.*

Sherisse is ready to go to school but can't help going over to the stove one more time. She's already checked the stove seven times, but her mother made pancakes this morning; she feels compelled to check the stove again to make sure the gas burner is off. If the stove isn't turned off, who knows what terrible things could happen? There might be a gas leak while she's at school, and her mother could be killed by the fumes. Or a fire could start. It would spread quickly throughout the kitchen and then the whole house, killing her mother. And her cats could die, too. Sherisse returns to the stove to make sure it's off. She leaves for school, but as she walks, she continues to doubt whether she checked the stove well enough. Maybe the gas looked like it was off, but it wasn't really. Sherisse is halfway to school but has to run home to check the stove just one more time. She arrives home, telling her mother she forgot something. She runs to the stove to check it again. It is now 9:05 a.m. Sherisse is late for school for the third time this week.

Ch.4

RECOGNIZING COMPULSIONS IN THE SCHOOL SETTING

If school personnel are to play an integral role in recognizing OCD, they must be aware of the compulsions in which young people frequently engage and how they may manifest in the school setting. Following is a description of rituals commonly reported by children and adolescents with OCD and their potential impact in school.

Washing/cleaning rituals

Fears of contamination frequently lead to washing or cleaning rituals, the most common of which is hand washing. Individuals who engage in washing or cleaning compulsions may feel compelled to wash extensively and according to a self-prescribed manner (e.g., washing the front of the hands first, then the back; manipulating the water faucet only with the elbows so the hands do not become "contaminated" by the faucet) for minutes to hours at a time. Others may be less thorough about hand washing but engage in the act an astounding number of times – sometimes hundreds of times a day. Some cleaning rituals involve washing clothes (washing a pair of jeans three times before they are "clean"); furniture (washing first the left side of a desk, then the right side, then the center); and other items in the environment.

Washing and cleaning rituals may appear in the school setting in ways not obviously or immediately related to washing or cleaning. For example, the student who frequently asks to be excused from the classroom under the guise of voiding actually may be seeking a private area in which to carry out cleaning rituals (e.g., washing hands or cleaning the sink, mirror, and walls of the bathroom). A more obvious sign of excessive washing is the presence of dry, chapped, cracked, and even bleeding hands. Individuals have been known to wash with a number of different cleaning agents, including isopropyl alcohol, bleach, and combinations of chemicals, to rid themselves of "contaminants." Eczema may be suspected, when, in fact, OCD is the culprit.

It is important to remember that OCD manifests in extremely idiosyncratic ways. Thus, while contamination fears frequently lead to excessive washing, they lead to other rituals, as well. For example, fears of contamination may result in a child's refusal to bring "dirty" school books into a "clean" home. Or, upon arriving at home after school, a child may insist that school books be baked in the oven to remove the "contaminants." Some children feel compelled to wear a helmet at school or hold their breath when they come into contact with other students to avoid germs. Young people with contamination fears may come to school with untied shoes, slovenly clothing, and dirty hair. In these cases, a fear that clothing or body parts are contaminated may result in the individual's compulsive refusal to touch them. Or it may be that cleaning rituals initially performed in response to the contamination fears may have become too difficult to complete. A combination of excessive hand washing and apparent sloppiness in other areas of grooming often has been reported.

Checking rituals

Checking rituals usually are performed to prevent some future disaster or calamity. Obsessive concerns about harm or fears of being responsible for something bad happening frequently lead to checking compulsions, including repetitively checking doors, windows, light switches, electrical outlets, and appliances. A child may be extremely anxious, for instance, that if she fails to lock a door, an intruder may enter the house and kill her family members. Obsessive doubting also may lead to compulsive checking. The girl who doubts that the iron really is unplugged or the adolescent who isn't absolutely certain he locked his father's car may feel compelled to perform checking rituals that consume inordinate amounts of time.

Whether precipitated by a fear of harm, obsessive doubting, or other sensory phenomena, checking rituals can create serious problems for the school-aged child. In the process of getting ready for school, a child may check his backpack over and over again – even risking tardiness – to ensure that all the necessary books and items are there. Once in school, a student may feel compelled to call or return home to check something yet another time. Children have been known to call parents at home or work multiple times each day to check on their well-being. School personnel also should be alert to such rituals as checking and rechecking answers on assignments to the point that they are submitted late, if at all, and repeatedly checking a locker to see if it is locked. In addition, checking rituals may result in a student's working late into the night on homework assignments that should have taken one or two hours to complete, because each item must be examined for accuracy over and over again.

In some cases, checking may take the form of compulsive reassurance seeking. In the school setting, children with OCD continually may ask teachers, other school personnel, and even peers, for reassurance that there are no germs on the drinking fountain, for example, or that they have not made any errors on an assignment.

Repeating rituals

Children and adolescents with OCD commonly perform rituals that involve repeating an action, sometimes for extensive periods of time. In some cases, these rituals are triggered by fears that something terrible will happen unless they perform an action over and over again. Like compulsive checkers, individuals typically perform repeating rituals to prevent something bad from happening. Checking rituals, however, frequently are shaped by the nature of their fears (e.g., a fear of the house burning down leads to excessive checking of the stove, oven, and iron), whereas repeating behavior often is unrelated to the obsession. For example, a child may feel compelled to tap his desk multiple times to prevent harm from coming to his family. Or a fear of making a mistake may compel a student to write a numeral on her math sheet repeatedly until it is "perfect."

In other cases, repeating rituals are driven by various sensory phenomena, including feelings triggered by visual, auditory, or tactile sensations (e.g., buttoning and rebuttoning a sweater until it feels "just right"). An inner sense that something is incomplete or isn't "just right" also may trigger the repetition of a behavior (e.g., touching a tree until it feels complete or "just right"). In yet other situations, repeating behavior is preceded neither by obsessions nor by sensations of feeling, but rather by a need or urge to perform a repetitive behavior.

In many cases, repeating rituals are connected to number obsessions or magical numbers: the child must repeat an action a certain number of times. Of note is that when individuals are in the process of repeating an action a given number of times, a disruption in the process can result in the need to start the ritual over again. Thus, the young girl who feels compelled to trace each uppercase "B" 12 times on every worksheet will, if interrupted on repetition number 11, have to start the ritual from the beginning.

Whether driven by anxiety, sensory phenomena, or magical numbers, repeating rituals can be very problematic for children and adolescents with OCD in the school setting. A student may need to walk up and down a hallway in a particular fashion repeatedly, get in and out of a desk or chair several times in a row, or go back and forth through a doorway in a self-prescribed manner (e.g., the doorway must be entered with the body in a certain position or while the child is touching the top of the door frame). A child may feel compelled to read and reread sentences or paragraphs in a book or sharpen a pencil multiple times. On written assignments, the student may endlessly cross out, trace, or rewrite letters or words, or erase and reerase words on an assignment to the extent that holes are worn in the paper.

Lock combinations can represent a serious difficulty for students with repeating rituals because a combination may need to be repeated a certain number of times, or until it is "just right." To avoid becoming "stuck" at their lockers, students actually have been known to carry all their books and other school paraphernalia from one class to another in a box rather than contend with their lockers. Scantron answer sheets for computer-scored tests may be a nightmare for students with repeating rituals, because they must fill in the circles or squares on the answer sheets until they are "just right." As a result, tests may be incomplete and do not represent a student's true ability. A child may experience repeating rituals outside the school building, as well, e.g., touching the playground equipment or bumping up against a wall a particular number of times.

Symmetry and arranging rituals

As previously indicated, symmetry and order rituals may be driven by anxiety: "If I don't straighten this rug perfectly, my dad will have a car accident and die." In other cases, sensory phenomena trigger these rituals. A child may insist upon having the silverware lined up by his plate, for instance, until it is "just right." Or an adolescent may have an urge to have things balanced and therefore has to place her worksheet in the center of her desk, with the same amount of empty space above, below, and on each side of the paper.

Children who engage in symmetry-related rituals may feel the need to have both sides of their bodies identical. For example, a child may spend an inordinate amount of time in school tying and retying shoelaces so each side of the bow is perfectly even. Symmetry rituals may involve taking steps that are identical in length or speaking with equal stress on each syllable in a word. Books on a shelf, items on a desk, or problems on a page may need to be arranged in a precise manner. Before completing a math assignment, for example, a student first may need to rewrite the math problems on a separate sheet of paper so they are "even." Or if the week's spelling words appear on the left side of a worksheet, a child may feel compelled to color in the right side of the paper before completing it. Consider the student who is following along with the class as the teacher goes over the answers to a math test. He pauses for a moment to get a pencil out of his desk. Seeing the disorganized contents of his desk triggers a need to arrange and rearrange all of the items in it. His arranging rituals cause him to lose his place, so he turns to the girl next to him and asks her what problem they are on. Annoyed by his inappropriate talking, the teacher reprimands him in front of the entire class and informs him that he will be punished by losing outdoor recess...

Counting rituals

As previously noted, obsessions and sensory phenomena related to numbers sometimes lead to counting compulsions. A child may be trying to avert harm when she attempts to neutralize or "undo" a bad number by counting up to a good number. Another child may have to count up to a particular number to feel "just right." Other young people experience an urge to count everything they see: doors and windows in the classroom, words in a book, objects on a wall. It is difficult to imagine the degree to which counting rituals interfere with task completion when a student has to count how many letters appear in every line of text he reads or when a student feels compelled to mentally count how many words the teacher has just written on the board.

Scrupulosity rituals

Individuals who fear they have sinned (religious scrupulosity) must find ways to neutralize, undo, or atone for their sins. They may feel the need to pray constantly or say a specific prayer or religious mantra a certain number of times, either aloud or mentally. Some people who experience religious scrupulosity have a compelling need to confess constantly. Children may tell their parents every "bad" thought they have and ask for reassurance regarding their religious concerns (e.g., "Are you sure God won't punish me if I didn't pray hard enough?"). An individual's religious background also may shape the nature of his or her rituals. Members of various religious groups feel compelled to engage in specific penance rituals to atone for their "sins," e.g., an individual of the Catholic faith may feel compelled to go to confession every day.

People who worry that their behavior has breached moral boundaries (moral scrupulosity) also engage in rituals to make amends for their perceived misdeeds. Children with moral scrupulosity, like those with religious scrupulosity, may feel compelled to tell their parents everything they have done or thought that might have been a violation of moral standards – but at most, was an insignificant mistake. They also may ask for reassurance or constantly apologize (e.g., "I didn't mean to touch the boy's arm on the bus today. Did I do something wrong?" or "I'm sorry if I had an angry thought about my teacher"). A child who receives help with homework from a parent may feel compelled to throw the homework away, believing that he or she has cheated by accepting the parent's assistance. A boy who looks up at the teacher during a test may be convinced that he inadvertently caught a glimpse of a classmate's test, and thus, has cheated. To atone for this transgression, the student may rip up his test. He even may write an incorrect answer on the test purposely to prove he didn't cheat. Or upon completing the test, the student may scrutinize his test answers to determine whether he may have cheated in some way.

Children and adolescents who experience religious or moral scrupulosity may exhibit observable behaviors in the classroom, which, in some cases, appear unusual – if not bizarre – to classmates, e.g., the student who rips up his test in class. In other cases, scrupulosity obsessions and rituals may be completely covert. An adolescent male who has a sexual obsession during class may become disturbed and frightened by the obsession and feel compelled to say a mental prayer repeatedly to undo the anxiety. The disruption and interference generated by scrupulosity obsessions and compulsions can be significant, and little, if any, attention may be available for academic tasks.

Rosalia, who is plagued by scrupulosity, is very fearful of having bad thoughts about God. As she is completing a reading assignment, an "evil" thought about God pops into her head, and she becomes extremely anxious. In order to reduce her anxiety, she must say a mental prayer five times. While Rosalia is mentally reciting the prayer for the fourth time, the teacher starts speaking to the class, interrupting her *mental recitation. She **must** do this ritual, however, and starts saying her prayers from the beginning. She finally finishes and tries to continue her reading assignment when a bad thought about Jesus pops into her head. Once again, Rosalia engages in praying rituals to neutralize the anxiety associated with this thought. Suddenly, the recess bell rings. She has completed only a fraction of her reading and receives a grade of "F" on the assignment.*

From: Adams, G. B. (2004). Identifying, assessing, and treating obsessive-compulsive disorder in school-aged children: The role of school personnel. TEACHING Exceptional Children, 37(2), 50.

Compulsive avoidance

Individuals with OCD frequently respond to obsessions and sensory phenomena with compulsive avoidance. They may go to great lengths to avoid objects, substances, or situations that trigger fear or discomfort. Children and adolescents with contamination fears may avoid touching items such as books, markers, basketballs, or even door knobs, because of the possibility that classmates who handled them were ill. In a similar vein, children may refuse to use school bathrooms or dress in gym locker rooms because of contamination concerns. Students also may avoid objects commonly found in the classroom such as paint, glue, paste, clay, tape, ink, and pencil lead, because they are "contaminants."

Students with fears of harming themselves or others may avoid using scissors, compasses, or other sharp tools in the classroom. Or a child may circumvent a particular doorway that triggers repeating rituals. A student with symmetry rituals may avoid going into a classroom with a tile floor because seeing the tiles precipitates the need to trace the edges of each tile with his eyes. Avoidance also may be evident with numbers. The child whose bad numbers are 3 and 5 may avoid doing any problems on a math worksheet containing those numbers. A girl with several bad numbers may be unable to answer questions on a multiple-choice test, because the letters a, b, c, and d are equivalent to 1, 2, 3, and 4. Students with scrupulosity concerns also use avoidance tactics. They may avoid answering an individual's question for fear of telling a lie or keep their heads down in one position during a test to avoid the possibility of cheating.

Note: Chapters 3 and 4 have provided a discussion of numerous obsessions and compulsions reported by children and adolescents with OCD and how they may present in the school setting. The reader is referred to Chapter 15 in Part IV for additional examples of school-based ritualistic behaviors associated with various obsessions and sensory phenomena.

An important note on hoarding obsessions/sensory phenomena and compulsions

Some children and adolescents with OCD engage in hoarding – the excessive acquisition of and failure to discard items or possessions that appear to be useless or of limited value. And although hoarding traditionally has been associated with OCD, there are a number of differences between OCD-based hoarding and hoarding unrelated to OCD — *Mataix-Cols et al., 2010.*

First, OCD-based hoarding is driven mainly by classic obsessions. Fears of contamination, for example, may result in an individual's being unable to touch an item that is contaminated, resulting in an accumulation of objects on the floor. Superstitious thoughts that something bad may happen if an item is discarded or intense feelings of incompleteness also may drive OCD hoarding. Second, OCD-based hoarding behavior generally is unwanted and very distressing; the individual derives no pleasure from it. Third, the individual shows no interest in most of the saved items – they have no sentimental or intrinsic value. Fourth, excessive acquisition usually is not associated with OCD hoarding. Excessive collections may result, however, if the individual has to purchase items in multiples of a particular number, for example, or feels compelled to buy something because he or she has touched – and thus is responsible for contaminating – the item.

Hoarding unrelated to OCD, by contrast, is *not* characterized by intrusive, distressing, or unpleasant obsessions. Hoarding thoughts are part of the individual's normal train of thought, are not repetitive in the same way typical obsessions are, and usually do not create distress. In addition, there is no ritualistic quality associated with hoarding (i.e., it is not an active attempt to neutralize unwanted thoughts, images, or impulses). Moreover, this type of hoarding frequently is associated with positive feelings of excitement and pleasure, if not exhilaration (distress may result from the product of hoarding behavior: clutter). Indeed, individuals who engage in non-OCD hoarding do form attachments to items and may experience distress (e.g., grief, anger, anxiety) at the prospect of discarding them. Because of its distinction from OCD hoarding, non-OCD hoarding likely will be included as a distinct disorder, provisionally called "Hoarding Disorder," in DSM-5 (successor to DSM-IV-TR) — *Mataix-Cols et al., 2010*.

Ch:5

OTHER CHARACTERISTICS OF OBSESSIONS
AND COMPULSIONS

Childhood OCD across cultures and ethnicities

Interestingly, the manner in which OCD appears during childhood and adolescence is very similar across cultures. The most common obsessions (e.g., fears of contamination; fears of harm, illness, or death; symmetry obsessions and sensory phenomena) as well as the most frequent compulsions (e.g., washing, repeating, checking) have been reported in the United States, Denmark, India, Israel, Japan, Spain, Turkey, Australia, and other countries. Prevalence rates of OCD among children and adolescents also have been found to be remarkably similar in various parts of the world. One researcher who examined 15 clinical samples of individuals with OCD from different continents found that cultural variation had very little influence on lifetime prevalence rates of OCD — *Pallanti, 2008*.

Although prevalence rates of OCD appear to be very similar worldwide, a person's culture may have an impact on the type of OCD symptoms an individual exhibits. Cleaning rituals, for example, may assume different forms, depending upon an individual's culture or religion. Research also has indicated that religious obsessions and compulsions may be more prevalent in cultures or countries with codes of conduct based upon strict religious beliefs and practices — *Pallanti, 2008*.

Although evidence suggests no differences in OCD prevalence rates with regard to ethnicity or geography, OCD is found more commonly among Caucasian than African-American children in *clinical samples*. One explanation for this disparity is the difficulty associated with recruiting minority families into pediatric mental health centers or OCD clinics. In addition, a recent study of 21 clinical, randomized trials of OCD among children and adults in the U.S. and Canada revealed that African-American, Hispanic, and Asian minorities were underrepresented in North American OCD trials — *Williams, Powers, Yun & Foa, 2010*.

Underrepresentation of minorities is a critical issue within the field of OCD that must be addressed in the future. Without participants of all races and ethnicities in clinical studies, treatments for OCD cannot be fully evaluated for safety and effectiveness. It is imperative that research include individuals who represent the diversity of the populations to which study results will be applied.

Symptom dimensions

OCD is not a unitary disorder but rather a heterogeneous disorder often categorized into subtypes based upon an individual's obsessions and compulsions. Research on OCD frequently refers to these subtypes, which have distinct but overlapping features, as "symptom dimensions." Although there are differences among studies on symptom categories in adults with OCD, much of the research points to four obsessive-compulsive symptom dimensions:

1. contamination/cleaning (sometimes includes checking);

2. symmetry/ordering/repeating/counting;

3. sexual/religious/aggressive/somatic (sometimes includes checking); and

4. hoarding obsessions and compulsions — *Stewart et al., 2007*.

It is important to note that, as indicated in Chapter 4, an increasing body of evidence supports a distinction between hoarding as a symptom of OCD and as a discrete disorder – Hoarding Disorder.

Recent research findings have indicated that basically the same OCD subtypes or dimensions are found in children and adolescents. In fact, one group of researchers concluded that, although not a perfect fit, the four-factor, category-based model of OCD symptom dimensions is adequate for use across all age groups — *Stewart et al., 2008*. The *frequency* with which children, adolescents, and adults exhibit symptoms of the four subtypes does differ, however. For example, one age group may have a higher reported rate of cleaning compulsions than others, while a different age group may have fewer reported hoarding symptoms (variability exists across studies with regard to the frequencies of these symptoms across age groups). Nonetheless, symptom dimensions have been found to be similar across the life span. Interestingly, a recent study found the same four OCD subtypes among a group of Japanese patients, suggesting that symptom dimensions may be stable even across cultures — *Matsunaga et al., 2008.*

Information about subtypes of OCD may play an important role in guiding future research. Knowing whether certain symptom dimensions correlate with particular kinds of treatment outcomes, co-occurring disorders, brain imaging findings, and genetic vulnerability could be extremely beneficial to researchers and clinicians. The results of a recent study examining the impact of various features on pediatric OCD (e.g., age of onset, gender, co-occurring disorders), for example, suggested that certain OCD subtypes were associated with particular characteristics — *Masi et al., 2010*. Specifically, the order/symmetry subtype was more frequent in males and occurred most frequently with tics. The contamination/cleaning subtype was more common among females, occurred with higher rates of comorbid generalized anxiety disorder and separation anxiety disorder than the other subtypes, and was linked with the least functional impairment. The hoarding subtype was associated with the most functional impairment and presented more frequently with social phobia and bipolar disorder. Information about various subtypes could serve to inform the choice of the most appropriate pharmacological and/or psychosocial interventions.

In another study of children with OCD who had hoarding symptoms, researchers found that hoarding often was associated with poor insight (i.e., symptoms were not viewed as being senseless or irrational) — *Storch, Lack, et al., 2007*. The investigators also noted that children with poor insight sometimes exhibited a strong negative reaction to their parents' attempts to throw away some of their items. The authors suggested that poor insight may be connected to higher levels of externalizing behavior observed in these young people. As a result, they may require more intensive and multidisciplinary treatment (e.g., parent training, special education services for disruptive behavior, etc.).

PART III: Important Issues Related to Childhood OCD

Ch: 6

PREVALENCE, AGE AT ONSET, AND GENDER ISSUES

Prevalence of childhood OCD

OCD is far more prevalent than once thought. In a 2001 World Health Organization mental health report, it was estimated that in the year 2000, OCD was among the top 20 causes of illness-related disability, worldwide, for individuals between 15 and 44 years of age. Moreover, numerous other research reports cite OCD as the fourth most common mental illness after phobias, substance abuse, and major depression.

In the past, OCD was considered rare among children and adolescents. Research conducted over the past several years, however, has indicated that the *lifetime* prevalence of OCD in youth, worldwide, is approximately 1-2% (lifetime prevalence of OCD refers to the percentage of individuals in a given statistical population who, at some point in their lives, have experienced a case of OCD). Research suggests that the prevalence rate for OCD is lower among young children and increases during childhood and adolescence. Another commonly cited figure in the body of information on OCD – sometimes referred to as the OCD literature – is that *at any one given point in time*, OCD affects approximately 1 in 100 children. Overall, research has identified OCD as one of the most common psychiatric illnesses affecting children and adolescents — *Stewart et al., 2004*. Therefore, it is probable that the vast majority of school personnel have encountered and/or will encounter students with OCD during their professional careers.

It should be mentioned that although it is considered one of the most common psychiatric illnesses in childhood, OCD frequently goes unrecognized. In fact, several studies of children and adolescents have found that OCD is underidentified and undertreated. Factors such as incorrect diagnosis, insufficient access to treatment, the secretive nature of OCD, and a lack of awareness among the community at large – including school personnel – have been proposed as possible reasons for this trend.

Age at onset/gender

Sources vary with regard to the reported age of onset for OCD. Some suggest two peak ages of onset: an early onset between the ages of 6 and 15 years of age and a late onset between 20 and 29 — *Gilbert & Maalouf, 2008*. Another source suggests:

1. a first peak in OCD between approximately 10 and 12 years of age – a period characterized by puberty-related biological changes in the brain and body as well as increased stress related to academic and social performance, and

2. a second peak during early adulthood, which also may be a time of developmental transitions and high levels of school and/or work-related stress — *Stewart, 2008*.

Interestingly, the onset of OCD has been reported in children as young as two years of age and, although uncommon, in individuals over 50 years.

Another factor associated with age of onset is gender. Differences in methods of conducting studies contribute to discrepancies in research findings (e.g., some studies are conducted with community samples, while others are conducted with clinical samples). The majority of the OCD literature, however, indicates that early-onset OCD is characterized by a predominance of males, whereas later-onset OCD is marked by a preponderance of females. Some research suggests that the age of onset for males is between 3 and 15 years of age and 20 and 24 for females — *Keeley, Storch, Dhungana, & Geffken, 2007*. By later adolescence or adulthood, there is no substantial difference between genders with regard to the prevalence of OCD.

The literature on OCD indicates that early-onset OCD is characterized not only by a predominance of males but also by higher levels of heritability, i.e., for relatives of individuals with early-onset OCD, the risk of developing OCD is significantly higher than the population at large. In addition, increased rates of attention-deficit/hyperactivity disorder (AD/HD) and tics have been found among children with early-onset OCD.

Research conducted with very young children with OCD (less than 7 years of age) suggests they may experience great difficulty articulating their obsessions because of their language and cognitive levels — *Choate-Summers et al., 2008*. The presence of compulsions without identified obsessions, therefore, may be common. In addition, very young children either may see no connection between obsessions and subsequent compulsions or cannot express them verbally. Moreover, they may not be capable of distinguishing obsessive thoughts from other normal thoughts or images. Sensory-related compulsions, such as the need to touch or tap objects until it feels "just right," also appear to be more common among the youngest children with OCD. These characteristics must be taken into account when designing treatment programs. Very importantly, it is crucial to differentiate OCD behaviors from developmentally normal rituals, which are very common in this age group (see Chapter 2).

Ch:7

CAUSES OF OCD

Many of the early theories proposed to explain the causes of OCD favored a psychological orientation. These theories inaccurately held parents accountable for the disorder, suggesting an overabundance of parental perfectionism, inappropriate toilet training, underparenting, or impaired receptivity to parenting during early childhood. Neither deep-seated conflicts nor problems in early childhood, however, appear to be the root cause of OCD. Indeed, to date, no definitive cause of OCD has been identified. It is believed, rather, that OCD likely is the result of some combination of biological, genetic, behavioral, cognitive, and environmental factors that trigger the disorder in a specific individual at a particular point in time.

Biological factors

A substantial amount of empirical evidence suggests that the abnormal metabolism of serotonin, one of the major neurotransmitters (chemicals that transport signals in the brain), plays a key role in OCD. The "serotonin hypothesis" primarily is supported by evidence that medications such as fluoxetine (Prozac), fluvoxamine (Luvox), sertraline (Zoloft), and clomipramine (Anafranil) – all of which increase serotonin levels at specific sites in the brain (synapses) – are effective in reducing OCD symptoms. Serotonin alone, however, likely is insufficient to explain the biochemistry of OCD, and tests examining serotonin levels are neither reliable nor correlate well with a child's response to medication — E. Storch, personal communication, September 4, 2010. Studies have indicated that other neurotransmitters, including dopamine and glutamate, also may be involved in OCD.

Brain circuitry, or neurocircuitry, is another biological factor that has been implicated in OCD. Data from numerous brain-imaging studies suggest patterns of atypical functioning in areas of the brain known as the orbitofrontal cortex, striatum, thalamus, and basal ganglia. Feedback loops or circuits involving these areas of the brain, which integrate motor and cognitive functioning, are believed to be associated with intrusive thoughts and repetitive behaviors. It appears that overactivity in these circuits generates symptoms of OCD. Hyperactivity in specific areas of these circuits has been identified via magnetic resonance imaging (MRI – more specifically, functional MRI). Data from another type of magnetic resonance imaging, volumetric MRI, also have suggested that the volume of certain regions of the brain involved in these circuits is different from that of individuals who do not have OCD. Of note is that research has indicated that medication and behavioral treatments can reverse these abnormalities in the brain.

A third biological factor related to OCD has come to light over the past two decades. Research has provided evidence for cases of sudden-onset OCD or tics (or the exacerbation of already-existing OCD symptoms or tics) that are linked to the Group A Streptococcus (GAS) infection. Known as Pediatric Autoimmune Neuropsychiatric Disorders Associated with Streptococcus, or PANDAS, this subtype of childhood-onset OCD is thought to be triggered by GAS, which, in turn, triggers the production of antibodies. The antibodies generated by the immune system in response to the infection cross react with cellular components of the basal ganglia in the genetically-vulnerable child, setting off an inflammatory reaction that results in OCD and/or tic symptoms. Research suggests that infection-related OCD probably accounts for no more than 10% of early-onset cases — *Trifiletti & Packard, 1999*. Following are the current diagnostic guidelines for PANDAS.

Current diagnostic guidelines for PANDAS include:

1. Presence of obsessive-compulsive disorder and/or a tic disorder

2. Pediatric onset of symptoms (age 3 years to puberty)

3. Episodic course of symptom severity

4. Association with group A Beta-hemolytic streptococcal infection (a positive throat culture for strep or history of Scarlet Fever)

5. Association with neurological abnormalities (motoric hyperactivity, or adventitious movements, such as choreiform movements)

National Institute of Mental Health (n.d.). PANDAS. Retrieved from www.intramural.nimh.nih.gov/pdn/web.htm.

Case reports indicate that aggressive treatment of the infection may lead to a reduction or elimination of the symptoms over time. Intriguingly, some research has linked cases of anorexia nervosa, age-inappropriate separation anxiety disorder, and late-onset AD/HD with PANDAS — *Larson, Storch, & Murphy, 2007.*

The PANDAS issue is not without controversy. Some researchers believe there is not enough evidence to support the link between GAS and OCD. Results of studies that provide backing for the GAS-OCD connection, however, continue to accumulate. Additional research on PANDAS clearly is warranted.

Genetic factors

Research has indicated that genetics plays an important role in the genesis of OCD — *Grados & Wilcox, 2007*. Family studies demonstrate that OCD is significantly more frequent among relatives of children with OCD than in the relatives of controls (controls are the individuals in the studies' comparison groups who do not have OCD). Thus, family history is a strong predictor of a child's developing OCD. Of note is that children often experience symptoms *different* from their parents or other family members, arguing against the idea that OCD is the result of imitating others' symptoms. A family history of tics or Tourette Syndrome also has been shown to increase the risk for OCD. In addition, first-degree relatives (i.e., parents, siblings, and children) of individuals with OCD experience a significantly higher risk of developing OCD than the population at large.

Studies of twins provide additional support for a genetic link to OCD. Some research has indicated that if one twin has OCD, the other is more likely to have OCD when the twins are identical, rather than fraternal. Research also has indicated that when a child has blood relatives with OCD, anxiety disorders other than OCD, or tic disorders, the child is at greater risk of developing any of these disorders.

In general, studies of twins with OCD estimate that genetics contributes approximately 45-65% of risk for developing the disorder — *van Grootheest, Cath, Beekman, & Boomsma, 2005*. Thus, while genetics appears to be a risk factor for OCD, environment also plays a vital role. Although much progress has been made in the study of genetics as it relates to OCD, no single gene for OCD has been discovered. More recent research, in fact, has suggested that genes related to the neurotransmitters serotonin, dopamine, and glutamate may be involved in OCD. Currently, several large-scale studies are being conducted to examine the role of genetics in the development of OCD.

Behavioral factors

Learning theorists suggest that behavioral conditioning plays an important role in developing and maintaining obsessions and compulsions. More specifically, they believe compulsions are learned responses that help an individual reduce or avoid the anxiety or discomfort associated with obsessions. A child who experiences an intrusive obsession regarding contamination, for example, may engage in hand washing to reduce the anxiety precipitated by the obsession. Because the ritual temporarily reduces the anxiety, the probability that the child will engage in hand washing when a contamination obsession occurs again is increased. Unfortunately, this reduction in anxiety increases reliance on compulsive behavior in the future. As a result, ritualistic behavior not only persists but actually become excessive. The learning theory model of OCD has received the most empirical support and corresponds best with the leading treatment for OCD in children and adolescents: cognitive-behavioral therapy (see Chapter 11).

Cognitive factors

Cognitive models, which are important to a discussion of the causes of OCD, suggest that dysfunctional beliefs and interpretations of intrusive thoughts lead to the creation of obsessions and compulsions. Building upon the work of other cognitive theorists, Rachman (1997) proposed a well-known theory of obsessions. According to Rachman, intrusive thoughts are experienced by virtually all human beings. It is the *misinterpretation* of the significance of intrusive thoughts as being personally important, revealing about one's character, or having catastrophic consequences, that leads to the formation of obsessions. Compared to the more common variety of intrusive thoughts, obsessions are more distressing (individuals have described their obsessions as immoral, sinful, criminal), intense, and longer lasting. Thus, one new mother may view an intrusive thought about harming her baby as strange and even somewhat frightening, but is able to dismiss it quickly from consciousness; the thought is a nuisance. A second mother, however, may dwell upon such thoughts, misinterpreting them as evidence that she is a potential murderer, an evil human being, and a despicable mother who likely will be locked away. These obsessions are so upsetting that the individual intensely tries to resist, block, or neutralize them. The individual also may engage in avoidance behavior or other compulsions to reduce distress.

Rachman (1997) also has discussed the role of intrusive *images* in OCD. Intrusive images – mental pictures that intrude unexpectedly into an individual's consciousness – frequently reflect common obsessional themes (e.g., contamination, sexual, blasphemous). As with intrusive thoughts, people may misinterpret intrusive images as having deep, negative, personal meaning that reflect a serious character flaw (e.g., "I must be a terrible person to have these images in my head"). Such misinterpretations increase the likelihood that intrusive images will become obsessional images, which are recurrent and distressing.

Like Rachman (1997), the Obsessive-Compulsive Cognitions Working Group (OCCWG), an international group of researchers interested in the cognitive underpinnings of OCD, has proposed that the onset and maintenance of OCD are associated with inappropriate interpretations of intrusive thoughts. The OCCWG has identified six types of dysfunctional beliefs associated with OCD, several of which dovetail with Rachman's theory.

Six Types of Dysfunctional Beliefs Associated with OCD

1. Inflated responsibility—a belief that one has the ability to cause and/or is responsible for preventing aversive outcomes;

2. Overimportance of thoughts (i.e., thought-action fusion);

3. A belief that it is both essential and possible to have total control over one's own thoughts;

4. Overestimation of threat—a belief that aversive events are very probable and will be bad;

5. Perfectionism—a belief that one cannot make mistakes and that imperfection is unacceptable;

6. Intolerance for uncertainty—a belief that it is essential and possible to know, without any doubt, that aversive outcomes will not transpire.

From: Obsessive Compulsive Cognitions Working Group (1997). Cognitive assessment of obsessive-compulsive disorder. Behavior Research and Therapy, 35(7), 667-681.

Empirical evidence supporting the relationship between cognitions and obsessive-compulsive symptoms does exist, but this is an ongoing area of research.

Environmental factors

A number of environmental factors may contribute to the genesis and maintenance of OCD. Although some research suggests that no link exists between negative life events and OCD, the literature reports numerous cases in which childhood OCD has been precipitated by a specific, often traumatic, occurrence, including the death of a loved one; the loss of a pet; a divorce in the family; a change in schools (e.g., going from elementary to middle school); a move to a new location (usually involving a change in schools); or unhappiness at school. Also, as previously noted, cognitive models support the notion that stress – which is omnipresent – can increase intrusive thoughts, increasing the risk of obsessions. Furthermore, a recent study indicated that one to two years prior to the onset of symptoms, both children and adults who develop OCD experience more adverse life events than controls — Horesh, Zimmerman, Steinberg, Yagan, & Apter, 2008. Taken together, these results suggest that stress or trauma can play a role in the development of OCD among certain individuals. Given the extraordinary levels of stress students sometimes experience in the home, school, and community, these findings are extremely important for education professionals.

Injuries also have been associated with OCD. In one study, 80 children and adolescents who suffered a traumatic brain injury were examined — Grados et al., 2008. It was found that almost 30% of these children experienced new onset obsessive-compulsive symptoms within one year after the serious injury. The results of this study indicated that obsessive-compulsive symptoms appeared more commonly in females than males.

Another environmental factor that often has an impact on OCD is the involvement of the family. In general, evidence specifically linking the *onset* of childhood OCD to family factors is absent. With regard to the *maintenance* of OCD symptoms, however, family members (including parents, siblings, and others) commonly play an important role.

In an attempt to decrease distress or symptom-related impairment, family members frequently accommodate the behaviors of children with OCD. Family accommodations may assume many forms, such as:

1. providing verbal reassurance to excessive reassurance
   -seeking requests;

2. conducting rituals with or for the child (e.g., helping check
   a stove, doing laundry);

3. providing items necessary to carry out rituals (e.g., supplying
   soap for hand washing);

4. allowing/helping the child avoid stimuli that serve as triggers;
   and

5. tolerating delays associated with ritual completion (e.g.,
   waiting in the car to drive to school while the child completes
   washing rituals).

Although usually well-intentioned, family accommodation often leads
to more severe symptoms and impairment. Accommodating a child
not only may have a negative impact on family dynamics but also may
reinforce the child's future involvement in rituals and avoidance. Thus,
the child's symptoms are worsened, rather than improved. A worsening
of OCD symptoms also can occur when family members respond to
a child's rituals with criticism or hostility. The reader is referred to the
section regarding the impact of family involvement on cognitive-
behavioral therapy in Chapter 11.

Future research undoubtedly will expand our current knowledge base
about the causes of OCD. One recent study, for example, found that
mothers of children with OCD experienced significantly higher rates of
prenatal illness requiring medical attention and difficulties at birth (e.g.,
forceps delivery, prolonged labor), compared to children without OCD
— Geller et al., 2008.

In sum, although the definitive cause or causes of obsessive-compulsive
disorder have not yet been pinpointed, ongoing research hopefully will
provide answers to many of our current questions. It is likely, however,
that a delicate interplay between various risk factors over time is
responsible for the onset and maintenance of OCD.

Ch:8

COMORBIDITY

When two or more disorders occur simultaneously in an individual, they are referred to as "comorbid" disorders. In the OCD literature, there is wide variation among cited prevalence rates for comorbid disorders. Because children with two or more disorders likely are treated at a clinic, for example, studies using clinical samples of children and adolescents will, in all probability, report higher rates of comorbidity than studies using community samples. Nonetheless, comorbidity is quite common in childhood OCD; it has been estimated that as many as 75-80% of children and adolescents with OCD have at least one comorbid disorder — *Flament, Geller, Irak, & Blier, 2007; Gilbert & Maalouf, 2008.*

Comorbidity is extremely important to a discussion of OCD, because the presence of comorbid disorders can affect its severity, course, and treatment. Several studies have shown that OCD symptoms are more severe when comorbid conditions exist. The results of other studies have indicated that children with OCD as their sole diagnosis responded better to medication for OCD than did children with certain comorbidities. Still other studies have demonstrated that children with OCD and no comorbid disorders responded better to behavior therapy than those with OCD and certain co-existing disorders.

Among children and adolescents, some of the most common comorbid disorders are anxiety disorders (e.g., separation anxiety disorder, social phobia); mood disorders (e.g., major depressive disorder, bipolar disorder); attention-deficit/hyperactivity disorder; disruptive behavior disorders (e.g., oppositional defiant disorder, conduct disorder); and tic disorders, including Tourette Syndrome. The following section contains a description of these and numerous other disorders that may occur with OCD. The descriptions are based largely upon information from the DSM-IV-TR, which, as previously noted, is considered the gold standard for providing diagnostic criteria for mental disorders, particularly in the United States. It is essential to keep in mind that for most of the disorders in the DSM-IV-TR, specific criteria are included with regard to:

1. the duration of the symptoms (e.g., symptoms must be present for a given length of time); and

2. the requirement that the symptoms cause sufficient distress to interfere significantly with an individual's normal routine (e.g., work, school, social activities).

Very importantly, whenever school personnel observe symptoms of any of the following disorders, they should bring them to the attention of pertinent school staff members and parents. The interested reader is referred to Appendix A, which contains a listing of websites, including websites dedicated to each of these disorders.

Anxiety disorders

School personnel likely are familiar with anxiety disorders, which have substantially high rates of comorbidity with OCD. Potentially less well-known is that a number of disorders other than OCD fall under the umbrella of anxiety disorders. Following is a discussion of anxiety disorders that may co-occur with OCD.

Generalized Anxiety Disorder (GAD). GAD is characterized by excessive worry or anxiety about a number of ordinary issues, e.g., school or work performance, excessive worry about the future. Individuals with GAD find their worry uncontrollable and may experience physical symptoms such as restlessness, irritability, fatigue, muscle tension, or difficulties with sleep or concentration.

Separation Anxiety Disorder. Separation anxiety disorder, which manifests prior to 18 years of age, is marked by excessive, developmentally-inappropriate anxiety associated with being separated from home or individuals to whom the person is attached (e.g., mother, father). Other characteristics of separation anxiety disorder include: severe distress upon anticipation of or actual separation from attachment figures; worries that attachment figures will be harmed or will leave; school refusal; excessive and continuous fear of being alone; reluctance or refusal to go to sleep without major attachment figure(s); nightmares about separation; and physical symptoms (e.g., nausea, headaches) upon anticipation of or separation from attachment figures.

Panic Disorder. Individuals with panic disorder experience recurring and unexpected panic attacks. Panic attacks are periods of extreme fear or discomfort during which the individual may experience many different physical symptoms, including heart palpitations, shaking, sweating, shortness of breath/smothering sensation, chest discomfort or pain, nausea, dizziness, or feelings of choking. The individual also may experience serious fears of going crazy, dying, or feelings of moving in slow motion or being detached from oneself. These symptoms develop suddenly and usually peak within about ten minutes. Individuals with panic disorder frequently develop persistent fears that they will experience another panic attack and therefore avoid certain situations that may trigger one. Although panic disorder is characterized by unexpected panic attacks, panic attacks may occur independently of panic disorder and within the context of any other anxiety or psychiatric disorder.

Social Phobia. Individuals with social phobia experience excessive fear that they will be humiliated or embarrassed in one or more social or performance situations in which unfamiliar people will be present or if there is a possibility they will be scrutinized by others. When exposed to the feared situation, an individual may experience anxiety that manifests in the form of a panic attack. Children in these situations may cry, have tantrums, freeze up, or withdraw. Feared social situations are avoided; when they cannot be avoided, the individual experiences extreme distress.

Specific Phobias. Individuals with specific phobias have an excessive and persistent fear that is triggered either by the presence or the anticipation of a particular object or situation. Exposure to the object or situation produces extreme anxiety or, in children, crying, tantrums, clinging, or freezing up. Common phobias include fears of flying, heights, and animals (e.g., snakes, spiders). As is the case with social phobia, stimuli associated with specific phobias are avoided or endured only with great anxiety or distress.

Agoraphobia. While not a specific disorder in and of itself, agoraphobia refers to anxiety related to being in situations or places from which an individual would have difficulty escaping. The individual also may fear that help would be unavailable in the event of panic or a panic attack. Agoraphobic fears may include being in a crowd, on a bridge, in a bus, train, etc., or outside the home alone. Situations that may trigger anxiety frequently are avoided; if they cannot be avoided, the individual experiences extreme distress or fears having a panic attack. In some cases, having a companion alleviates the anxiety. Specific disorders that relate to agoraphobia include Panic Disorder Without Agoraphobia, Panic Disorder With Agoraphobia, and Agoraphobia Without History of Panic Disorder.

Mood disorders

Major Depressive Disorder. Many educators have encountered students who are depressed. Depression can manifest in a myriad of ways but frequently is associated with subjective reports of feeling sad or empty. Observations made by others – that an individual is tearful, for example – also may be indicative of depression. Other characteristics of depression include a decreased interest in or enjoyment of activities, weight gain or loss, too much or too little sleep, fatigue, feelings of worthlessness or guilt, and a diminished ability to concentrate. Children and adolescents may exhibit an irritable, rather than a depressed, mood. For many children with OCD, depression is secondary to the hopelessness and feelings of isolation associated with OCD. When children and adolescents with OCD have comorbid depression, appropriate treatment is critical; suicidal ideation, suicide attempts, and suicide completions all have been reported among these young people.

Bipolar Disorder. Bipolar disorder, previously known as manic depression, is characterized by severe changes in one's mood, energy level, behavior, and thinking. It is referred to as bipolar disorder because the mood of the individual can vary, or swing, between two poles: *depression* (sad, hopeless, depressed mood) and *mania* (an elevated or irritable mood). These changes in mood occur in cycles and are referred to as "episodes." Individuals may experience mixed episodes, in which features of both mania and depression are present at the same time. Mood changes can last for hours, days, weeks, and even months. A number of different categories of mood disorders fall under the umbrella of bipolar disorder (e.g., a category for individuals who are experiencing a first episode of mania, another for those who have recurrent mood episodes).

Attention-Deficit/Hyperactivity Disorder

Attention-deficit/hyperactivity disorder, or AD/HD, is well-known among education professionals. There are three different types of AD/HD:

1. AD/HD, predominantly inattentive type;

2. AD/HD, predominantly hyperactive-impulsive type; and

3. AD/HD, combined type.

The inattentive type of AD/HD is marked by characteristics such as failing to attend to detail, making careless mistakes, having difficulty with organization, losing items necessary for the given task, not listening when spoken to, not following through on instructions, and being forgetful and distracted. Children with the hyperactive-impulsive type of AD/HD may display signs of hyperactivity such as fidgeting, running around or climbing in settings where it is inappropriate to do so, having difficulty playing or participating in free-time activities quietly, getting out of their seats when they are supposed to remain seated, talking excessively, or moving constantly. Impulsivity may manifest in difficulty awaiting turns, interrupting others, and blurting out answers instead of waiting for an appropriate point to speak. Children with the combined type of AD/HD exhibit a combination of both inattentive and hyperactive-impulsive symptoms.

Several studies have indicated that among children with comorbid OCD and AD/HD, AD/HD brings to bear a number of difficulties over and above those related to OCD. One study found that compared to controls, children with OCD only were impaired in many areas of adaptive functioning and emotional adjustment. Children with both OCD and AD/HD, however, experienced additional problems with regard to school functioning, school difficulties, and self-reported depression — *Sukhodolsky et al., 2005*. Another study indicated that in addition to exhibiting greater functional impairment than children with OCD only, children with comorbid OCD and AD/HD showed less clinical improvement on treatment follow-up as well as higher rates of certain comorbid disorders — *Masi et al., 2006*. A third study found that compared to children with OCD only, youth with both disorders had more severe and persistent OCD symptoms — *Walitza et al., 2008*. Of note is that AD/HD and OCD co-occur quite commonly; some reports suggest that as many as 50% of young people with OCD also have AD/HD — *Sukhodolsky et al., 2005*. In addition, OCD may be misdiagnosed as AD/HD, especially when rituals are mental, rather than overt. Because obsessions and compulsions are distracting and interfere with attention and concentration, OCD may be misconstrued as AD/HD.

Disruptive behavior disorders (DBDs)

Disruptive behavior disorders such as oppositional defiant disorder (ODD) and conduct disorder (CD) may co-exist with OCD. In some cases, the symptoms associated with disruptive behavior disorders may lead to greater impairment than the OCD symptoms themselves. Indeed, some experts recommend addressing symptoms of a disruptive behavior disorder (using, for example, parent management training) *prior* to implementing cognitive-behavioral therapy (CBT) for the OCD — *Lehmkuhl, et al., 2009; Storch, Merlo, Larson, et. al, 2008*. Following is a description of oppositional defiant disorder and conduct disorder.

> Note: Some sources include AD/HD as a DBD, while others do not. For the purposes of this discussion, AD/HD is treated separately – see previous section.

Oppositional Defiant Disorder. ODD is a disorder that usually arises during childhood or adolescence. Youth with ODD exhibit, as its name implies, oppositional, defiant, and negative behavior. They frequently lose their tempers, argue with adults, refuse to comply with adults' requests, purposely irritate others (and are easily irritated by others), blame others for their misbehavior or mistakes, and are angry and resentful, or spiteful or vindictive. These behaviors occur more frequently among individuals with ODD than in others of similar age and developmental levels.

Conduct Disorder. Although CD, like ODD, typically emerges during childhood or adolescence, it has been known to occur in preschool-aged children. Individuals with conduct disorder violate the basic rights of others or important rules or norms established by society. Behaviors associated with CD include destroying others' property, setting fires, stealing, lying, demonstrating aggression or cruelty toward people (e.g., bullying, robbery, mugging, forced sexual activity) and animals, and committing major rule violations (e.g., running away from home, being truant from school).

Eating disorders

Eating disorders, which are characterized by severe disturbances in eating behavior, generally include two disorders: anorexia nervosa and bulimia nervosa. Eating disorders frequently co-occur with OCD; there is even evidence that they may be related.

Anorexia Nervosa. Anorexia nervosa is a condition in which one's body weight fails to reach a level considered minimally normal, based upon age and height. Individuals with anorexia nervosa have serious fears of becoming fat or gaining weight, even though they are underweight.

There also may be a distortion in the way they view their bodies or shape, a denial of the severity of their low weight, or an excessive emphasis on body weight or shape in self-evaluations.

Bulimia Nervosa. Like people with anorexia nervosa, individuals with bulimia nervosa may place undue emphasis on body shape and weight in self-evaluations. A distinctive characteristic of bulimia, however, is eating excessively during a given period of time; the person feels he or she cannot control the amount of food consumed. In response to overeating, the individual engages in various behaviors to prevent weight gain, including self-induced vomiting, inappropriate use of laxatives and diuretics, excessive exercise, or fasting.

Individuals with anorexia and bulimia nervosa commonly experience obsessions and compulsions. When the obsessions are related only to food and body image, and the corresponding restricting or purging rituals are conducted to lose weight or prevent weight gain, the individual may have an eating disorder *to the exclusion* of OCD.

Autism spectrum disorders (ASDs)

Autism spectrum disorders, also known as pervasive developmental disorders (PDDs), usually are first diagnosed in early childhood. ASDs comprise a range of disorders from autism, which may be more severe, to Asperger's Syndrome, a much milder form of ASD. Also included among ASDs are two rarer disorders: childhood disintegrative disorder and Rett's Syndrome. When a PDD does not meet the criteria for any of these specific disorders, it may be referred to as a pervasive developmental disorder not otherwise specified (PDD-NOS).

All children with ASDs exhibit deficits in social interaction and verbal/nonverbal communication, as well as repetitive behaviors or interests. Symptoms may range from mild to severe. In addition, children with ASDs often have atypical responses to sights, sounds, and other sensory experiences. Despite these commonalities, children with ASDs demonstrate very unique patterns of behavior.

ASD traits are quite common among children and adolescents with OCD, largely as a result of comorbid autism spectrum disorders. These traits also have been found in young people who have OCD with other comorbidities such as Tourette Syndrome and AD/HD. Compared to controls, however, higher levels of autistic traits have been found even in individuals with OCD and no comorbid disorders, suggesting the possibility of some underlying relationship between OCD and ASDs — *Ivarsson & Melin, 2008*.

Obsessive-compulsive personality disorder (OCPD)

Not to be confused with OCD, OCPD is a personality disorder characterized by a preoccupation with perfectionism, orderliness, and mental and interpersonal control. Individuals with OCPD may be so engrossed in details, order, and rules, that the major purpose or theme of an activity may be lost. They may be dedicated to working and being productive to the extent that they do not participate in free-time activities or interact with friends. Other characteristics of OCPD include a bent toward perfectionism, miserly spending habits, rigidity, and stubbornness.

A major difference between OCD and OCPD is that individuals with OCD usually are extremely frustrated by their behavior; they know it is irrational yet feel compelled to carry out rituals. By contrast, people with OCPD perceive themselves and their excessive need for order and rules as normal. Friends, family, and colleagues of individuals with OCPD, however, may become aggravated by the inflexibility and stubbornness characteristic of OCPD.

Obsessive-compulsive spectrum disorders

A number of disorders share many similarities with OCD, including:

1. repetitive thoughts and behaviors (obsessions and compulsions);

2. similar brain activity, as evidenced by neuroimaging studies; and

3. comparable responses to certain treatments (e.g., medication, behavior therapy).

As a result, these disorders commonly are referred to as obsessive-compulsive spectrum disorders (OCSDs). OCSDs co-occur among individuals with OCD at rates higher than those in the general population. Interestingly, the relationship between OCD and OCSDs, autism spectrum disorders, and other disorders has prompted discussions as to whether OCD is better characterized as an OCSD rather than an anxiety disorder. In the forthcoming DSM-5, OCD ostensibly will be grouped in a class of disorders labeled "Anxiety and Obsessive-Compulsive Spectrum Disorders." — *E. Storch, personal communication, September 4, 2010.*

Discrepancies among sources exist as to the specific disorders included among the OCSDs. Indeed, Ravindran, da Silva, Ravindran, Richter, and Rector (2009) indicated that "The breadth of the spectrum, and which conditions should be included in it, remain contentious" (p. 332). For the purposes of this discussion, OCSDs include Tic Disorders/Tourette Syndrome, Trichotillomania, Body Dysmorphic Disorder, and compulsive skin picking and nail biting.

Tic Disorders/Tourette Syndrome. Tic disorders and Tourette Syndrome occur quite frequently in children and adolescents with primary OCD. Tics are sudden, rapid, recurring motor movements (motor tics) or vocalizations (vocal tics). Motor tics range from simple movements such as eye blinking, head jerking, and wrinkling of the nose to more complex and longer-lasting motor movements, e.g., jumping, touching, and twirling while walking. Similarly, vocal tics range from simple vocalizations such as sniffing and throat clearing to complex vocalizations, e.g., spontaneously expressing a phrase or repeating one's own words. An individual has a Chronic Motor Tic Disorder when he or she experiences motor tics but not vocal tics for a period of more than a year; a Chronic Vocal Tic Disorder is characterized by the presence of vocal tics only for over a year. Tourette Syndrome involves both motor and vocal tics for more than a year. These disorders are neurobiological in nature and begin before 18 years of age.

When OCD co-exists with tic disorders or Tourette Syndrome, it commonly is referred to as "tic-related OCD," or in some cases, "Tourettic OCD" — *Mansueto & Keuler, 2005.* Family studies have shown that a substantial degree of tics occurs not only in individuals with OCD but also their first-degree relatives. Higher rates of OCD also have been found in individuals with tic disorders, compared to the population at large. Thus, it has been suggested that the disorders are related and may be a different expression of the same genes.

Tic-related OCD, a subgroup or subtype of OCD that overlaps with early-onset OCD, is characterized by several features. Tic-related OCD, as compared with OCD unrelated to tics, usually is associated with:

1. an earlier age of onset;

2. a predominance of males;

3. higher frequencies of certain types of obsessive-compulsive symptoms, including intrusive aggressive and sexual images or thoughts, hoarding and counting rituals, and concerns about symmetry and exactness; and

4. higher frequencies of sensory phenomena (e.g., general feelings, urges, or bodily sensations) occurring prior to or with compulsions.

Trichotillomania (TTM). The distinguishing feature of trichotillomania is the repeated pulling out of one's own hair to the extent that there is observable hair loss. The scalp and face (e.g., head, eyebrows, eyelashes) are common hair-pulling sites, but any part of the body covered with hair may be involved (e.g., arms, pubic region). An individual with TTM may be aware of an escalating sense of tension prior to pulling hair (or when trying to avoid pulling) and a sense of relief or pleasure while pulling it out. Some people with TTM, however, particularly children, report they do not experience this tension/pleasure pattern; they are unaware of their pulling and do it without thinking.

Body Dysmorphic Disorder (BDD). Individuals with BDD are preoccupied with a defect in their appearance that either is imagined or very minor. Although any part of the body may be a focus of concern, common complaints involve imagined or slight flaws of the face or head, including some aspect of the nose, mouth, teeth, etc. In response to these concerns, people with BDD frequently engage in repetitive behavior, including checking mirrors repeatedly, asking others for reassurance, covering the "defective" body part with clothing, and even seeking plastic surgery to fix the imperfection. Of note is that individuals with BDD typically have poor insight into their disorder; they do not recognize that their concerns are excessive or unreasonable.

Important Issues Related to Childhood OCD

Part III

57

Many observers believe the late Michael Jackson had body dysmorphic disorder, a condition that frequently paralyzes its sufferers with shame, embarrassment, and even disgust. Michael Jackson was only one of many who have struggled with this disorder. But certainly few cases of BDD have gained the notoriety Michael Jackson's did. Only someone with BDD would be able to appreciate the depth of anguish he may have felt when he looked in the mirror.

Some cases of BDD are mild – in many cases, it would never be suspected that a particular individual had it. But BDD is very real and has the potential to inflict tremendous pain – not only upon the individuals who have it but also those who love them.

Body dysmorphic disorder probably doesn't even come close to explaining all the eccentricities displayed by Michael Jackson. But understanding even this much about the famous "Man in the Mirror," an oft-changed face that was recognizable in perhaps nearly every country of the world, may, at least, shed some more light on the complexity of the one who would be called The King of Pop.

Skin Picking/Nail Biting. Problematic skin picking and chronic nail biting are categorized as impulse control disorders in the DSM-IV-TR (specifically, Impulse-Control Disorders, Not Otherwise Specified) and occur at higher rates among individuals with OCD compared to the general population. Compulsive skin picking is a condition involving repetitive behavior that leads to the destruction of one's own skin. Although any part of the body may be involved, the face is a major target of skin picking. Individuals with compulsive skin picking may feel compelled to pick at, open, or squeeze even the smallest of pimples, either with one's fingers or with an object such as tweezers or needles. This behavior frequently results in the presence of many scars, red sores, and scabs.

Compulsive nail biting also involves repetitive behavior. With compulsive nail biting, the individual continuously bites his or her nails to the point that the fingernails and frequently the surrounding skin and cuticles are damaged or destroyed. Nail biting is quite common in the general population, and most people occasionally pick at or bite pieces of a rough nail or cuticle. Individuals who engage in compulsive nail biting, however, bite their nails past the nail bed and cuticle, frequently until they are bleeding. This behavior may lead to bruises, infections, and even permanent damage to the fingers.

People sometimes engage in compulsive skin picking or nail biting automatically while watching TV or reading a book without an awareness of what they are doing. In other cases, individuals are fully aware of their behavior and will even interrupt other activities to pick their skin or bite their nails.

Learning disabilities and nonverbal learning disabilities

Although the DSM-IV-TR includes a discussion of Learning Disorders, a learning disability typically is considered an educational, rather than a mental health, diagnosis. Learning disabilities, which commonly occur with OCD, are neurological in nature and affect an individual's ability either to interpret what is seen and heard or to link information from different parts of the brain. These difficulties interfere with a person's capacity to listen, think, speak, read, write, spell, or do mathematical calculations. Learning disabilities are not the result of other disabilities (e.g., blindness, intellectual disability) or environmental, cultural, or economic disadvantage. By definition, individuals with learning disabilities have average to above average intelligence levels.

Nonverbal learning disabilities (NVLDs) also may co-exist with OCD. NVLDs are characterized by distinct patterns of strengths and deficits in neuropsychological, academic, and social-emotional functioning. According to Telzrow and Bonar (2002), primary characteristics and indicators of the disorder include:

1. higher verbal compared to nonverbal (performance) abilities as measured on IQ tests;

2. difficulties with psychomotor skills (e.g., skipping, riding bike) and perceptual motor skills (e.g., writing, coloring);

3. better performance in reading and spelling than arithmetic;

4. better performance on rote memory tasks than tasks requiring integration and synthesis;

5. difficulties with problem-solving skills, inflexibility, and changes in routine;

6. weaknesses in the social and interpersonal domains; and

7. problems with psychosocial adjustment (e.g., high prevalence of anxiety and depression during adolescence).

Implications for school personnel regarding comorbidity

The presence of high rates of comorbidity among students with OCD has important implications for school personnel. When a child is diagnosed with OCD or is suspected of having OCD, school personnel must be vigilant for symptoms of other disorders. The child or adolescent with OCD and various comorbidities may experience more difficulties with academic, social, and behavioral functioning than the student for whom OCD is the sole diagnosis. Moreover, the presence of comorbidities renders collaboration with outside mental health providers (whenever possible) crucial in terms of coordinating treatment to enhance school performance.

Ch:9

Children and adolescents with OCD frequently experience a number of difficulties in addition to comorbid disorders. Following is a discussion of some of the more significant problems.

Sleep problems

The results of the first study examining sleep problems in a large sample of children and adolescents with OCD indicated that 92% of the youth experienced at least one sleep-related problem (SRP), and an astounding 27.3% had five or more SRPs — *Storch, Murphy, Lack, et al., 2008*. The most commonly reported SRPs were being overtired, having nightmares, a need to sleep next to someone in the family, and child and parent reports of having trouble sleeping.

Younger children (ages 8-11) had more sleep problems in general, and nightmares, specifically, than older children (12-17 years of age). Older children were reported as having higher rates of the problem "sleeps more than most kids." Females had significantly more reported SRPs than males. Females also had higher rates than males of being overtired and sleeping more than most kids. Importantly, the results of the study indicated that rates of sleep problems decreased following treatment with behavior therapy.

The data from this study support anecdotal reports of sleep difficulties among children and adolescents with OCD. These young people frequently spend an inordinate amount of time engaging in rituals, which often interfere with sleep. Some children stay up until the early hours of the morning completing rituals (e.g., checking and rechecking answers on homework). Others awaken several hours prior to the start of school to complete washing, dressing, and eating rituals. Many experience elevated levels of general or OCD-related anxiety that impede their ability to fall or stay asleep.

The implications for school personnel are great. Educators must be sensitive to the fatigue youth with OCD frequently experience along with other sleep-related difficulties, including arriving at school on time, staying awake in class, being able to concentrate, and completing assignments.

Somatic symptoms

It is not uncommon for children to report somatic, or physiological, complaints such as headaches, shakiness, dizziness, stomach aches, and chest pains. Evidence suggests that somatic complaints occur at a higher frequency among youth with psychiatric illnesses, including anxiety disorders. The presence of somatic problems specifically among youth with OCD, however, only recently has been examined.

The results of a study conducted on 85 children and adolescents with OCD revealed that somatic symptoms were extremely common among this population — *Storch, Merlo, Keeley, et al., 2008*. Almost 97% of the participants reported at least one somatic symptom; approximately 67% indicated 5 or more symptoms. Symptoms reported most frequently by children were tenseness and restlessness. Females reported significantly higher levels than males on 6 symptoms, including tenseness, jumpiness, feeling strange, restlessness, shaky hands, and getting sweaty. Of note is that of the 62 children and adolescents in this study treated with cognitive-behavioral therapy, a significant pre- to post-treatment reduction in somatic symptoms was reported by the youth and their parents.

Psychosocial functioning

The results of several recent studies have shown an association between OCD and impaired levels of psychosocial functioning. The first U.S. study to examine the psychosocial functioning of children and adolescents with OCD investigated potential difficulties in three domains:

1. home/family;

2. school/academic; and

3. social — *Piacentini, Bergman, Keller, & McCracken, 2003*.

This study indicated that almost 90% of parents and children reported a significant problem in at least one of the domains; almost half of the parents and children reported at least one substantial problem in all three domains. Of great importance is that the top two concerns reported by parents and children across all three domains were:

1. doing homework and

2. concentrating on work.

This study was repeated by a different group of researchers with children and adolescents in Norway and Sweden — *Valderhaug & Ivarsson, 2005.* The results of this research confirmed the results of the U.S. study: parent and child reports revealed that the majority of children and adolescents with OCD experienced significant impairment – especially in the home/family domain, but also in the school and social domains. Intriguingly, within the school domain, the top two concerns reported by parents and students alike were *identical* to those reported in the U.S. study: doing homework and concentrating on work. It is evident that these two school-related issues are of paramount importance to school personnel (see sections on homework and concentration in Chapter 18).

Using a different set of measures, another group of researchers found that children with OCD were more impaired than controls in several areas of adaptive functioning and emotional adjustment. OCD was associated with difficulties in school and social functioning and self-reported depression and anxiety — *Sukhodolsky et al., 2005.*

A recent study examined variables that might be associated with child- and/or parent-reported functional impairment among youth with OCD — *Storch, Larson, et al., 2010.* The results indicated that a number of factors were directly related to impairment, including symptom severity, depressive symptoms, and family accommodation of the child's symptoms. In addition, insight into one's disorder – the ability of an individual to recognize that his or her concerns are excessive or unreasonable – was inversely related to functional impairment: the less insight the child possessed, the greater the impairment.

In addition to providing support for functional impairment in youth with OCD, i.e., the child's ability to perform typical, age-appropriate tasks in school, at home, and in social realms is compromised, research also suggests that OCD may negatively affect a child's quality of life. Varni, Burwinkle, Seid, and Skarr (2003) defined quality of life as "a patient's perceptions of the impact of disease and treatment functioning in a variety of dimensions including physical, mental, and social domains." The results of a recent study — *Lack et al., 2009* suggested that OCD symptoms had a significant and pervasive negative impact on the quality of life of children and adolescents with OCD.

Teasing and bullying are inherently related to the psychosocial problems of young people with OCD. These issues are addressed in greater depth in the section on teasing/bullying in Chapter 19.

Executive functioning

Although not a new term, "executive functioning" (EF) has received increased attention in the fields of education, psychology, neuropsychology, and psychiatry over the recent past. Acknowledging that varying definitions of this term are found in the literature, the Council for Exceptional Children (2008) defines EF as "the cognitive processes that enable individuals to engage in goal-directed or problem-solving behaviors. Thus, EF may include goal setting or identifying a problem, developing a plan, the ability to execute the plan, flexibility, attention and memory systems to guide the individual (e.g., working memory), and evaluation or self-monitoring." Problems with executive functioning can have a negative effect on a student's academic, social, behavioral, and emotional functioning.

Difficulties in EF commonly have been ascribed to individuals with learning and attention problems (e.g., learning disabilities, AD/HD). The connection between EF and OCD has not received as much attention in the literature, however. The majority of research related to EF in individuals with OCD has been conducted on adults. Although the results have been mixed, there is considerable evidence to suggest that adults with OCD exhibit problems with executive functioning tasks compared to controls — *Zandt, Prior, & Kyrios, 2009.*

Although problems in executive functioning have been hypothesized in children and adolescents with OCD, scant data on this topic exist. Moreover, the results of the studies that have been conducted are inconclusive — *Zandt et al., 2009.* Some studies have shown that children with OCD do exhibit problems on certain tasks of executive functioning, while others have indicated that these children perform similarly to controls on a range of executive functioning tests. It has been suggested that problems with EF may not appear as frequently in children with OCD as they do in adults, because children do not have fully matured prefrontal networks in the brain – the area responsible for EF – and have less-developed executive functioning. Many executive and memory functions show the greatest progression after the age of 12 years — *Savage & Rauch, 2000.*

Additional research undoubtedly is needed to clarify the connection between EF and OCD in children and adolescents. Because some difficulties in this area have been suggested, however, and also because a considerable number of children with OCD have comorbid AD/HD and/or learning disabilities, school personnel should be aware of the potential for problems with EF among students who have OCD.

Family stress

It is essential that educators recognize family stress as a potentially debilitating situation that commonly occurs with OCD. Indeed, the results of a recent study examining the parental experience of having a child with OCD indicated that parents experience considerable distress regarding their child's OCD — *Storch, Lehmkuhl, et al., 2009*. Parents were anxious not only about the disorder itself but also how it would affect their child's future – e.g., the ability to pursue an education, maintain a job, and develop relationships.

Families of children with OCD are subject to the daily stressors all families experience, e.g., financial and job-related problems. In addition, they frequently experience OCD-related difficulties that wreak havoc with their lives. Witnessing a child's rituals can be very disturbing to family members. Situations in which family members are "forced" to participate in a child's rituals are perhaps even more stressful. The child may insist, for example, that a parent repeatedly check a door or wash a piece of silverware. In other cases, family members are prohibited from going outside so they do not bring germs or other "contaminants" into the home. Family members unwillingly participate in these rituals in order to "keep the peace." Indeed, parents often report that their child has "meltdowns" when OCD symptoms are not accommodated.

Additional stress results when parents take their child to multiple physicians, only to receive an incorrect diagnosis each time. Indeed, parents frequently consult with a number of professionals before their child is correctly diagnosed. In many cases, years have passed between the onset of the disorder and the time an appropriate diagnosis has been rendered. Currently, large-scale efforts are underway to educate the public – professionals and non-professionals alike – about OCD. Greater awareness should lead to earlier and more accurate diagnosis and intervention. An understanding of OCD is particularly important for school personnel, who represent a first line of defense in the identification of OCD due to their extensive interactions with students on a consistent basis.

Parents of children with OCD sometimes experience stress due to feelings of guilt that they are in some way responsible for their child's disorder. Parents increasingly are becoming educated about OCD and are aware, for example, that OCD has a strong genetic component. As a result, one or both parents may fear they have transmitted the illness.

Another contributor to family stress is the frustration parents experience trying to distinguish involuntary behavior (i.e., OCD-related behavior that is outside the child's control) from voluntary behavior (i.e., behavior that is unrelated to OCD and thus within the child's control). Determining if and when limits and consequences should be applied can be very difficult. Moreover, parental concerns and differences in opinion related to the management of the child with OCD frequently surface and may lead to marital tension.

Like parents, siblings of children and adolescents with OCD frequently experience high levels of stress. In some cases, they are ridiculed because of their brother's or sister's bizarre behavior. They even may be reluctant to invite friends into their homes. Moreover, siblings sometimes feel neglected by their parents; they feel the child with OCD "gets all the attention." And indeed, caring for a child with this disorder frequently requires an inordinate amount of parents' time and energy. Very importantly, siblings may harbor fears that they, too, will fall prey to OCD. Therefore, when a child suffers from OCD, it is important to attend to the needs of siblings, as well.

Note: The interested reader is referred to OCD: New Hope for the Family (Gravitz, 2004) in Appendix B for a more in-depth discussion of OCD and its impact on the family.

Ch:10

School personnel play a significant role in helping identify OCD in children and adolescents (see Chapter 16 for information on the contributions of school professionals to the identification and assessment of OCD). Because OCD is a psychiatric illness, however, they are not in a position to make a formal diagnosis; that responsibility falls to trained clinicians. A thorough psychiatric, developmental, and medical history ideally should be performed to make an accurate diagnosis of OCD and any comorbid disorders. Care also needs to be taken to distinguish OCD behavior from normal, developmentally-appropriate behavior (see Chapter 2). Although there are no biological tests for OCD, a complete physical exam may uncover some of the consequences of repetitive behavior (e.g., excessive hand washing, hair pulling). Because of the complexity of the diagnostic process, clinicians typically use a number of different instruments to make an assessment of OCD. Following is a brief description of some of the more commonly-used measures.

Diagnostic interviews

Mental health professionals frequently use diagnostic interviews to determine the presence of OCD. These interviews, which also are useful in determining the existence of comorbid disorders, generally have good reliability and validity. They must be administered by extensively-trained professionals, however, and may be time-consuming and expensive.

Two diagnostic interviews regularly used to diagnose OCD in children and adolescents are the Anxiety Disorders Interview Schedule for DSM-IV: Child and Parent Version — *Silverman & Albano, 2004* and the Schedule for Affective Disorders and Schizophrenia for School-Age Children-Present and Lifetime version — *Kaufman et al., 1997*. Both instruments are based upon the Diagnostic and Statistical Manual of Mental Disorders, Fourth Edition, and include screening questions to determine the presence of a number of childhood psychiatric disorders other than OCD.

Measures of OCD severity

Once a diagnosis of OCD has been established, it is important to ascertain the level of impairment and distress the OCD is causing. The most frequently used instrument, or "gold standard," for this purpose is the Children's Yale-Brown Obsessive-Compulsive Scale, or CY-BOCS — *Scahill et al., 1997*. Administered by a clinician to the parents and child, the CY-BOCS is a semi-structured inventory that assists in determining which OCD symptoms are present (i.e., obsessions and compulsions) and the severity of those symptoms. Although used less commonly, the Yale Children's Global Stress Index — *Findley et al., 2003* is another measure administered by a clinician to parents and the child to determine the child's level of psychosocial distress.

Child- and parent-report measures

Child- and parent-report measures frequently are used in the assessment of OCD in children and adolescents, for a variety of reasons. First, they can be completed quickly, with minimal training on the part of clinicians, and administered to several individuals at one time. As a result, they are useful as screening devices. Second, these measures can be re-administered throughout or after treatment to determine the effects of the treatment. Third, individuals sometimes are more comfortable completing questionnaires and will report symptoms more candidly without the health professional present. Self- and parent-report measures, however, are subject to potential concerns. Individuals may differ with regard to the interpretation of certain items or be careless about completing the measures. Moreover, the questionnaire may not contain specific OCD symptoms an individual experiences.

It is beyond the scope of this book to describe, in detail, each of the self- and parent-report measures used to assess OCD. Examples of some of the more commonly-used questionnaires, however, are the Children's Obsessional Compulsive Inventory — *Shafran et al., 2003*, Obsessive Compulsive Inventory, Child version — *Foa et al., 2010*, Children's Florida Obsessive-Compulsive Inventory — *Storch, Khanna, et al., 2009*, Child Obsessive Compulsive Impact Scale — *Piacentini, Peris, Bergman, Chang, & Jaffer, 2007*, and Family Accommodation Scale — *Calvocoressi et al., 1999*.

Teacher questionnaires

An OCD assessment is incomplete unless it includes information regarding a child's school functioning. School-aged children spend approximately 1,100 hours per year in the school setting. Moreover, teachers and other school personnel are a critical source of information with regard to their students. And yet in many cases, this vital resource remains untapped.

Although no validated teacher rating scales for OCD currently exist, the Florida Obsessive-Compulsive Student Inventory as well as a revised version of the Obsessive-Compulsive Scale from the Child Behavior Checklist (a tool commonly used in school settings) may be useful in providing information about a child's school functioning. The reader is referred to the section on teacher questionnaires in Chapter 16, in which these instruments are discussed in greater detail.

Although they frequently feel overwhelmed by what seems like mountains of paperwork, school personnel represent an invaluable resource in identifying OCD. Therefore, it is crucial that they complete rating scales or questionnaires for students undergoing an evaluation to assist in making an appropriate diagnosis.

71

Ch11

Within the body of literature on OCD in children and adolescents, two treatments consistently have been shown to be effective:

1. cognitive-behavioral therapy, or CBT, and

2. a class of medications called serotonin reuptake inhibitors (SRIs).

In 2008, the results of an extensive review of the literature on treatment for OCD in children and adolescents were published — *Watson & Rees, 2008*. The researchers who performed this review found 127 reports documenting the treatment of pediatric OCD, including the use of hypnosis, psychodynamic therapy, and homeopathic agents. Of these studies, 13 used randomized, controlled methodology, the "gold standard" for conducting research. Medication in the form of SRIs and/ or CBT were the only treatments for childhood OCD studied using this methodology, and both were found to be significantly superior to controls. Moreover, new practice parameters for the treatment of pediatric OCD developed by the American Academy of Child and Adolescent Psychiatry (in press) recommend CBT as the first line of treatment for children and adolescents with mild to moderate cases of OCD. A combination of CBT and medications is recommended in severe cases of OCD. This chapter addresses cognitive-behavioral therapy; Chapter 12 provides a discussion of medication.

What is cognitive-behavioral therapy?

CBT is a type of psychological treatment based upon both learning and cognitive principles. According to the cognitive-behavioral model of OCD, people engage in rituals to reduce the anxiety or discomfort associated with obsessions. Because rituals temporarily reduce anxiety/ distress, an individual's reliance on compulsive behavior persists and even becomes excessive. Moreover, relying on rituals prevents the individual from making a realistic assessment of the actual threat posed by the feared stimuli. Cognitive-behavioral therapy is designed to break this cycle.

A vast literature on cognitive-behavioral therapy for children and adolescents exists. Therefore, it is beyond the scope of this text to provide a comprehensive discussion of this process. Readers interested in more information on CBT are referred to four texts:

1. OCD in Children and Adolescents: A Cognitive Behavioral Manual — *March & Mulle, 1998,* written for clinicians;

2. Talking Back to OCD — *March, 2007,* which contains a step-by-step program for helping parents and teens use CBT to overcome OCD;

3. Freeing your Child from Obsessive-Compulsive Disorder — *Chansky, 2000,* written for parents of children and adolescents with OCD; and

4. Treatment of OCD in Children and Adolescents: Professional's Kit — *Wagner, 2007,* which contains valuable information on childhood OCD and CBT for clinicians.

A brief overview of CBT, however, is provided below.

The main components of CBT are exposure, response prevention, and cognitive therapy. With exposure, the individual is placed in situations that precipitate his or her fears, anxiety, or discomfort. Response prevention, also known as ritual prevention, involves having individuals refrain from engaging in rituals they typically perform to reduce their anxiety or distress. These two components form the core of CBT: exposure and response prevention (E/RP). The purpose of cognitive therapy is to identify and help the individual correct dysfunctional beliefs or maladaptive appraisals of intrusive thoughts.

Prior to beginning E/RP, the therapist educates both the child and the family about what OCD is and explains it as a neurobiological problem. The therapist also provides a detailed description of the treatment process.

The first step in E/RP consists of developing a rank-ordered list, or hierarchy, of all the child's fears and rituals as well as the situations in which these symptoms are likely to be triggered. The child then is systematically exposed to these situations, starting with situations that provoke minimal levels of anxiety or discomfort, and gradually working on tasks associated with increasing levels of anxiety or distress.

Exposures are followed by response prevention, in which the child is encouraged to resist carrying out rituals (at least for a period of time) to decrease the anxiety or distress. The child learns that the anxiety or discomfort created by the exposure will gradually decrease on its own, even without performing rituals that were thought to be necessary – a process known as "habituation." Habituation has been likened to what happens when an individual jumps into a swimming pool with cold water: while uncomfortable at first, the body acclimates to the temperature of the water, and, over time, the individual feels better – even though the temperature of the water has not changed. When habituation occurs within the context of E/RP, situations that previously triggered OCD symptoms are associated with less anxiety/distress and a reduced urge to ritualize.

For example, a child whose contamination fears have resulted in excessive hand washing may be asked to perform the next task on his predetermined hierarchy: pick up and handle a piece of paper retrieved from a wastebasket (exposure). The child then is asked to refrain from washing his hands for perhaps an hour (response prevention). Over time, the child may be asked to wait increasingly greater periods of time before washing. As this E/RP exercise is repeated, the anxiety associated with the "contaminant" lessens, as does the urge to ritualize. To reinforce E/RP performed in the therapist's office, the child is given homework assignments to complete between sessions with the clinician.

Cognitive therapy is used as an adjunct to E/RP to challenge maladaptive thinking or cognitions. For example, if the child with hand washing rituals has an inflated sense of responsibility for harm, he might be asked to challenge his current thinking – "If I touch that piece of paper from the wastebasket, I'll get a disease and then give it to everybody in my family" – and taught to replace his faulty thinking with a more valid alternative, e.g., "I've seen people touch paper in wastebaskets many times, and they've never gotten sick."

Impact of family involvement on CBT

As previously indicated, family members may have a significant impact on a child's OCD symptoms (see section on environmental factors in Chapter 7). They may accommodate the child or adolescent by participating in rituals or exacerbate OCD symptoms by being critical or hostile. Therefore, involving family members in treatment – especially when family members engage in the child's rituals – is key to the success of treatment. It is very important that family members be taught to:

1. decrease their involvement in the child's rituals, and

2. provide positive attention and support for the child's efforts during the CBT process (a process that can be fraught with challenges and frustration) for completing E/RP tasks and for other positive behaviors.

Although not directly related to the CBT process, two other important issues related to family functioning must be addressed to optimize the success of a child's CBT treatment. First, parents frequently blame themselves and carry a tremendous burden of guilt for their child's illness. Supporting parents and helping them move beyond these feelings may allow them to be more effective partners in the treatment process. Second, when other family members have OCD, it is important that they seek treatment, as well.

Success of CBT

Although there is variation among studies, it has been suggested that 57-88% of children and adolescents who receive CBT for OCD respond to this form of treatment — *Lewin, Storch, Geffken, Goodman, & Murphy, 2006*. Moreover, treatment gains associated with CBT frequently are maintained over time. By contrast, follow-up studies have indicated that treatment gains associated with medication often do not continue with the cessation of medication. The results of one study, for example, indicated that at 9-month follow-up, approximately 5% of a group of children treated with group CBT for 12 weeks relapsed, whereas 50% of a group of youth treated with medication for 12 weeks experienced a relapse — *Flament et al., 2007*. More recent research underscores the long-term durability of CBT for children and adolescents with OCD. In one study, treatment gains continued to occur 24-36 months after original treatment — *Shalev, et al., 2009*. The results of another study indicated that cognitive-behavioral family treatment for young people with OCD was effective 7 years after treatment — *O'Leary, Barrett, & Fjermestad, 2009*.

A number of factors have been studied to determine their potential impact on the effectiveness of CBT. In general, research has indicated that neither age nor gender has a significant effect on the success of CBT in children and adolescents. A number of other factors appear to be associated with a poorer response to treatment, however, including:

1. a higher number and severity level of obsessions and compulsions;

2. greater OCD-related academic and functional impairment;

3. the presence of hoarding and sexual/religious symptoms (although some research has indicated that response to CBT does not differ substantially across OCD subtypes);

4. greater parental stress, negative family interactions, and family dysfunction;

5. the presence of OCD or another anxiety disorder in a parent;

6. impaired cognitive level (e.g., very young, developmental delay, cognitive disability);

7. poor insight regarding the senselessness of symptoms; and

8. comorbidity with certain disorders (e.g., disruptive behavior disorder, AD/HD) — Keeley, Storch, Merlo, & Geffken, 2008; Storch, Merlo, Larson, et al., 2008.

Several factors have been associated with a good response to CBT, including fewer and less-disabling OCD symptoms and the presence of insight into the disorder. Treatment also results in better outcomes when the child is willing to participate in CBT, developmentally capable of monitoring and reporting symptoms, and motivated to eliminate rituals and other symptoms. Family involvement in CBT also appears to be associated with better results: of the studies examining CBT for children and adolescents with OCD, those in which families were actively involved in CBT reported among the highest levels of improvement — Keeley et al., 2008; Storch, Merlo, Larson, et al., 2008.

Delivery of CBT services

Traditional CBT typically is delivered on an individual basis by a trained therapist via one-hour, weekly sessions for approximately 12-16 weeks. The duration of treatment may vary, however, depending upon the individual. Follow-up, or "booster," sessions are provided after treatment.

Alternatives to this traditional service delivery model have been explored. Some research indicates that CBT provided in group settings is as effective as individual sessions. Researchers also have compared intensive family-based CBT (14, 90-minute sessions over three weeks) to more traditional, weekly, family-based therapy (14, weekly, 90-minute sessions) — *Storch, Geffken, et al., 2007*. The results showed that youth treated with either intensive or weekly therapy showed marked improvement in symptoms (with some slight advantages for intensive therapy immediately after treatment), and gains largely were maintained over time.

The success of intensive CBT (I-CBT) has important implications for treating children and adolescents with OCD. Despite its documented efficacy, traditional CBT has been unavailable to a substantial segment of the population for a number of possible reasons. First, the number of qualified mental health professionals trained in CBT for OCD is limited; indeed, overall awareness of this approach is limited. It may be that clinicians-in-training receive inadequate exposure to cognitive-behavioral therapy, in general, and CBT for OCD specifically. Second, the typical mental health professional may not see a sufficient number of cases of pediatric OCD, as compared to other anxiety disorders, to warrant receiving CBT training for OCD. This is particularly true in more rural areas (CBT frequently is more readily available in areas associated with major medical centers). Third, there may be some reticence on the part of therapists to abandon older, preferred approaches, in favor of newer techniques. Because of the limited availability of CBT, clinicians frequently prescribe medication for OCD.

Intensive CBT may help reduce the frequency with which OCD is treated with medication alone. Because I-CBT is shorter in duration than traditional CBT (e.g., 3 weeks compared to 14 weeks), families may be willing and able to work their schedules around a few weeks of treatment, especially when treatment centers are more distant. As a result, clinicians could provide services to greater numbers of children and adolescents with OCD. In addition to increasing access to treatment, another benefit of I-CBT is that improvement in OCD symptoms occurs more rapidly. Moreover, intensive forms of CBT have been shown to be effective for individuals who are treatment refractory, i.e., they have not experienced success with other, previous treatments for OCD (e.g., traditional CBT, medication, etc.). Preliminary research even has indicated that I-CBT is effective in treating the PANDAS subtype of OCD — *Storch, Murphy, Geffken, et al., 2006* (see Chapter 7 on causes of OCD for a discussion of PANDAS).

CBT for young children

The vast majority of research on CBT in children and adolescents has been conducted on young people over 7 years of age. To address this concern, a group of researchers developed a CBT program that considers the unique characteristics of very young children (5-8 years of age) with OCD — *Freeman et al., 2007*. Although this system is adapted from other, well-established programs for youth with OCD, it includes many elements that focus on the specific needs of very young children. For example, emphasis is placed upon the therapist's role in carefully distinguishing OCD symptoms from normal, developmentally-appropriate rituals, which are very common in this age group. The therapist also uses age-appropriate language, visual imagery, examples, and metaphors (e.g., "OCD is a monster you have to boss back") to facilitate explanations. Exposure and response prevention exercises occur within the context of play sessions, and rewards for completing these exercises (e.g., verbal praise and encouragement, tangible rewards, and privileges) are carefully built into the program.

Perhaps the highlight of this program is that parent involvement gradually is increased so that by the end of treatment, parents are actually guiding exposure completion during therapy sessions with the support of the therapist. As a result, parents are able to translate treatment from the office to home more effectively. Parents also are taught how to tolerate the anxiety they experience as a result of their child's distress. Although traditional CBT programs for children and adolescents with OCD include parental involvement, they are characterized by a greater focus on one-to-one interaction between the therapist and the child.

The results of the first study in which a group of children were treated using the early childhood version of CBT indicated that 69% of the children in the program attained a clinical remission, as compared to 20% of the children in the control group, who received relaxation training — *Freeman et al., 2008*. Another large-scale study examining the effectiveness of early childhood CBT currently underway also is likely to yield good results — *E. Storch, personal communication, September 4, 2010*.

Intervention at a very early stage is vital to helping young children with OCD learn skills to reduce their symptoms before patterns of problematic behavior are developed. If these skills are in place when important transitions such as the beginning of formal schooling occur, the potential impact of OCD on learning and behavior may be minimized.

Ch:12

MEDICATION TREATMENT OF OCD

A number of studies have demonstrated that CBT is more effective than medication in treating pediatric OCD. CBT also has been shown to be more durable than medications (i.e., the positive effects of treatment are longer-lasting) and safer (drugs always carry the potential for side effects). However, as previously indicated, large numbers of individuals do not have access to CBT. Moreover, in some cases, individuals are unwilling to participate in CBT (e.g., they do not see the senselessness of their obsessions and compulsions; they have difficulty engaging in exposures), or they are unresponsive to CBT. In these cases, medications may be prescribed to treat OCD. Importantly, many individuals are more willing to engage in CBT after being on medication for a period of time.

Medications used to treat childhood OCD

Clomipramine (Anafranil) is an older medication that has been used to treat children and adolescents with OCD for many years. Anafranil is a type of drug known as a serotonin reuptake inhibitor (SRI), which causes the neurotransmitter serotonin to be more available at the neuron level in the brain (more specifically, the synapse). It belongs to a class of drugs known as tricyclic antidepressants and has been approved by the FDA for use with children 10 years of age and above.

Several controlled studies have shown that Anafranil is effective in treating childhood OCD. It has been associated with many potentially harmful side effects, however, including seizure risk, weight gain, and negative cardiovascular effects. The serious side effect profile of Anafranil has led experts to recommend another class of antidepressant medications, the *selective* serotonin reuptake inhibitors, as the first line of medication treatment. Selective serotonin reuptake inhibitors, or SSRIs, are associated with fewer side effects than Anafranil.

Like Anafranil, the SSRIs make serotonin more available at the synapse level. Three SSRIs have been approved by the Food and Drug Administration (FDA) for use with children: sertraline (Zoloft), for children 6 years of age and over; fluoxetine (Prozac), for children aged 7 years and above; and fluvoxamine (Luvox), for children 8 years of age and over. In some cases, a medication is used "off-label" when it is administered to treat a condition or an age group not specifically listed on its prescribing label as an FDA-approved use. Thus, although certain SSRIs, e.g., paroxetine (Paxil) and citalopram (Celexa) – as well as non-SSRI medications such as venlafaxine (Effexor) – are not FDA approved for treating childhood OCD, physicians do prescribe these drugs for that purpose.

Side effects of OCD medication

Like all drugs, SSRIs have potential side effects. Side effects such as nausea, increased anxiety, jitteriness, and insomnia are relatively common, especially during the initial phase of treatment. Although side effects subside in many cases, they may occur throughout treatment. Beginning with low doses of medication and gradually or slowly increasing the dose until the optimal level is reached may help reduce the presence of side effects.

One potential side effect of antidepressants in children and adolescents is a phenomenon known as behavioral activation. Behavioral activation encompasses a variety of symptoms, including agitation, aggression, irritability, impulsivity, hyperactivity, increased depression or anxiety, and, among a small fraction of youth, an increased risk for suicidality – suicidal thinking and behavior. Indeed, in October of 2004, the Federal Drug Administration issued a black box warning (i.e., a warning that appears on the package insert of prescription drugs) alerting health care providers to the potential risk of increased suicidality among young people taking antidepressants. Studies have indicated that this risk pertains not only to children and adolescents with depression but also to those with OCD and other anxiety disorders. Multiple treatment studies have provided evidence, however, that the benefits of using SSRIs to treat pediatric OCD generally outweigh the risks. Whenever a child or adolescent is taking an antidepressant, rigorous clinical monitoring for suicidal ideation, suicidal behavior, and other troubling behaviors is essential. Potential safety concerns associated with medication lend support to the implementation of cognitive-behavioral therapy prior to medication as an intervention for pediatric OCD.

Other medication-related issues

Research has not yet supported the efficacy of one SSRI over another. Therefore, the choice of SSRI should be determined carefully by considering the child's medical history, the potential side effects of each SSRI (e.g., Prozac has been associated with more agitation; Zoloft may have more gastrointestinal effects such as loose stools), and the possibility of a negative interaction with another drug the child is taking.

Experts generally recommend that a child or adolescent take an SSRI for 12 weeks at an adequate dose before another SSRI is tried. Some individuals may not experience an initial response to a drug for 6-8 weeks, and a maximal response may take 20 weeks. During medication treatment, the child should be monitored carefully, especially during the early phases. Some experts recommend that when a good medication is found, the child should stay on it for at least a year. At that point, it should be tapered slowly and discontinued only after two years have passed.

As previously indicated, a substantial number of individuals experience a return in symptoms once medication is withdrawn. Moreover, it has been estimated that individuals taking medication for OCD experience only about a 30-40% reduction in OCD symptoms — *The Pediatric OCD Treatment Team, 2004*, leaving the majority of patients who respond to drugs with residual symptoms. Many experts believe that adding CBT to medication, whenever possible, is the best strategy for improving treatment outcomes. Indeed, a recent study of 30 youth with a primary diagnosis of OCD who responded either partially or not at all to two or more medication trials received 14 sessions of intensive family-based CBT — *Storch, Lehmkuhl, et al., 2010*. At both post-treatment and follow-up, 80% of the participants were considered improved, and the severity of OCD symptoms was reduced by 54%.

When children and adolescents are treatment refractory, or unresponsive to CBT and trials with a number of different SSRIs, clinicians sometimes add another drug to produce a more potent effect, overall (also known as augmentation therapy). There is scant research, however, regarding drug augmentation therapy in youth with OCD.

Of note is that there are several residential treatment facilities that provide treatment for children and/or adolescents with OCD who fail to benefit from outpatient therapy. Information on these facilities is available at the website for the International Obsessive-Compulsive Disorder Foundation: *www.ocfoundation.org*.

ch:13

Treating childhood OCD: CBT, medication, or both?

A large body of literature addresses treatment for childhood OCD, most of which focuses on CBT and/or SRIs. And indeed, these two forms of therapy represent the cornerstone of OCD treatment not only for children and adolescents but also for adults. What do experts recommend, however, as best practice for treating young people with OCD? Two landmark reports provide significant guidance on this question.

First, the American Academy of Child and Adolescent Psychiatry (AACAP) publishes practice parameters for numerous disorders (e.g., AD/HD, autism, depressive disorders) to assist clinicians in providing highly-effective assessment and treatment that reflect the best available scientific evidence and clinical consensus. The new AACAP practice parameters for the treatment of pediatric OCD (in press) recommend CBT as the first line of treatment for children and adolescents with mild to moderate cases of OCD; a combination of CBT and medications is recommended for severe cases of OCD.

Second, in 2004, The Pediatric OCD Treatment Study Team released the results of the first, large-scale study to compare the effects of CBT, medication (the SSRI Zoloft), or the combination of CBT and medication. Known as POTS I, this randomized, controlled trial was conducted at three academic centers in the U.S.: Duke University, the University of Pennsylvania, and Brown University. It involved 112 children and adolescents aged 7 through 17 with a primary diagnosis of OCD (97 of the original 112 participants completed the full 12 weeks of treatment). The results of the study indicated that patients treated with CBT alone or in combination with Zoloft showed the highest probability of improvement. Of note is that although the Duke University results favored combination therapy over CBT alone, the results for CBT alone at the University of Pennsylvania site were excellent – as good as combined treatment. On the basis of these findings, the researchers concluded that children and adolescents with OCD should begin treatment with CBT alone or CBT plus an SSRI.

Other treatments for childhood OCD

Although CBT and/or medication represent the cornerstone of treatment for children and adolescents with OCD, there are many other critical pieces in the treatment "pie." Although not every component will be part of the treatment plan for all young people and their families, each of them should be considered carefully.

Supportive psychotherapy. It is important to note that currently, there is no evidence to support a number of "talk therapies" for treating pediatric OCD, including psychoanalytic, relaxation, insight-oriented, supportive, or play-based therapies. It is equally important to note, however, that supportive therapy may help children manage conflicts due to OCD, including difficulties with school, peers, and family members. Family members also may benefit from supportive therapy (most CBT approaches involve families in treatment). A parent may need direction in terms of how to handle angry struggles with the child, for example, or cope with family disruption and stress that often accompany OCD.

Support groups. Many individuals with OCD and their family members find OCD support groups extremely valuable. There are a number of different types of support groups for OCD; some are free of charge while others (especially those led by professionals) charge a fee. Professionally-assisted support groups are led by mental health professionals and provide a form of group therapy. Another type of support group is the mutual self-help group, which typically is run by individuals who have recovered from OCD and presently are managing their symptoms. Mutual self-help groups are educational and supportive in nature rather than therapeutic. A third type of support group is the 12-step group. A network of Obsessive Compulsive Anonymous groups, which are run similarly to Alcoholics Anonymous, is available throughout the United States. Giving Obsessive-Compulsives Another Lifestyle (G.O.A.L), a fourth type of support group, is designed to prevent OCD relapses by working on exposure and response prevention tasks in group therapy. Although G.O.A.L. groups are professionally-led, clinicians provide technical information only; the group is run by the members themselves.

While many individuals prefer attending support groups in person, others prefer the ease and anonymity of online support groups. The website for the International OCD Foundation (*www.ocfoundation.org*) contains a wealth of information regarding in-person and online support groups.

Patient advocacy groups. Another facet of OCD treatment is not-for-profit patient advocacy groups, many of which have been established over the years. Advocacy groups generally work to increase public and professional awareness of OCD, educate and support people with OCD and their families/friends, and encourage research into new treatments and a cure. Perhaps the most well-recognized advocacy group is the International OCD Foundation (currently located in Boston, MA), which has affiliates in several different states. The website for the International OCD Foundation (*www.ocfoundation.org*) contains information on each of its affiliates. Another excellent patient advocacy group is OCD Chicago. The website for this group (*www.ocdchicago.org*) contains a special segment specifically designed for school personnel.

Educational interventions. Whenever a child or adolescent has OCD, it is critical to assess his or her functioning at school. For some young people, OCD is mild and poses no difficulties in the school setting. For others, however, OCD has a significantly negative impact on educational, social, and behavioral performance. Unless and until OCD-related school issues are addressed, treatment for OCD is incomplete. Part V of this book is devoted entirely to OCD in the schools.

Long-term outcome of OCD in children and adolescents

In 2004, the results of a large meta-analysis (an analysis of combined past studies) of the long-term outcome of OCD in children and adolescents were published — *Stewart et al., 2004*. This meta-analysis included only studies in which follow-up periods were at least one year in duration. The results indicated that the combined, average persistence rate was 41% for full-blown OCD and 60% for the presence of *any* OCD. Thus, there was an overall remission rate (i.e., criteria for full or subthreshold OCD were not met) of 40%. Persistence of OCD at follow-up was predicted by an earlier age of onset, longer duration of OCD symptoms at baseline (prior to treatment), and inpatient status. Severity of symptoms after initial treatment and psychiatric comorbidity also appeared to be associated with a poorer long-term outcome.

A more recent study examined a cohort of 45 young adults with childhood-onset OCD who had been treated an average of 9 years earlier — *Bloch et al., 2009*. The results of this study indicated that at follow-up, 44% of the adults had subclinical obsessive-compulsive symptoms. A number of factors were associated with the persistence of OCD, including the presence of hoarding symptoms, female gender, and severity of childhood symptoms.

Taken together, the results of these studies:

1. point to a number of factors associated with the persistence of OCD symptoms into adulthood, and

2. suggest that a higher number of childhood cases of OCD improve or remit by adulthood than previously thought.

Indeed, earlier studies of childhood OCD indicated that OCD usually was a chronic and debilitating disorder. Moreover, as previously indicated, up to 80% of adults with OCD report onset of the disorder during childhood. Because estimates of the prevalence of OCD are very similar in pediatric and adult OCD, logic dictates that in some children and adolescents, OCD becomes subclinical or even remits over time.

Although outcomes may have improved over the years, OCD continues to be a significant disorder for a substantial percentage of young people. Particularly if left untreated, OCD has the potential to become a chronic disorder that not only is characterized by substantial impairment in family, social, and educational functioning but also poses a higher risk for other psychiatric problems in adulthood. Without a formal diagnosis, young people are unaware that they have obsessive-compulsive disorder – a real disorder with a real name. In many cases, they believe they are the only ones on the entire planet who could possibly be thinking such "crazy" thoughts or engaging in such bizarre behaviors. These beliefs can exacerbate the feelings of isolation and loneliness they already are experiencing. Thus, pediatric OCD deserves close attention from school personnel, health professionals, and parents alike – individuals who have the potential to make a huge difference in preventing childhood OCD from becoming a chronic disorder with severe long-term effects on mental health and well-being.

Future treatment of childhood OCD

Although it can be managed – and in many cases, managed extremely
well – there currently is no cure for OCD. Ongoing research hopefully
will lead to a long-awaited cure. New ideas and methods for improving
OCD treatments for children and adolescents continually are emerging,
however, begging a number of questions: "What does the future hold
for the treatment of childhood OCD?" Will cognitive-behavioral therapy
regularly incorporate virtual reality into exposure and response
prevention exercises? Do vitamin supplements play a potential role in
treating pediatric OCD? Will physical exercise be incorporated into
every treatment plan for young people with OCD? Will future genetic
studies reveal children who are more vulnerable to OCD and lead to
the implementation of prevention programs? Will CBT be used as an
intervention for early signs of OCD in children and adolescents, before
it becomes a disorder? What role, if any, will deep brain stimulation
(a procedure in which electrodes that emit electrical signals are
permanently implanted in a person's brain to alter brain circuitry) play
in treating children and adolescents with OCD? The future is certain
to hold answers to these and many other questions that hopefully will
improve the quality of life for hundreds of thousands of young people
all over the world who struggle with OCD.

ch:14

THE IMPACT OF OCD IN THE SCHOOL SETTING

What are the Effects of OCD on School Functioning? How Can School Personnel Help?

Part IV

92

As with all disorders, there is a range not only in the severity level of OCD but also the contexts in which it occurs. A child's OCD symptoms may be very mild and interfere minimally with functioning at home, school, or in the community. Some children with OCD experience symptoms at home but not at school; school actually may keep them busy and provide a respite from the intrusion of the disorder. For others, OCD triggers are more challenging at school than at home. For many young people, however, OCD encroaches upon every aspect of their lives at home, in school, and in the community.

Children sometimes are able to suppress or hide their symptoms at school or substitute mental rituals for overt rituals (e.g., mentally repeating a specific number pattern may take the place of hand washing). These students work diligently, expending an enormous amount of energy – even to the point of becoming extremely fatigued – just to "keep it together;" so much so, in fact, that school personnel may be surprised to learn that they have OCD.

Suppressing symptoms during the school day may come at great cost to these students. Once they arrive home, they sometimes engage in a frenzy of ritualizing — Adams & Burke, 1999, even to the point of "making up" rituals that weren't performed at school. This situation has the potential to set the stage for conflict between parents and educators. Parents and other family members may be drained by the child's OCD symptoms at home, while school personnel are witnessing no problems at school. It even may be difficult for school professionals to believe that parents are providing an accurate account of the situation at home. In these circumstances, it is critical that school staff take parents at their word and offer as much support as possible.

What does it feel like to have OCD at school?

To appreciate the extent to which OCD can impair school functioning, an account of one young boy's struggles with OCD in school is provided here. This story is excerpted from the book *It's the Thought that Counts* by Jared Kant, a young man with OCD. The following represents just a sample of Jared's real-life struggles with OCD in middle school.

Locker Room Meltdown

One day, it went too far even by OCD standards—and that's far indeed. I was running later than usual, and everyone else had already scuttled out the double doors leading from the locker room. I began changing into my gym clothes, but somewhere along the line, the anxious thoughts looping through my brain took over, and I lost track of everything else. When I finally snapped out of it, I realized, much to my confusion and distress, that I wasn't wearing any clothes except my socks and shoes. Standing there nearly nude in the middle of the floor, I panicked.

I was terrified that the other students would return to change back into their regular clothes and find me still semi-naked. Yet I had to fight with my brain for several minutes to put on even a marginally decent number of clothes. Finally, I collapsed onto the floor, crying. Unable to shake my mind free from obsessions, I felt mentally stuck and physically rooted to the ground. Unless someone I trusted could assure me that it was perfectly fine to keep dressing, I wasn't going to budge from that spot. I needed reassurance from a person of authority that a cataclysm wasn't going to happen, or if it did, that it would have little or nothing to do with the way I got dressed.

Eventually, I started yelling to see if anyone—by that point, it didn't matter who—would hear me and come to bail me out from my personal jail. My voice became hoarse from yelling so much. I sobbed on the dirty floor, and I wondered if I was doomed to stay on that nasty spot until I starved to death or caught some fatal illness from the filth.

At that moment, the coach happened to go into his office, and he heard me cry out. He came into the locker room, concerned and confused. Although he didn't know much about OCD, the coach, like all the faculty, was aware that I had something wrong with my head, that I would get scared for no apparent reason, and that I would often need the help of adults, whether I liked it or not.

Looking back, I think the coach must have been considering the rules about contact with a student, as it was rather obvious that what I really needed was a hug. In the end, I think he weighed the risk and decided to hell with it. He came over, knelt beside me, and wiped my tears until I looked up in choking sobs. Then he asked me what had happened. To be honest, I didn't really know, and I told him as much.

What are the Effects of OCD on School Functioning? How Can School Personnel Help?

Part IV

93

Just Following Orders

I wonder in retrospect how that must have sounded. I was crying on a grimy locker room floor, disoriented and anxious. Unaware of how I had reached the point of immobility, I was still clinging to the orders in my head that said to stay put until someone else told me what to do.

I cried for a long time. Another student—a good-hearted friend who cared about my condition and wanted to help—wandered into the locker room. Ironically, I think he was hoping to skip out of extra laps around the gym for some insubordination. Luckily for him, good Samaritans are more in demand than discipline cases. The coach told my friend to contact the other gym teachers and explain that the boys' locker room was temporarily closed and gym students would be excused from other classes until they could change.

The coach sat with me and coached me through getting dressed. He assured me that no harm would befall me or anyone else if I opened my locker and finished putting on my clothes. When I was finally dressed, I felt a ripple of fatigue wash through my body. It's incredibly draining to put that much effort into anything. I collapsed against the coach and cried. He asked what else he could do to help, and I thanked God for this man who had wandered through by sheer providence and helped me overcome the immobilizing effects of anxiety.

At last, I was ready to leave. Unseen by the other students, I exited the locker room and went to my advisor's office, where I could catch my breath and get my bearings. After I was gone, the locker room was reopened. My classmates changed into their regular clothes without ever realizing how close they had come to witnessing one of my less-than-stellar moments. That was the scariest part of the whole disease for me. OCD was unpredictable, awkward, and embarrassing. It would crop up in the most inconvenient places—although I think it's safe to say there's really no such thing as a good place for an OCD attack.

THE THOUGHT THAT COUNTS — *By Kant, Franklin & Andrews (2008) 806w from pp. 52-54. By permission of Oxford University Press*

What are the Effects of OCD on School Functioning? How Can School Personnel Help?

Part IV

94

OCD simulations

One technique commonly used to facilitate an understanding of how it feels to have a certain disability is the use of simulation exercises. Participants in such exercises may be asked to put on a pair of glasses smeared with lotion to simulate low vision or to wear a blindfold to get a sense of being blind. Or an individual may be placed in a wheelchair and instructed to maneuver around a room in an attempt to replicate an orthopedic disability. These exercises have been criticized for their lack of authenticity and the atmosphere of levity with which they often are associated. Furthermore, simulations have been criticized for promoting negative reactions among participants that reflect pity (e.g., "How terrible it must be to be deaf"), superiority, sadness, or even misunderstanding – all of which undeniably are unintended consequences – instead of promoting an appreciation for what it might be like to have a particular disability.

Despite these criticisms, this author has used OCD simulations with school personnel for a number of years as empathy-building exercises. And they do appear to convey a measure of understanding that cannot be communicated via facts and figures. In that spirit, the following simulation activities are provided to promote an appreciation for how OCD may interfere with a student's school functioning.

Simulation 1
••••••••••••••••

Directions: Copy the following set of simple math problems on a separate piece of paper and complete them. There is one glitch, however. You happen to be a student with OCD who experiences severe number obsessions. For you, 7's and 9's are "bad" numbers; 2's and 4's are "good" or "safe" numbers. Therefore, as you complete the problems, any time you see a 7 or 9, you must find a 2 or 4 somewhere on your sheet to reduce the anxiety associated with seeing a 7 or 9. If you have to write a 7 or 9, you must write a 2 or 4 somewhere on the paper, once again to neutralize or undo the anxiety created by having to write a 7 or 9. Give yourself one minute to do these math problems. When you are done, ask yourself the questions below the problems.

6278	882	7606	3540	5683	508
x 47	+966	-5102	-1368	+2977	x 62

Questions to ask yourself:

1. What were you thinking as you were doing the problems?

2. How were you feeling as you were doing the exercise?

3. Did your simulated OCD affect your ability to complete the task?

4. How many of these (simple) problems were you able to complete in 1 minute?

Simulation 2
. . . .

Directions: Below is the opening passage from the novel *Through the Looking-Glass* by Lewis Carroll. Simply read the passage silently. However, you have OCD and fear that if you don't count every lowercase "a" in each line, something terrible will happen to your family. Therefore, as you read, be sure to keep track of how many lowercase a's appear in each line. You have 2 minutes to complete it (set a timer to keep track of your time). When you're done, ask yourself the questions below the passage.

CHAPTER I. Looking-Glass house

One thing was certain, that the WHITE kitten had had nothing to do with it:--it was the black kitten's fault entirely. For the white kitten had been having its face washed by the old cat for the last quarter of an hour (and bearing it pretty well, considering); so you see that it COULDN'T have had any hand in the mischief.

The way Dinah washed her children's faces was this: first she held the poor thing down by its ear with one paw, and then with the other paw she rubbed its face all over, the wrong way, beginning at the nose: and just now, as I said, she was hard at work on the white kitten, which was lying quite still and trying to purr--no doubt feeling that it was all meant for its good.

What are the Effects of OCD on School Functioning? How Can School Personnel Help?

Part IV

96

What are the Effects of OCD on School Functioning? How Can School Personnel Help?

Part IV

97

But the black kitten had been finished with earlier in the afternoon, and so, while Alice was sitting curled up in a corner of the great arm-chair, half talking to herself and half asleep, the kitten had been having a grand game of romps with the ball of worsted Alice had been trying to wind up, and had been rolling it up and down till it had all come undone again; and there it was, spread over the hearth-rug, all knots and tangles, with the kitten running after its own tail in the middle.

'Oh, you wicked little thing!' cried Alice, catching up the kitten, and giving it a little kiss to make it understand that it was in disgrace. 'Really, Dinah ought to have taught you better manners! You OUGHT, Dinah, you know you ought!' she added, looking reproachfully at the old cat, and speaking in as cross a voice as she could manage--and then she scrambled back into the arm-chair, taking the kitten and the worsted with her, and began winding up the ball again. But she didn't get on very fast, as she was talking all the time, sometimes to the kitten, and sometimes to herself. Kitty sat very demurely on her knee, pretending to watch the progress of the winding, and now and then putting out one paw and gently touching the ball, as if it would be glad to help, if it might.

THROUGH THE LOOKING-GLASS — *By Lewis Carroll*
The Millennium Fulcrum Edition 1.7

Questions to ask yourself:

1. What were you thinking as you read this passage?

2. How were you feeling as you were doing the exercise?

3. Did your simulated OCD affect your ability to complete the task?

4. How far were you able to read in 2 minutes?

5. How well did you comprehend what you read?

Impact of OCD on academic performance

The above simulations reveal a very important fact: OCD can exact a heavy toll on the academic performance of children and adolescents with OCD – young people who typically have average to above-average intelligence levels. Obsessions can be extremely intrusive and interfere with normal thinking or information processing. Attention is a limited resource, and short-term (working) memory is limited in duration – approximately 5-20 seconds, depending upon the individual. If the majority of one's attention and working memory is devoted to obsessive thoughts and the need to ritualize, few, if any, cognitive resources are available for academic assignments.

Students experiencing obsessions and compulsions may appear to be "stuck" or fixated on certain points and lose the need or ability to go on. OCD may interfere with the student's capacity to listen in class, follow directions, and concentrate on school assignments. Moreover, students who leave the classroom to carry out rituals (e.g., go to the bathroom to wash hands) may miss out on potentially important academic information. The interference created by obsessions and compulsions may delay or halt work completion, lead to a decrease in work production, and result in poor or failing grades. In some cases, deterioration of academic performance may be abrupt and dramatic.

It is important to mention that OCD symptoms may be mistaken for inattentiveness and even AD/HD. In reality, the child is paying attention, but not to the task at hand. Indeed, he or she may be unable to disengage attention from obsessions and compulsions. As aptly stated by a group of OCD researchers, "Cognitions associated with OCD might best be described as an inability to inhibit and direct attention from distressing thoughts and images toward more pleasant or less distressing mental experiences" — *Björgvinsson et al., 2007, p. 365*. As noted in the section on psychosocial functioning in Chapter 9, research supports attention-related difficulties among children and adolescents with OCD: researchers in two independent studies (one conducted in the U.S. and the other in Norway) found that one of the top two school-related problems reported by both parents and children was concentrating on work.

What are the Effects of OCD on School Functioning? How Can School Personnel Help?

Part IV

98

Students with OCD also may appear as if they are noncompliant. During an OCD episode, they may not be able to follow the teacher's directions, but they are complying with OCD's demands – dutifully carrying out rituals, for example, in order to prevent something terrible from happening. Moreover, these students sometimes appear to the outside observer as if they are daydreaming, unmotivated, or – worse yet – lazy. When one considers the mental torment that many of these students endure, it is evident that such characterizations are inappropriate and unwarranted.

In addition, tardiness and school absenteeism may have a negative impact on the school performance of youth with OCD. Rituals can be tedious, time-consuming, and interfere with sleep, sometimes resulting in a child's being late to school (see section on sleep problems in Chapter 9). Students may become so frustrated having to complete certain rituals before school day after day that they opt to skip school entirely. In some cases, children and adolescents are distressed by peer ridicule to the point that they cannot bear going to school. In other instances, students avoid school because they fear school-based stimuli that trigger obsessions and compulsions. Tardiness and absenteeism can result in significant gaps in instruction which, in turn, may lead to serious academic problems. A child who misses instruction in important skills is likely to have difficulty learning concepts and new information that build upon those skills.

Impact of OCD on social functioning

Social competence, which is closely linked to academic performance, can be severely affected by OCD. Studies of children and adolescents with OCD report that many of these young people are withdrawn and isolated from peers and have few, if any, friendships. Several factors may contribute to social difficulties.

First, OCD symptoms may render interaction with peers extremely difficult. Fears of being contaminated due to touching others, for instance, may preclude involvement in contact sports (e.g., football, hockey). Second, some children and adolescents have little time for friends, family, or social activities because ritualizing devours so much time outside of school. In addition to performing rituals they normally complete at home, they also may carry out rituals suppressed at school. Moreover, homework may consume a huge chunk of the child's time due

What are the Effects of OCD on School Functioning? How Can School Personnel Help?

Part IV

99

to OCD symptoms. Third, many children are physically and mentally exhausted by their obsessions and compulsions, especially when they suppress them during the school day. The energy students expend concealing OCD at school can be draining, and they simply are too fatigued to participate in sports or other social activities. Fourth, because OCD rituals may involve behavior that appears peculiar to others (e.g., holding one's breath to avoid being contaminated; hoarding scraps of paper, stones, glass, etc., picked up from the playground; walking on the sidewalk in a circuitous fashion to circumvent cracks), some children and adolescents prefer to retreat from peers rather than risk social rejection, humiliation, or bullying. Finally, OCD rituals sometimes disturb or disrupt other students in the classroom. When rituals are interrupted by peers or classroom events, students with OCD may become agitated or even panicked, leading to verbal outbursts. Such incidents can have an extremely negative effect on social acceptance.

What are the Effects of OCD on School Functioning? How Can School Personnel Help?

Part IV

Ch:15

GENERAL AND SPECIFIC EFFECTS OF OCD ON SCHOOL BEHAVIOR

Although OCD is very idiosyncratic and may manifest in a myriad of
ways, it is important that school personnel be aware of some of the
more common manifestations of OCD at school. Following is a list
of a number of general difficulties students with OCD experience.

General school-related problems associated with OCD

• Difficulty with transitions during the school day

• Difficulties with changes or interruptions in school routines

• Habitual tardiness (e.g., engaging in eating, dressing, washing
rituals before school)

• School absenteeism/school avoidance (e.g., contamination
concerns at school; fear of being teased/bullied; fear harm will
come to family if student leaves home)

• Difficulty maneuvering/getting around school (e.g., fear of
becoming contaminated by others or objects; touching rituals;
walking rituals)

• Poor attention and concentration

• Outside appearance of being inattentive, distracted, noncompliant,
lazy

• Outside appearance of being fidgety and distracted (engaging in
rituals, e.g., opening and shutting book bag to make sure all books
and writing utensils are there)

• Working very slowly/difficulty completing school assignments, tests,
homework (e.g., checking answers, rewriting answers, rereading
questions, erasing, writing letters/numbers until they are "perfect")

• Working quickly and impulsively to guard against the intrusion
of OCD symptoms

• Procrastination (e.g., avoiding work because it has to be done
perfectly)

• Difficulty taking notes (e.g., poor concentration, rechecking,
rewriting; doubting what teacher said)

What are the Effects of OCD on School Functioning? How Can School
Personnel Help?

Part IV

102

- Writing difficulties

- Reading difficulties

- Classroom disruption due to OCD symptoms (e.g., disruption of lessons due to compulsive questioning); may include outbursts, arguments (e.g., if a ritual is interrupted by a peer or an activity)

- Dropping out of or avoiding sports/social activities

- Low self-esteem; feelings of demoralization, depression

- General somatic complaints (e.g., stomach ache)

- Memory problems

- Fatigue/drowsiness (e.g., lack of sleep, staying up late, or getting up early to do rituals)

Following is a list – by no means exhaustive – of specific behaviors that may be exhibited by students with OCD. For convenience' sake, it is organized by common obsessions/sensory phenomena. It must be emphasized, however, that a number of different obsessions/sensory phenomena can lead to certain OCD behaviors. Students with OCD who avoid touching other students, for example, may do so because they fear contamination. On the other hand, a student may avoid peers because of fears that he somehow may harm them. The reader is urged to keep this in mind while examining the following list.

Specific school-related problems associated with OCD

Contamination obsessions

- Difficulty walking through hallways (e.g., fear of being contaminated)

- Making frequent trips to bathroom/staying in bathroom for extended periods of time

- Engaging in frequent/excessive hand washing (potential presence of dry, cracked, chapped, bleeding hands)

- Repeatedly using hand sanitizers or anti-bacterial wipes

What are the Effects of OCD on School Functioning? How Can School Personnel Help? | Part IV

103

What are the Effects of OCD on School Functioning? How Can School Personnel Help?

Part IV

104

- Covering hands with clothing, gloves, shirttails, cuffs, tissue, or paper towels to open a door or turn on a faucet

- Covering face (e.g., with a mask, shirt sleeve), hiding face (e.g., in shirt), or holding breath to avoid becoming contaminated

- Opening doors, lockers, books, etc., with elbows

- Holding hands in air to avoid touching anyone/anything that might be contaminated

- Refusing to handle/touch tissues (even one's own)

- Refusing to bring "contaminated" school books into the "clean" home

- Asking for reassurance that someone or something isn't dirty or contaminated

- Avoidance behaviors; avoiding:

    - Bathroom at school (e.g., may be contaminated)

    - Other areas of school that may be contaminated, e.g., cafeteria gymnasium, chemistry lab

    - Objects at school that have been touched by others: books, toys, crayons, sports equipment

    - Peers in classroom (e.g., fear of becoming contaminated or contracting illness)

    - Groups of people, e.g., group projects, assemblies

    - Certain materials in class that are "gummy" or "sticky:" glue, paint, clay, paste

    - Chemicals/cleaning products or objects/substances that are "smelly," e.g., magic markers, cleaning spray for white-boards, perfumes/lotions used by teacher, peers

Harm, illness, or death obsessions

- Calling parents/family members from school to check on their safety

- Checking to make sure that doors, windows are locked

- Asking for reassurance that doors, windows, are locked

- Checking that desk, paper, materials are not close to an electrical outlet

- Asking school personnel or peers for reassurance that they are safe from harm

- Asking for reassurance from school personnel or peers that they have not hurt/offended them

- Avoidance behaviors; avoiding:

    - Peers (e.g., for fear of causing harm/offending them)

    - Sharp objects in the classroom, e.g., scissors, compass (student may fear being harmed or experience taboo obsessions related to inflicting harm upon others)

    - "Unsafe" areas such as playground, gym

"Just right" obsessions/sensory phenomena

- Writing letters, words, numbers, until they are "perfect"

- Drawing items, objects until they are "perfect"

- Erasing and reerasing words, numbers, letters, to the extent that holes are worn in the paper

- Reading and rereading words, sentences, paragraphs in a book

- Working slowly to ensure no mistakes are made

- Starting assignment over from beginning if any errors are found

- Asking for reassurance that everything has been completed correctly

What are the Effects of OCD on School Functioning? How Can School Personnel Help?

Part IV

105

- Checking work repeatedly to ensure no mistakes have been made

- Checking homework until the early hours of morning

- Handing in work late; not handing in work at all

- Filling in circles/squares on scantron (bubble) sheets repeatedly

- Remembering/memorizing everything about a topic/what has been read

- Asking a question/soliciting an answer repetitively

- Repeating a lock combination over and over

- Getting in and out of a seat numerous times

- Going in and out of a doorway again and again

- Taking off and putting on shoes excessively

- Buttoning and rebuttoning clothing over and over

- Counting items in school (e.g., windows in classroom, tiles on a floor; bricks in a wall of the school)

- Counting words as they are spoken by the teacher or peer; counting one's own words while reading

- Counting the number of steps between classes

Symmetry or order obsessions/sensory phenomena

- Repeating tasks until they turn out even, e.g., must have an even number of numerals in math responses; even number of letters in a sentence; even number of items on each side of a drawing

- Arranging, rearranging, ordering, or lining up books on a shelf, items on or in desk

- Arranging and rearranging items alphabetically, by size or color

- Touching or tapping items symmetrically

- Tying and retying shoelaces until balanced or "even"

What are the Effects of OCD on School Functioning? How Can School Personnel Help?

Part IV

106

- Taking steps that are identical in length

- Speaking with equal stress on a syllable

- Rewriting problems from a math worksheet/book on a separate sheet so they appear symmetrical to the student

- Holding a paper or book with even pressure on both sides

- Placing a paper or book on the desk so it appears symmetrical to the student

Scrupulosity (religious/moral) obsessions

- Asking for reassurance that the student has not sinned/done anything wrong

- Frequently praying for transgressions (may be imagined or minor); student may fear that a bad word was verbalized or an inappropriate gesture was made

- Repeating phrases, mantras to atone for "sins" (overt, subvocally or mentally)

- Frequently apologizing for no obvious reason

- Confessing all of one's thoughts/actions

- Refusing to answer questions for fear of telling a lie or making the "wrong" decision

- Throwing homework away if parent has helped

- Throwing test away (e.g., for fear that student has cheated)

- Making errors purposely (e.g., on tests) to preclude the possibility that student has cheated

What are the Effects of OCD on School Functioning? How Can School Personnel Help?

Part IV

107

Sexual obsessions

- Repetitively praying for having thoughts or images about sex or incest

- Distracting oneself to keep from thinking sexual thoughts

- Asking for reassurance regarding gender identity (even though student is heterosexual)

- Avoidance behaviors; avoiding:

    - Peers (for fear of molesting them, bumping into "private parts")

    - Material in books, magazines, TV shows, etc., with any sexual content (e.g., people kissing)

Hoarding obsessions/sensory phenomena

- Refusing to throw away any old school papers, notes (e.g., may avoid them because of need to check or read through each paper before discarding it; may avoid due to fear of losing important information)

- Filling up desk/locker with gum wrappers, rocks, worn-down pencils, other useless items (e.g., may fear something bad will happen if they are discarded; may result from feelings of incompleteness)

- Accumulation of objects due to fear of contaminating others who may touch them if they are discarded

- Purchasing items in a store that student has touched (and therefore contaminated) for fear that another individual who touches them may become contaminated

- Avoiding spending money for fear that something bad will happen or money will run out

- Collecting items in multiples of a particular number (e.g., may be student's "good" or "magic" number)

Part IV | What are the Effects of OCD on School Functioning? How Can School Personnel Help?

108

Number obsessions/sensory phenomena

- Repeatedly counting up to a particular number

- Using only "good," "safe," "magical" numbers; may be related to odd or even numbers

- Touching an item a certain number of times

- Reading words, paragraphs, pages, a given number of times

- Going in and out of a doorway a specific number of times

- Repeating an action a certain number of times; must start over if interrupted before number is reached

- Avoidance behaviors; avoiding:

    - "Bad" numbers (may be related to odd or even numbers)

    - Numbering items on a page or pages in a series, with a "bad" number (e.g., if "3" is a bad number, will write "1, 2, 4, 5, 6…" resulting in an incorrect sequence)

    - Worksheets, pages in a book, etc., with certain numbers on them

    - Looking at or writing specific numbers

Obsessive doubting

- Checking locker to be sure all items are there

- Checking backpack to be certain all items are there

- Checking lock on locker repeatedly to be sure it is secured

- Calling home and leaving messages due to uncertainty that the answering machine worked previous time(s)

- Asking to leave classroom to check something (e.g., locker, making call to parents to check safety)

What are the Effects of OCD on School Functioning? How Can School Personnel Help?

Part IV

109

Ch:16

HOW CAN SCHOOL PERSONNEL HELP?

Thousands of students with OCD struggle, on a daily basis, in classrooms all over the world. Held hostage by OCD, they cannot perform tasks they have the ability to do. Unable to complete assignments, these students frequently receive poor and even failing grades. Moreover, their social competence often is compromised because of the intrusion of OCD. Is there hope for these students, or are they doomed to academic and social failure?

Fortunately, school personnel can play an integral role in the process of identifying, assessing, referring, and treating children and adolescents with OCD. The next sections provide a discussion of how school staff may assist in this process. Adaptations at the local level will be necessary, because the make-up of student services teams and the roles of individual members understandably will vary from one school district to another.

Identification

School personnel may encounter one of several different scenarios related to students with OCD. In some cases, a student already has been formally diagnosed with OCD and is under the care of one or more mental health professionals. In addition, the parents have taken a proactive stance and have conferred with relevant school personnel regarding the child's situation. This scenario is optimal, because a partnership among the student, parents, school personnel, and clinicians is likely to provide the best possible support for the child.

In other cases, a student has been diagnosed with OCD and is receiving outside professional help. However, the family has opted not to share information about OCD with school personnel. It may be difficult to understand why parents would choose such an option. There are a number of reasons, however, why they may have reached this decision.

First, parents sometimes fear that if they disclose their child's OCD, he or she may be labeled or stigmatized. Although much progress has been made, misconceptions and stigma surrounding mental illness still abound — *Burke & Adams, 1999*. In some cases, it is the student who prefers school personnel not be informed for fear that he or she will be singled out or receive special treatment from the teacher. Second, some parents have concerns that if school personnel learn about the child's illness, they will immediately try to persuade the family to put the child on

What are the Effects of OCD on School Functioning? How Can School Personnel Help?

Part IV

111

What are the Effects of OCD on School Functioning? How Can School Personnel Help?

Part IV

112

medication – a decision many parents are reticent to make. Third, parents sometimes fear that the information they disclose will not remain confidential, and privacy will be breached. Finally, many parents have been counseled by clinicians, either directly, or indirectly via various publications, etc., that there is no real need to inform school personnel about their child's OCD if it isn't impairing school performance and symptoms aren't present at school.

A caveat regarding such advice, i.e., not to inform school personnel, is that OCD symptoms tend to wax and wane. The possibility always exists, therefore, that symptoms will occur in the future. If difficulties do arise, teachers who lack background information about the student understandably may rely upon faulty explanations and make incorrect assumptions about those difficulties (e.g., the child is inattentive, noncompliant, unruly, etc.). Students even may be punished for OCD behavior because it was interpreted as aggressive or disruptive. Educators who are informed about a student's OCD are in a much better position to understand his or her behavior and provide supports that are crucial to successful school functioning.

Yet another scenario school personnel may encounter is that the child has not been formally diagnosed with OCD but is experiencing symptoms at home, at school, and/or in the community. In certain cases, the onset of symptoms may be sudden – as if they occurred overnight. Sudden-onset OCD has been linked to Pediatric Autoimmune Neuropsychiatric Disorders Associated with Strep, or PANDAS. As its name implies, this form of OCD is thought to be triggered by strep infections (see section on biological factors in Chapter 7).

When students do not have a formal diagnosis but exhibit symptoms that suggest OCD, classroom teachers and other school personnel can play a key role in the identification process, for a number of reasons. As previously noted, parents may not be the first to recognize that their child has a problem. In addition, teachers generally are very effective at identifying youth at risk for academic, social, emotional, or behavioral problems. Moreover, teachers and other school professionals are uniquely positioned to interact with and observe students for extended periods of time on a consistent basis. Before school personnel can successfully identify OCD, however, they first must become knowledgeable about the disorder.

Two researchers who have examined school-related issues in children with OCD have noted, "The key to successfully identifying OCD in schools is to educate classroom teachers and other school personnel on the nature of anxiety disorders. Even a brief, hour-long lecture by the school psychologist or a local clinician can help teachers to learn about the common signs of these highly prevalent disorders" — *Ledley & Pasupuleti, 2007, pp. 340-341*. Informed school staff members can play a pivotal role in the early detection of OCD. And early identification followed by appropriate treatment can mean the difference between a child who has learned to manage the symptoms of OCD and one whose childhood is fraught with emotional pain and suffering.

Educators can learn about OCD by keeping abreast of current information and literature on OCD and by attending lectures, seminars, and conferences that feature information on the disorder. A number of mental health organizations sponsor conferences on various illnesses, including OCD, some of which provide continuing education credit. Another option is to have the school psychologist, social worker, counselor, school nurse, or another staff member assume responsibility for disseminating literature on OCD and posting information regarding lecture, workshop, and conference opportunities. It also may be helpful to establish, within a school library or resource center, an area where information on OCD (and other disorders) is placed and easily accessed by faculty. In addition, school districts are urged to invite health care providers or other individuals with expertise on OCD to provide professional development workshops. Moreover, a wealth of information on various disabilities, mental illnesses, and other conditions now is available on the Internet. The reputability of these sources always should be checked, however. Several well-known Internet resources are listed in Appendix A.

What are the Effects of OCD on School Functioning? How Can School Personnel Help?

Part IV

114

Assessment

Because OCD is a psychiatric illness, it is the responsibility of health professionals, rather than school personnel, to formally diagnose the disorder. But gathering information regarding a student's academic, social, and behavioral functioning is essential both to the clinical diagnostic process and future educational programming decisions. Input from school personnel therefore is extremely important.

Observing student behavior. Friend and Bursuck (2006) suggest that school personnel consider a number of issues to determine whether a student's academic performance or behavior triggers concern. They recommend that school professionals note *specific* examples or instances of a student's difficulties; vague concerns and hunches should be supported by explicit information.

It is vital that school professionals keep detailed, objective, written records of observations of student behavior. It is much more effective to write "The student is walking up and down the aisle next to his seat," for example, than "The student is disrupting the class." It also is important to record what the student *is* doing rather than what he or she *is not* doing: "The student is tracing and retracing letters on his worksheet," rather than, "The student is not completing his work." Such specificity can be extremely helpful in determining whether behavior is related to OCD. Documenting that a student has come to class the last four days without homework and said "It wasn't good enough to turn in," is far more informative than writing "The student isn't turning in homework." The former notation suggests the student may need to do things "just right."

Written observations also should include specific details regarding the date and time the behavior was observed, the setting (e.g., math period), and ongoing activity (e.g., independent worksheet). Furthermore, it is extremely beneficial to document any event/s that preceded or set the stage for the student's behavior (antecedents) and event/s that occurred after or followed the student's behavior (consequences). Such information may be helpful in determining potential patterns regarding triggers for a behavior (e.g., student starts to cry every time the teacher asks him to sit on the floor) or what follows it (e.g., each time student cries, the teacher verbally reprimands him for not sitting on the floor). In addition, any social impact the behavior has on peers, others in the room, or the classroom climate, should be recorded (e.g., peers laugh when teacher repeats her directive) (see section on functional behavioral assessment and positive behavior interventions and supports in Chapter 22). Finally, any adaptations, modifications, or interventions that have been tried with the student should be documented.

Friend & Bursuck (2006) also describe certain factors that may raise a red flag about student behavior, including:

1. a chronic pattern of behavior that has a negative impact on learning;

2. an increase in the severity of the difficulty over time; and

3. functioning that differs significantly from that of classmates.

When a student's behavior does elicit concern, it is important that school personnel gather additional information, which should include, but is not limited to, input from parents and appropriate school personnel.

Information from parents. Some parents welcome the opportunity to speak with school personnel about problems they are experiencing with their child at home. Other parents are more reticent to acknowledge a problem exists. Nonetheless, it is important that parents be contacted early in the information-gathering process. Family members often can provide important insight into a child's difficulties.

Several general guidelines for conferring with parents regarding potential OCD symptoms may be helpful. First, it is extremely important to begin a conversation by sharing positive feedback with parents about the student's behavior and relating other strengths exhibited by the child. Parents frequently receive only negative feedback, so it is critical that they hear "what's right" with their child. Moreover, starting a conversation in this manner may be conducive to the parents' being more receptive to information about the child's difficulties. Second, it is important to provide parents details about a student's behavior. As noted above, a discussion of specific examples of student behavior and objective information are much more meaningful to parents than subjective impressions. Third, parents frequently experience great emotional pain and frustration as they grapple with their child's difficulties. Therefore, it is important to approach parents with an

What are the Effects of OCD on School Functioning? How Can School Personnel Help?

Part IV

115

What are the Effects of OCD on School Functioning? How Can School Personnel Help?

Part IV

116

attitude of caring and concern. Blaming parents for a child's symptoms is unwarranted and inappropriate. It also is extremely important to listen carefully and empathically to parents as they describe what may be very sensitive concerns. Fourth, it is vital that school personnel avoid using educational jargon and acronyms that may confuse parents (e.g., IDEA, IEP, OHI). Such language should be used only if it has previously been explained to parents. Fifth, communication should embody respect not only for parents and their child but also for their culture. Parents may feel very uncomfortable discussing certain issues because of cultural or social values. Finally, it is always important that school personnel be familiar with local and state regulatory constraints and privacy laws governing communication among parents, school personnel, and the student.

If a conversation with parents is not going well, it is important not to force parents to continue. The National Eating Disorders Association (2008) offers educators several suggestions for ending a difficult conversation with parents. Although written for the benefit of students with eating disorders, these guidelines are equally appropriate for students of all types – including those with OCD.

Tips for Ending a Difficult Conversation with Parents/Guardians

Don't persist with a conversation that isn't going well. This may damage future communication. To end a conversation that isn't going well:

- acknowledge that you sense it must be difficult to talk about;

- affirm that the choice not to talk about it is OK;

- reiterate the school's concerns for their son/daughter;

- leave the door open by reassuring them that you are available to talk anytime;

- let them know that you will contact them again soon to check in; and

- you may also want to let them know about the school's duty of care to its students.

Reprinted with permission from the National Eating Disorders Association. For more information: www.NationalEatingDisorders.org.

Information from school personnel. A number of different school professionals may provide important information about a student's performance. Classroom teachers can be an excellent resource regarding the child's grades, attendance patterns, academic and social behavior, and very importantly, the student's strengths and talents. School psychologists, social workers, counselors, and other student services providers may play a key role in gathering information, e.g., conducting direct observations of the student in the school setting, soliciting information from school staff, parents, and/or the student via questionnaires, checklists, rating scales, etc.

Although validated teacher rating scales of OCD currently do not exist, one questionnaire, the Florida Obsessive-Compulsive Student Inventory (FOCSI) — *Merlo & Storch, 2005*, may provide extremely useful information. The FOCSI consists of a checklist of 15 different OCD-related behaviors a teacher might observe as well as a 15-item school impairment rating scale (see Appendix D). The items for this inventory were modified from several current measures and the authors' clinical experience with children and adolescents who have OCD.

One checklist frequently used in school settings that provides information on a broad range of competencies and behavioral/ emotional difficulties in children and adolescents is the Child Behavior Checklist (CBCL) — *Achenbach & Rescorla, 2001*. Various versions of the CBCL are designed for different informants, including parents, teachers, and children 11-18 years of age. Of note is that researchers have developed a revised version of the Obsessive-Compulsive Scale from the CBCL that appears to provide a highly-effective screen for OCD in children and adolescents — *Storch, Murphy, Bagner, et al., 2006*.

As noted in the section on teacher questionnaires in Chapter 10, school staff frequently feel overwhelmed by the paperwork involved in working with students, especially those with disabilities. It is crucial, however, that OCD rating scales or questionnaires be completed thoughtfully to assist not only with a clinical diagnosis but also educational programming decisions.

What are the Effects of OCD on School Functioning? How Can School Personnel Help? | Part IV

117

Referral

If it is determined from the assessment/information-gathering stage that the student's behavior does, indeed, warrant further attention, a referral may be made to the prereferral or instructional assistance team. The team may decide that a full assessment for possible special education services is necessary (see Chapter 21 on IDEA and Section 504).

If a student exhibits symptoms of OCD but has not been evaluated clinically, it is critical that he or she be seen by a physician or outside mental health professional (e.g., psychologist, psychiatrist) to determine if OCD and/or other disorders are present. Due to school liability issues, however, teachers are not in a position to make a direct, formal recommendation to parents to seek a medical evaluation for their child.

One way school personnel may approach parents is to share with them behaviors their child has displayed at school that have raised concern, noting that these are common symptoms of OCD. Alternatively, school staff might say they have seen or had other students (*never* revealing the names of the other students, for confidentiality reasons) who exhibited behaviors similar to their child, which were symptomatic of OCD. School personnel may suggest that the parents consult their child's physician and discuss the school staff's observations. Such observations may be put in writing and shared with the health professional, who, in turn, could direct the parents to various services, as appropriate. If parents request information from school personnel regarding mental health providers, the staff may provide names and contact information of therapists in the area *who have experience treating children with OCD.* Not all mental health professionals are familiar with how to diagnose and treat OCD in children and adolescents appropriately. Names of such health care providers are available through the International OCD Foundation (*see www.ocfoundation.org*). Information on therapists also may be found at the website for the Anxiety Disorders Association of America (ADAA) (*www.adaa.org*)

With the appropriate releases of information from pertinent school personnel (e.g., school psychologist, social worker, counselor), parents, outside therapists/physicians, and the student (if over 12 years of age), information regarding the student's functioning can be shared among all involved parties. Parents should have the name of a contact person at school if the therapist needs additional information for diagnostic purposes.

Part IV | What are the Effects of OCD on School Functioning? How Can School Personnel Help?

118

Ch:17

INTRODUCTION TO SCHOOL-BASED TREATMENT
FOR STUDENTS WITH OCD

Chapters 11 and 12 were devoted to the clinical treatment of children and adolescents with OCD. It was noted that cognitive-behavioral therapy, alone or in combination with medication, represents the cornerstone of treatment today. A number of other treatments complement CBT and medication, including supportive psychotherapy for the child and his or her family, support groups, and patient advocacy groups (see Chapter 13). Very importantly, for the child or adolescent who struggles with OCD at school, *an educational intervention is a fundamental part of treatment*. Indeed, unless and until OCD-related issues are addressed at school, treatment for young people with OCD is incomplete.

An important first step in school-based interventions

One of the most important ways school personnel can help their students is by knowing what OCD is, understanding that it is a disease with a neurobiological basis, and being compassionate. It is vital that students with OCD be educated in a safe environment in which school personnel refrain from lecturing or punishing them for OCD-related difficulties. This theme is recurrent throughout the literature on childhood OCD. Following is an excerpt from a book written Dr. Tamar Chansky, a leading expert on childhood OCD:

"The single most valuable thing a teacher can do for a child is to believe that the child is not crazy for having these fears and doubts and convey that belief to the child. Taking this as the starting point will naturally lead to a child feeling safe to be himself" — Chansky, 2000, p. 314.

Dr. John March, another renowned authority in the field of pediatric OCD, addresses parents about the role of school personnel:

"Where OCD interferes with school performance by taking up time, or when rituals directly interfere with school tasks, it's important for school staff to know that your child is struggling with an illness and what that illness entails. Teachers may even become active members of the treatment team, but at the very least you should expect the child with OCD to be treated with kindness and compassion at school, as at home" — March, 2007, p. 105.

In addition to being understanding and compassionate, educators must work to create a stable and non-threatening environment free from ridicule and stigma. It is common knowledge that teasing and bullying are all too frequent in our schools, and students with disabilities are particularly vulnerable (see section on teasing/bullying in Chapter 19).

It also is of paramount importance that school personnel themselves model positive social interactions with all students. Unfortunately, the literature contains many examples of teachers calling attention to the behavior of a student with OCD and overtly reprimanding – or worse yet, humiliating – the student in front of classmates. Although the behavior of a student with OCD may be challenging, ridicule and harsh words are harmful and have no place in the educational environment.

In addition, school staff are encouraged to minimize the stress level for students with OCD to the greatest extent possible. Stress undeniably is a part of the human condition, and it is impossible to create an environment free of stress. But knowing about potential stressors can help school personnel prepare for situations in which a student's OCD symptoms may be heightened. A number of environmental factors can have a negative impact on a student's OCD, including anxiety, fatigue, illness, and life and school transitions. Making demands on the student that cannot be met due to OCD symptoms also creates tension. Moreover, even positive events – the excitement associated with birthdays, holidays, and vacations – can be stressful. School personnel may benefit from soliciting input from parents regarding triggers for their child's anxiety or discomfort and strategies they have used successfully to manage stress.

In general, structuring educational environments to keep stress levels at a minimum can go a long way toward managing the behavior of students with OCD. As noted by one school psychologist, "Well-structured classroom environments with clear expectations, smooth transitions, and a calm climate are helpful for all students, but especially for students who have OCD, whose symptoms may be exacerbated by stress" — Paige, 2007, p. 14.

The role of school personnel in the treatment of children and adolescents with OCD is multi-faceted. Therefore, various aspects of treatment will be discussed in separate chapters. More specifically, the following areas will be addressed: school-based accommodations and support strategies for students with OCD (Chapters 18); special issues related to the school-based treatment of students with OCD (Chapter

19); laws pertaining to educational services for students with OCD
(Chapter 20); categorizing students with OCD under IDEA (Chapter 21);
IDEA, discipline, and OCD behavior (Chapter 22); school-based
cognitive-behavioral therapy when an outside therapist is involved
(Chapter 23); and school-based interventions when an outside therapist
is not involved (Chapter 24).

SCHOOL-BASED ACCOMMODATIONS AND SUPPORT
STRATEGIES FOR STUDENTS WITH OCD

An overview of accommodations for students with OCD

The No Child Left Behind Act of 2001 and the Individuals with Disabilities of Education Act of 2004 require the participation of students with disabilities in standards-based instruction and assessments. To ensure that students work toward grade-level content standards, educators must implement an array of instructional strategies based upon the individual needs of their students. School personnel also must provide accommodations for students with disabilities during instruction and assessments to promote equal access to the general curriculum. School-based accommodations, which are practices and procedures that help "level the playing field" for students with disabilities, frequently are classified into four different categories
— *Council of Chief State School Officers, 2005:*

1. **Presentation accommodations** provide students alternatives to visual reading for accessing standard print, e.g., listening to a chapter in a text that has been recorded on a CD;

2. **Response accommodations** allow students to complete work, assignments, activities, tests, etc., in a variety of ways (e.g., giving responses to a test orally, using a word processor rather than writing by hand) or to solve or organize problems using an assistive device (e.g., calculator) or organizer (e.g., visual or graphic organizers);

3. **Setting accommodations**

   a. allow students to take a test or complete an assignment in a different location, or

   b. create a change in the conditions of the setting (e.g., wearing headphones, earphones, earplugs to reduce distractions); and

4. **Timing and scheduling accommodations** afford students additional time to complete an assignment or assessment or change the way in which time is organized (e.g., providing multiple breaks during an assignment or test).

Accommodations for students are provided when OCD interrupts the child's ability to access instruction and assessment in the traditional manner. A word processor, for instance, may provide the student who is compelled to write and rewrite words with the opportunity to complete an entire assignment and demonstrate his or her actual knowledge about a topic. If OCD symptoms subside or disappear, however (e.g., child improves as a result of clinical treatment), the accommodation should be modified or phased out. In a similar fashion, accommodations may be necessary during the waxing cycles of OCD (the symptoms of OCD are worse) but discontinued during waning cycles (the symptoms of OCD are better). Some teachers have found that students with OCD may make up missed assignments or even work ahead a bit during periods of milder symptoms, leaving some leeway for periods of symptom flare-up. Although accommodations for students with OCD generally are temporary, they may need to be continued if the child does not respond to treatment, or if he or she is chronically ill.

A number of factors should be considered when selecting accommodations for students. Inconspicuous accommodations are preferable to those that draw attention to the student's being "different." If possible, implementing a strategy with other students or the entire class may preclude singling out the student with OCD. Another consideration is whether the accommodation can be provided consistently over time. If not, more realistic interventions may need to be selected. In addition, school personnel must be aware of and take into account the types of accommodations allowed by individual states or locales, especially with regard to assessments.

One factor vital to selecting accommodations is the direct involvement of the student with OCD, as appropriate, for a number of reasons. First, students themselves frequently are an excellent resource in terms of accommodations. Children and adolescents can be extremely creative with regard to devising effective methods to accommodate their difficulties – methods that can be implemented easily in the school setting. Second, some students have had limited experience advocating for themselves and expressing personal preferences – especially when school personnel and other authority figures are involved. Self-advocacy skills are essential for students with disabilities, and having a voice in selecting accommodations provides an avenue for developing these skills. Moreover, when students are involved in making decisions about accommodations, they are more likely to use them.

School personnel who have worked with the student in the past also may be an excellent resource regarding accommodations that have been implemented successfully. In some cases, students, parents, school personnel, and the therapist – if one is involved – may need to brainstorm ideas about possible accommodations, keeping in mind the student's strengths and OCD-related challenges.

A caveat related to accommodation selection is to resist the urge to "fix" everything at once. If many accommodations are necessary, it is important to choose critical areas in which OCD symptoms are most intrusive and to prioritize interventions realistically.

Once specific accommodations have been selected, they should be implemented for a trial period and evaluated to determine if they are benefitting the student with OCD (e.g., improvement in grades, attitudes, behavior). Collecting data on the use and effectiveness of accommodations for instruction and assessment is extremely important. Such data can provide support for their continued use or the need to change them. Students, themselves, also should be involved in evaluating the success of accommodations, as appropriate. A website containing sample accommodation evaluation forms for both students and teachers is *www.specialconnections.ku.edu*. Because symptoms of OCD change, school personnel should be prepared to change accommodations to match a student's difficulties at any given point in time.

Students with OCD (as well as students with other disabilities) sometimes are reticent to use accommodations for fear they will feel even more "different" than they already feel. In these cases, it may be constructive to show students how various strategies might facilitate school functioning and assist them in achieving their goals. Helping students understand the potential benefits of these accommodations may outweigh their concerns about receiving "special treatment."

Finally, it is important to note that if a student is receiving special education services under IDEA, accommodations must be documented in the student's Individualized Education Program (IEP). For the student who receives services under Section 504 of the Rehabilitation Act of 1973, accommodations must be documented in the student's 504 plan (see laws pertaining to educational services for students with OCD in Chapter 20). Following are a number of valuable ideas related to selecting appropriate accommodations for students.

DO'S AND DON'TS WHEN SELECTING ACCOMMODATIONS

Do...make accommodation decisions based on individualized needs.

Don't...make accommodation decisions based on whatever is easiest to do (e.g., preferential seating).

Do...select accommodations that reduce the effect of the disability to access instruction and demonstrate learning.

Don't...select accommodations unrelated to documented student learning needs or are intended to give students an unfair advantage.

Do...be certain to document instructional and assessment accommodation(s) on the IEP or 504 plans.

Don't...use an accommodation that has not been documented on the IEP or 504 plans.

Do...be familiar with the types of accommodations that can be used as both instructional and assessment accommodations.

Don't...assume that all instructional accommodations are appropriate for use on assessments.

Do...be specific about the "Where, When, Who, and How" of providing accommodations.

Don't...simply indicate an accommodation will be provided "as appropriate" or "as necessary."

Do...refer to state accommodations policies and understand implications of selections.

Don't...check every accommodation possible on a checklist simply to be "safe."

Do...evaluate accommodations used by the student.

Don't...assume the same accommodations remain appropriate year after year.

Do...get input about accommodations from teachers, parents, and students, and use it to make decisions at IEP team or 504 planning committee meetings.

Part V | School-Based Treatment of OCD

127

> *Don't...make decisions about instructional and assessment
> accommodations alone.*
>
> **Do...provide accommodations for assessments routinely used for
> classroom instruction.**
>
> *Don't...provide an assessment accommodation for the first time on
> the day of a test.*
>
> **Do...select accommodations based on specific individual needs in
> each content area.**
>
> *Don't...assume certain accommodations, such as extra time, are
> appropriate for every student in every content area.*
>
> *Council of Chief State School Officers (2005). Accommodations Manual: How to Select,
> Administer, and Evaluate Use of Accommodations for Instruction and Assessment of
> Students with Disabilities. Washington, DC: Author.*
>
> *www.osepideasthatwork.org/toolkit/pdf/AccommodationsManual.pdf*

The reader interested in additional information about accommodations is referred to the website for the National Center on Educational Outcomes at *www.cehd.umn.edu/NCEO*. It includes a wealth of information on accommodations, including an online accommodations bibliography list.

One final issue related to accommodations for students with OCD (and other disabilities) deserves special mention. Educators and parents sometimes harbor concerns about implementing accommodations for students with OCD. They may believe the child is "getting off too easily" or the accommodations serve as a "crutch." Others are concerned that implementing accommodations to work around a child's OCD symptoms will not "fix" them. And it is entirely true that accommodations do not resolve these symptoms. But wheelchairs don't "fix" orthopedic disabilities, nor do hearing aids "fix" deafness. And yet students with these disabilities – outwardly visible disabilities – would be unable to function in the school setting or access the general education curriculum without them. Young people with OCD do not look "different," because their disability is hidden. But their need for educational supports is no less real than that of students with observable disabilities. Providing students with OCD accommodations and interventions (which usually are temporary) can make the difference between a student's keeping up with the class or falling hopelessly behind.

School personnel, parents, and mental health professionals who are apprehensive about providing accommodations for students with OCD sometimes raise the specter of "equal treatment for all." In other words, providing accommodations for some children is inherently unfair. The reality of the educational landscape is that children and adolescents exhibit exceedingly heterogeneous levels of skill, ability, and need. If the "equal treatment" principle were applied in school, asthma inhalers, walking canes, and glasses would be distributed to *all* students if even a single student required one of these aids. Equality and fairness are not synonymous. Fairness means providing students what they need to be successful in school, and for many students with OCD, this translates into accommodations. The distinction between equality and fairness is one that many school personnel already recognize and embrace; it is important that students be taught to understand the difference, as well.

Specific accommodations and support strategies for difficulties students with OCD frequently experience

Because OCD is an extremely heterogeneous disorder that includes many different subtypes (e.g., washing/contamination, symmetry/ordering/counting/repeating; see Chapter 5 for a discussion of symptom dimensions), it affects children and adolescents in an almost unimaginable number of ways. Therefore, when it comes to determining accommodations and other educational strategies to assist students with OCD, the "one size fits all" approach is inappropriate. Indeed, what may work beautifully with one student may be ineffective – if not a disaster – for another. Nonetheless, it is extremely important for educators to be knowledgeable about interventions that have been used with students who have OCD. To that end, the following section is provided. It contains numerous presentation, response, setting, and timing/scheduling accommodations as well as other support strategies for OCD-related academic, social, behavioral, and emotional difficulties. Of note is that the suggestions in this section may be helpful for students with other disabilities; indeed, some may be appropriate for *all* students.

Contamination/washing or cleaning

Contamination fears are very common among students with OCD. These students may fear becoming "contaminated" by a number of different sources, including classroom materials and people. Contamination concerns frequently lead to washing or cleaning rituals. Following are a number of different strategies school personnel can implement to help students with these difficulties.

- Allow the student to have a separate set of books at home if he or she fears contaminating the home environment with books that have been used in school.

- Allow the student to have his or her own set of materials at school (e.g., scissors, paint, glue) to avoid using materials handled by classmates (may be "contaminated").

- Allow the student to use a locker that is removed from those of other students.

- Give the student permission to be first in line in the cafeteria to avoid other students' "germs."

- Give the student permission not to be first in line in classrooms; this precludes the student's having to touch the door knob/ handle.

- Seat the student where he or she will be first to receive handouts to avoid classmates' "germs" (student will need to contend with only the teacher's "germs").

- Provide the student with an easy exit from a trigger situation (e.g., "contaminated" area such as a gymnasium) to "save face."

- Allow the student to use hand sanitizer in lieu of going to the bathroom to wash.

- Allow the student to use a bathroom infrequently used by other students if he or she is unable to use high-traffic bathrooms.

- Provide the student with an alternative to an activity if that activity is associated with contamination, e.g., if a student cannot participate in a sport due to contamination concerns, allow the student to assist with equipment, recordkeeping.

Doubting/checking

Students with OCD may experience excessive doubting, e.g., they doubt their own memories ("Did I really put everything I needed in my backpack?") or even their senses ("The door looked locked when I left for school, but was it really?"). Doubting often triggers checking rituals. Below are several strategies school personnel may use to address these concerns.

- Permit the use of calculator to check math answers one time only.

- Permit the use of spelling/grammar checker (limit # of times used) if the student has fears of making errors/doubts that something has been written correctly.

- Allow some time (set a limited time period) during the school day for the student to check his or her backpack/other materials to ensure that all necessary items are included.

Tardiness

Students with OCD sometimes are late to class because of OCD symptoms. Various morning rituals (e.g., washing, dressing, eating) may be slowing the student to the point of tardiness. In addition, many children and adolescents with OCD experience sleep related problems that affect their ability to awaken and get to school on time (see section on sleep problems in Chapter 9). *It is critical to be patient with and refrain from punishing these students.* That many of these students are even able to make it to school – given the extraordinary obstacles OCD frequently presents – is a testament to their perseverance and courage. As the student progresses in treatment, difficulties with tardiness should begin to diminish. When students with OCD experience difficulties with tardiness, however, school personnel may provide support in a number of different ways.

- Allow tardiness; do not apply negative consequences when the student is in the throes of OCD. Often, when students know there will be no penalty for tardiness, their stress and anxiety are reduced, and they are more likely to arrive at school on time.

- When a student with OCD is late to class, ignore his or her entrance as much as possible and continue with the lesson to avoid drawing attention to the student; do not react to the student's tardiness with negative remarks, frustration, or anger.

- Apply incentive systems for being on time when the student's symptoms improve (continue not to penalize the student for being tardy).

- Adapt the student's schedule (i.e., in middle/high school) to fit the student's needs, e.g., have the student start later in the day if morning rituals, sleep-related difficulties, etc., are leading to tardiness.

- Try to schedule classes to match the student's energy level, e.g., if symptoms worsen as fatigue sets in, schedule less demanding subjects in the afternoon.

- Provide accommodations for students when homework completion interferes with sleep (e.g., reduce length of homework assignments) (refer to the section on homework later in this chapter).

- Solicit information from parents about their child's sleep habits using the following sleep survey.

Sleep Survey

Name of Student: _____ Date: _____

Instructions: This form is to be completed by the parent or guardian. Please return this to me by _____.

ITEM	RESPONSE
How many hours of sleep does your child usually get each night of the school week?	
What time does your child usually go to bed on school nights?	
What time does your child usually fall asleep on school nights?	
What time does your child usually wake up for school?	
Once your child falls asleep for the night, does he sleep through the night or is sleep interrupted?	
Does your child wake up easily in the morning?	
Do you struggle to get your child up on school mornings?	
Does your child stay up late at night to do homework?	
Does your child sleep in the afternoon after school? If yes, how long does he sleep?	
Does your child maintain the same sleep pattern on weekends or when school is closed for vacation? If no, how is his sleep cycle different?	
Does your child set an alarm clock and wake himself up in the morning?	
Use the back of this page, if needed, to let me know about any of your child's sleep problems that may affect his alertness or mood in school.	

Reprinted by permission from Leslie E. Packer & Sheryl K. Pruitt, Challenging Kids, Challenged Teachers: Teaching Students with Tourette's, Bipolar Disorder, Executive Dysfunction, OCD, ADHD, and More (Bethesda, MD: Woodbine House, 2010), [page 299].

Transitions/changes in routine

Transitions can be very difficult for students with OCD. When transitioning from one class to another, for example, they may experience anxiety walking through hallways teeming with other students. The student with moral scrupulosity concerns may fear saying something inappropriate to another student. Or the student with contamination fears may worry about bumping into a peer and becoming ill. In other instances, students with OCD need to spend extra time at their lockers to ready themselves for the next class. Changes in schedules and transitions between in-class activities also may be stressful. Students with OCD sometimes get "stuck" on one task and have difficulty moving on to another. Following are some suggestions for assisting these students.

- Allow the student to leave class early (perhaps 3-5 minutes) to avoid crowded hallways during passing periods.

- Allow the student to leave class early (perhaps 3-5 minutes) if additional time is needed at the locker to prepare for the next class.

- If a student's OCD makes transitions from class to class extremely difficult, consider allowing the student to spend longer blocks of time in the same classroom, if possible, until symptoms improve.

- Provide the student extra time to make in-class transitions from one activity to another.

- Use a timer or other auditory device to signal that it's time to start a different task or make another transition.

- Try to keep classroom routines as predictable as possible without sudden changes. Whenever possible, plan in advance for transitions that will occur. Provide the student with cues/signals before a transition to prepare for the upcoming change (e.g., notify child of a fire drill prior to the fire bell ringing).

- Whenever possible, send a note home to alert the child/family to an upcoming change in schedule (e.g., substitute teacher, assembly) to give the student time to process/prepare for change.

- Reward successful transitions.

In addition to these suggestions, Packer (2004) indicates that some students who experience difficulty with transitions benefit from having a second work desk. The extra desk essentially provides a change in the environment and may help students leave the old task behind to start a new assignment. In addition, a second desk may be helpful for students whose rituals involve large motor movement or touching other students – it provides a "buffer zone" around the student.

Distractions in the classroom

Some students with OCD are distracted not only by internal stimuli (i.e., OCD symptoms) but also by other stimuli in the environment. If the student is sensitive to noise, smell, visual clutter, etc., it may be helpful to eliminate unnecessary distractions. School personnel may offer support in several ways.

- Provide the student an individual study area within the classroom, e.g., carrels or cubicles (other students should have access to these areas so the student with OCD is not singled out).

- Provide an alternative, quiet location for the student (e.g., library, resource room, section of classroom with less noise).

- Allow the student to use headphones, earphones, earplugs, etc., to block out background noise.

Concentration

Anecdotal records and research studies alike have underscored the difficulty students with OCD encounter concentrating on their work. When obsessive thoughts strike and the need to ritualize increases, little, if any, attention, is available for the task at hand. As a result, concentration suffers. In fact, difficulty concentrating was one of the top two school-related concerns reported by both students with OCD and their parents in two separate studies. For students experiencing these difficulties, school personnel may use a number of support strategies.

- Ask the student if providing a cue (e.g., code word, hand signal, physical proximity to student) would be helpful when he or she appears to be "stuck" in an obsessive cycle. If so, establish – with the student – the signal that will be used to help redirect attention.

- Seat the student closer to the teacher for the purpose of redirecting the student's attention, as necessary.

- Be available to check the student's progress and provide feedback as much as possible during the initial stages of independent seatwork.

- Allow the student to complete work in an altered sequence (e.g., math before reading; doing the last item first and working backward; easiest work first) if the usual sequence causes him or her to get "stuck."

- Allow the student to work with a partner or in a group; student interaction may keep the student from engaging in rituals.

- Pass worksheets out one at a time so the student does not become overwhelmed by too much work at once.

- Use learning materials and teaching methods that provide high levels of student engagement and opportunity to respond (e.g., Direct Instruction).

- Consider the following suggestions for giving class directions/ instructions

    - Give directions that are short and succinct rather than long and wordy.

    - Provide visual aids to accompany verbal directions/ instructions (e.g., write directions on board).

    - Capture students' attention prior to giving directions by telling them they need to listen to instructions about to be given. Watch for eye contact, modulate voice (e.g., state directions with increased volume), or provide a signal such as clapping hands.

Decision making

Many students with OCD have difficulty making decisions because they doubt making the "right" choice (or fear making the "wrong" choice). As a result, these students may be paralyzed by indecision and cannot move forward. Below are a number of different ideas that may be helpful.

- Limit the number of open-ended choices provided to the student.

- Assign a book, topic, etc., instead of asking student to make a choice.

- Give the student a choice from two alternatives.

Chansky (2000, p. 318) offers a number of excellent ideas for assisting students with OCD who have difficulty beginning creative writing assignments.

- Ask the student to tell you the most interesting or important facts about a given topic.

- Ask the student to imagine that he or she is describing information about a given topic to a friend rather than think of the writing task as a graded assignment.

- Ask the student what questions he or she has about a given topic and have the student find the answers to these questions.

- Give the student one minute to quickly write down as many important points about the topic as possible. Have the student circle the most important ideas, number them, put them into outline form, and begin to fill in information (this brainstorming strategy can be used again if the student gets stuck).

Class participation

OCD symptoms can hinder class participation. A student may fear
getting an answer wrong, for example, or saying something that might
be embarrassing. Obsessions and the need to ritualize also may
interfere with the student's concentration and ability to stay on task
during class discussions. In these cases, school personnel may use the
following strategies.

- Ask the student closed-ended (yes or no) questions rather than
  open-ended questions.

- Ask the student opinion questions rather than questions requiring
  a particular answer.

- Use a signal to let the student know that his or her turn is coming
  up (e.g., teacher lightly touches student's desk while circulating
  around the room).

- Call on the student for answers on topics about which he or she
  is knowledgeable or confident.

- Refrain from calling on a student who appears to be experiencing
  OCD symptoms.

- Prearrange with the student a system for participating in class.
  When the student raises his or her hand and shows an open
  hand, it means "Call on me." When the student raises his or her
  hand with a closed fist, it means, "Don't call on me" (this strategy
  makes it appear that the student is actively participating and
  helps him or her "save face").

Reading

Chansky (2000) sums it up beautifully with regard to how reading rituals
can affect a student with OCD: "For children with reading rituals,
reading is torture...These children may have to reread a sentence many
times, either because they didn't hear it 'just right,' or they messed up
a word and have to start over, or because they're not sure they 'got it.'

Perhaps they hit a trigger word, such as 'bad' or 'death,' and then have to undo the bad luck of that word. Still other children may need to count up the letters in each word and find a way for it to be divisible by 2, or to end up with an even number" (p. 318). For these students, the strategies below may be helpful.

- Allow another individual to read to the student (peer, aide, other), unless the student is uncomfortable with this arrangement.

- Photocopy a reading assignment. As the student reads, have him or her draw a line through the words that have been read with a dark marker to prevent rereading.

- Reduce the amount of material to be read: assign shorter reading assignments; provide a summary of a chapter; allow the student to use the CliffsNotes version of a book.

- Photocopy longer reading assignments, highlight the important sections, and have the student read only those parts.

- Suggest that the student read aloud; reading aloud sometimes prevents the intrusion of reading rituals.

- Give the student the page numbers containing the answers to questions in the assigned reading material.

- Allow the student to use a card/piece of paper to cover anxiety-provoking words in reading material (e.g., "death," "germs") but keep other words visible.

- Set time limits on the completion of reading assignments (may use a timer); have the student work until time is up.

- Allow the student to submit an assignment involving reading after the due date. Establish a contract delineating the modified due dates/times with students who have difficulty turning in assignments (this approach may benefit these students by providing structure and limits).

- Divide reading assignments into shorter segments and allow breaks in between.

Writing

Many students experience writing difficulties because of OCD symptoms. Rituals involving the need to:

- write/rewrite numbers, letters, and words repeatedly;

- cross out/rewrite endlessly;

- erase/reerase to the extent that holes are worn in the paper; or

- write/rewrite everything until it is "just so"

can seriously hamper the ability of these students to write if not immobilize them. For these students, school personnel may provide a number of different accommodations and support strategies.

- Allow the student to use a word processor rather than write by hand (for in-class assignments, tests, homework, etc.).

- Allow the student to print, if cursive handwriting is problematic, or vice versa.

- Have the student use an audio recorder to record lectures instead of writing notes.

- Permit the student to give responses orally/on an audio recorder.

- Have the student use a pencil without an eraser.

- Have the student use unlined paper, if the student feels compelled to write every letter perfectly on the lines of lined paper.

- Allow the student to dictate answers to another individual (e.g., paraprofessional, peer, parent) who writes down the information for the student (e.g., scribe).

- Have the student write on an outline of the lecture provided by the teacher.

- Allow the student to use a mechanical pencil if traditional pencils have to be sharpened perfectly.

- Allow the student to highlight the sentences/sections that answer the assigned questions on a photocopy of a reading assignment.

- Have the student write only the answers to questions rather than the questions and answers (e.g., questions at end of a history chapter).

- Set up a system in which a classmate provides a copy of his or her notes for the student (unless the student with OCD is uncomfortable with this arrangement).

- Provide the student with alternatives to written assignments, e.g., have the student do a picture, mural, model, poster, diorama, etc., to demonstrate his or her knowledge of a topic.

- Reduce the number of items the student is required to write (e.g., have the student complete 5 items on a test or worksheet instead of 10); have student complete odd- or even-numbered items (unless number obsessions are problematic), starred items, items marked with asterisk.

- Set time limits on completion of written assignments (may use a timer); have the student work until time is up.

- Divide written assignments into shorter segments and allow breaks in between.

- Allow the student additional time to submit an assignment involving writing. Establish a contract delineating the modified due dates/times with students who have difficulty turning in assignments (this approach may benefit these students by providing structure and limits).

- Refrain from complimenting the student on "perfect" work if he or she spends hours at home writing/rewriting assignments until they are "perfect."

Karen was a second-grader who was just learning to write in cursive. She was very proud of her ability to use this new form of handwriting. But one day, as she looked at an uppercase "𝒢" she had just written, a thought popped into her head that her mom somehow was inside the loop of the G. She thought about how silly that was and went on with her writing. But when she wrote a lowercase "𝓎," the thought that her father was in the loop intruded into her mind. Worse yet, Karen believed she had trapped her mother and father in the loops, and they couldn't get out. Before long, she was "trapping" all of her loved ones in every cursive letter she wrote. She became so distressed that she started refusing to use cursive. When asked by the teacher why she stopped using cursive, Karen stated that she didn't think her writing was good. Reassuring her that her cursive was very good, the teacher insisted that Karen start using it. Karen refused, bursting into tears and saying, "I'm not going to use cursive ever again!" Upset by her words, the teacher chided Karen, reminding her that she would receive a failing grade in handwriting if she didn't.

Because Karen exhibited other behaviors of concern, her parents had her evaluated by a psychologist, and she was diagnosed with OCD. The therapist planned to use cognitive-behavioral therapy to help her overcome her fears related to cursive writing. But there were more pressing behaviors that had to be tackled first in therapy. Until the psychologist was able to work with Karen on cursive writing, she was allowed to write using manuscript print. She successfully completed all of her assignments. In time, the therapist used exposure and response prevention to help Karen conquer her fears of trapping loved ones in the loops of cursive letters. The therapy was very successful, and within a short period of time, Karen was back to using cursive on a consistent basis.

Test-taking

Many students with OCD experience difficulty taking tests. Obsessive thoughts and rituals can significantly interfere with test completion. Tests may also provoke anxiety related to concerns about time limits and fears of making errors. And added anxiety can lead to an exacerbation of OCD symptoms. The following accommodations and support strategies may alleviate test-taking difficulties for these students.

- Provide extra time to complete a test.

- Allow the student to take a test over periods of time (e.g., do part in the morning and part in the afternoon).

- Provide breaks during a test.

- Permit the student to take a test in a different part of the room or in a location other than the classroom to avoid distractions and reduce the potential for ritualizing (some OCD rituals are triggered by other students, e.g., need to look at or touch a particular student).

- Allow the student to take tests orally (e.g., he or she may get stuck in writing rituals so that everything is written perfectly or "just so").

- Permit the student to write directly on the test booklet rather than fill in circles on computerized test sheets (bubble sheets). The student may circle or check the correct response on the test sheet/booklet.

- Supervise the correct placement of answers if the student does use bubble sheets.

- Provide multiple choice or short answer tests in lieu of essay tests if writing is problematic.

- Encourage students to review the entire test before answering any questions and do the easiest questions first to build confidence.

- Give open-book or take-home tests.

- Allow the student to submit an alternate product in lieu of a test (e.g., project, drawing).

- Be very cautious about timed tests (e.g., one-minute tests on addition facts); they are extremely anxiety-provoking for some students. It may be preferable to allow the student to complete the sheet without a time limit and inconspicuously record the student's beginning and ending times.

Please also refer to other sections in this chapter (e.g., difficulties with reading, writing, and concentration) for strategies that may be relevant to test-taking.

Organizational/study skills

Many students with OCD experience difficulties with organization and study skills, including organizing materials, studying (including studying for tests), taking tests, note-taking, and completing long-term assignments. In some cases, these difficulties are related to OCD symptoms. Students who feel compelled to have everything "perfect," for example, may procrastinate, especially when it comes to long-term projects. Although the results of research on executive functioning (e.g., cognitive skills such as goal setting, developing a plan, executing the plan, flexibility, attention, memory systems, and self-monitoring) in young people with OCD has been mixed, preliminary evidence suggests that some children and adolescents with OCD (especially older students) may experience difficulties with executive functioning. Moreover, a considerable number of students with OCD have comorbid AD/HD, which has come to be known as a developmental impairment in an array of executive functions. Below are a number of suggestions for students who experience difficulties with organization and study skills.

Organization

- Provide students *direct instruction* in organizational skills.

- Have the student use an assignment book that parents and teachers check daily. Provide space for teachers and parents to make comments, thus promoting communication.

- Have students use visual organizing systems such as color-coded folders (e.g., math folder is red; reading is blue) or sticky notes to keep assignments organized.

- Help the student set up a separate notebook with 3 individual pocket dividers for organizational purposes only: one divider is for "Work to be done," another is for "Completed work," and a third is for "Papers to save." Attach a weekly homework assignment sheet to the inside front cover of the notebook. Paperwork across all subjects (e.g., math, reading, social studies, etc.) goes into the appropriate divider in this notebook.

Long-term projects/longer assignments

- Provide students *direct instruction* in skills and strategies for planning and completing long-term projects (e.g., breaking longer tasks down into smaller, more manageable tasks).

- Try to establish limits on how much time should be spent on any part of a project; communicate with parents to enlist their help in determining and enforcing time limits.

- Write a contract with the student delineating how the project will be broken down and deadlines for each part; carefully monitor progress.

- Provide students charts, outlines, flow charts, and other graphic organizers that provide cues for completing various assignments, e.g., a five-paragraph essay contains an introductory paragraph, three supporting paragraphs, and a closing paragraph.

Note taking

- Provide students *direct instruction* in note taking strategies, e.g., Cornell System for taking notes.

- Provide students an outline of a lecture; students use a highlighter pen to follow along as the teacher lectures.

- Provide partial notes containing the main ideas of the lecture, leaving space for student notes.

- Give students cues, during the lecture, regarding the importance of specific ideas.

- Allow students to review positive models of notes (e.g., examples of good notes taken by other students).

- Have the student use an audio recorder to record lectures in lieu of writing copious notes.

Studying (including studying for tests)

- Provide students *direct instruction* in how to study, e.g., SQ4R study method.

- Communicate with parents to ensure that the student has an appropriate environment for studying at home. Encourage parents to schedule family activities, extracurricular activities, doctor appointments, etc., so they do not interfere with studying time.

- Suggest that the student study with a partner or in a study group.

- Encourage students to create various aids, e.g., flashcards, pictures, chapter summaries, etc., to help them organize and remember material.

- Encourage students to study using distributed practice (e.g., study for a period of time each day) rather than massed practice (e.g., "cram" the night before a test).

- Teach students mnemonic devices to aid memorization. Use acronyms, e.g., "HOMES," to remember all the great lakes: Huron, Ontario, Michigan, Erie, Superior. Use acrostics, e.g., take the first letter of each word in the sentence "All cows eat grass" to remember the spaces in the bass clef: A, C, E, G.

Strategies for completing tests

- Provide students *direct instruction* in how to take tests.

- Encourage students to read and/or listen to all test directions carefully before starting the test.

- Teach students to use time wisely on tests (try to budget time); the teacher may provide a suggested time limit for each section of a test.

- Encourage students to do the multiple-choice section of a test first if the test contains essay and multiple choice items (information on multiple choice items may be helpful in the essay section).

- Encourage students to review the entire test before answering any questions and do the easiest questions first to build confidence.

- Teach students specific strategies for answering various types of questions, e.g., multiple choice, true-false, short answer, essay.

Please also refer to other sections in this chapter (e.g., difficulties with reading, writing, and concentration) for strategies that may be relevant to organizational/study skills.

Homework

When homework is overwhelming, students with OCD and their parents can become extremely frustrated. Indeed, homework completion may take a toll on the entire family. Students with OCD who have worked hard to suppress or hide their symptoms at school may be extremely tired when they arrive home. Once at home, they may feel compelled to engage in rituals, including those they "missed" during the school day, leaving little time or energy for homework. While doing their homework, students may be plagued by reading, writing, or a whole host of other rituals that interfere with their ability to complete assignments. Difficulty doing homework was one of the top two school-related concerns reported by both students with OCD and their parents in two separate studies.

Homework completion is a process. According to Illes (2008), completing a homework assignment means the student must:

1. know and understand what the assignment is;

2. record the assignment;

3. bring the required materials home;

4. do the homework;

5. return the homework to a book bag or backpack;

6. take the homework to school; and

7. turn the assignment in to the teacher.

Students with OCD may have difficulty with any one or more of these areas. Following are a number of ways school personnel may provide homework support.

- Use a cue to signal that homework is going to be announced, e.g., use an auditory cue such as a bell, state homework assignment in louder voice.

- Write homework directions on the board in addition to announcing them verbally.

- Have a peer tutor, paraprofessional, or other individual cue the student when:

    - Homework is being assigned

    - The assignment needs to be recorded in an assignment book, notebook, etc.

- Post homework assignments on a homework hotline (telephone or online).

- Provide a specific time at the end of the day for organizing books and materials that need to go home. If the student has a second set of books/materials at home, ensure that appropriate materials stay in school.

- Have a peer tutor, paraprofessional, or other individual assist the student with organizing materials to take home/leave at school.

- Create a form for the student listing materials that need to go home/stay in school each day.

- Talk with parents to ensure that the student has an appropriate environment in which to do homework, e.g., appropriate amount of time allocated for homework, appropriate location.

- Reduce the amount of homework assigned, e.g., in lieu of completing every math problem, have the student complete every other item.

- Ask parents how much time their child spends on homework in the evening without undue stress (e.g., 20 minutes, half hour). Assign homework that can be completed within that time frame. As the student progresses in treatment, the time limit may be increased.

- Give the student estimates of how much time an assignment should take; such estimates will provide a rough guideline as to how detailed the assignment should be (even if the student needs more time to complete it).

- Tell students to work on an assignment for a certain period of time (e.g., 30 minutes or time period that is appropriate for the student) and to stop when that time period is over. As the student progresses in treatment, the time limit may be increased.

- Do not (as a rule) send home class work that has not been completed during the school day as homework.

- Suggest to the student that he or she try switching to another subject if he or she gets "stuck" on a particular assignment.

- Suggest to the student that he or she try doing homework with a friend, or assign the student to a peer tutor/study group (interaction with another student may prevent or reduce obsessions/rituals).

- Do not penalize the student for homework not submitted if OCD symptoms are interfering.

- Consider various options with regard to *grading* homework: grade assignments on the basis of content rather than neatness; allow some ungraded assignments; be flexible with due dates (e.g., provide a pre-determined amount of extended time without penalty); use only those parts of an assignment that have been completed as the basis for assigning a grade; and for students with perfectionism difficulties, grade rough drafts when they can't complete an assignment, or allow them to submit additional drafts of a project.

- Attend to comments made by the student when homework is/is not turned in, e.g., "I think I made a lot of mistakes," or "It wasn't good enough to turn in," for possible insight into the student's OCD.

- Communicate regularly with parents regarding homework completion and other homework issues via an assignment notebook, parent-teacher log, etc.

- Provide usual consequences for homework not completed for reasons *unrelated* to OCD.

Please also refer to other sections in this chapter (e.g., difficulties with reading, writing, and concentration) for strategies that may be relevant to completing homework.

Understanding the difficulties students with OCD (and other students) experience with homework is critical to providing the assistance they need. To that end, school personnel may have a parent or guardian complete the survey below on students' homework habits. This survey can provide school staff a wealth of information that may help them design effective strategies to support students with homework difficulties.

Homework Screening Survey — Parent Reporting Form					
Student's Name: _____					
Completed by: _____ Date: _____					

[N] never [R] rarely [S] sometimes [O] often [A] always					
ITEM	N	R	S	O	A
My child records all of his or her homework assignments independently in school.					
My child brings the homework planner or recorded assignments home.					
My child brings home the books or materials needed to complete the day's homework assignments.					
My child misplaces or loses schoolwork or homework.					
My child knows and understands the assignment(s).					
My child knows when the assignments are due.					
My child starts homework without reminding or nagging.					
My child leaves homework assignments until the last minute or is late in doing them.					
My child completes the homework without someone sitting with him or her.					
My child can shift or switch easily between homework assignments.					
My child packs up his/her school bag independently and correctly.					
The level of the homework is too difficult for my child to complete independently.					
The amount of homework is too great for my child to complete due to other factors (disabilities, after-school sports, medications, sleep problems, etc.)					
If you have to help your child with homework or supervise your child to make sure the homework gets done, how much time are you spending each day with your child on homework?					
How much time does your child usually spend doing homework each day?					
How often do you fight with your child about homework?					

Reprinted by permission from Leslie E. Packer & Sheryl K. Pruitt, Challenging Kids, Challenged Teachers: Teaching Students with Tourette's, Bipolar Disorder, Executive Dysfunction, OCD, ADHD, and More (Bethesda, MD: Woodbine House, 2010), [page 190].

It was a beautiful day in late May, and Gandira was getting off the school bus after a long day at school. He was looking forward to having his cousins over that evening to celebrate his 10th birthday. He'd have to finish his homework right after school to have the evening free. As he was running home, he took a shortcut through a neighbor's yard to save time. Just as he finished jogging through the yard, he saw a sign in the grass indicating it had been treated with chemicals. Terror engulfed Gandira. He hated chemicals. They can be poisonous and make you sick or even kill you. And when you get them on you, it's almost impossible to get them off.

When he arrived home, Gandira's mother knew something was terribly wrong. Before she had a chance to question him, he tore upstairs, ripping his shoes and clothing off along the way. He got into the shower and began washing – and washing and washing. His mother repeatedly came to the bathroom door, asking him to finish up because their company would soon be arriving. Gandira was deaf to her pleas. When his cousins arrived, he was still taking a shower. After 30 minutes, they left. Gandira finally got out of the shower, drained and shaking. As he started to put on new clothing, he saw something on his arm that looked like chemicals. He stepped back into the shower. This pattern was repeated throughout the entire evening. No company, no birthday celebration – not even any dinner.

Gandira arrived at school the next morning, exhausted and unable to concentrate. He received a zero for the previous night's homework...

Social and emotional functioning

As has been indicated throughout this text, students frequently experience social and emotional distress due to OCD. Following are several sections pertaining to accommodations and strategies school personnel may use to help students who are struggling in these areas.

Symptom/Emotional Buildup

- Prearrange a system in which a student signals the teacher regarding the need to leave the room because symptoms are building and he or she is starting to feel overwhelmed. The signal may be an index card (e.g. brightly-colored card; card that says "Leave," "Time," or another signal word), a hand signal (e.g., a student raises his hand with a closed fist), or another sign. The signal should be as inconspicuous as possible to avoid drawing classmates' attention to it. In addition, time limits for the break (e.g., 10 minutes) should be established with the student in advance. Interestingly, most students with OCD do not abuse this opportunity. When a student knows this option is available, anxiety may lessen, and he or she may not need to use it. Caution should be used, however, with regard to implementing this strategy with students who frequently use the bathroom.

- Provide an alternate location to which a student may go when he or she leaves the classroom to regroup or calm down, such as the nurse's or school psychologist's office. It must be emphasized that this is not a traditional time-out in which the student is punished by being removed from the current activity.

- Allow the student to leave the room briefly to get a drink of water, run an errand, etc., to help clear his or her mind of obsessive thoughts.

- Seat the student closer to the classroom door for an easy exit if and when it is needed.

- Provide a designated time (e.g., lunch, recess) during which the student may engage in rituals if he or she feels compelled to perform rituals at school.

Classroom disruption due to OCD symptoms

- Be creative about devising "face-saving" choices for the student when OCD symptoms become noticeable to peers.

- Seat the student in a location where OCD symptoms will be the least obvious to classmates.

- Continue to conduct class if the student with OCD engages in a ritual that is obvious to peers. Make advance arrangements with the student that he or she can join the rest of the class after completing a ritual. Stopping a lesson and focusing on the student with OCD can be extremely humiliating.

- Try to distract the attention of classmates away from the student with OCD when he or she is engaging in a ritual.

- Avoid trying to stop a ritual when the student is experiencing a high level of anxiety; a major conflict could arise. When anxiety levels accompanying a ritual appear to be lower, redirecting the student (e.g., making a verbal statement or using a hand signal) may be helpful.

- Interact with the student as calmly and neutrally as possible when disruptions do occur; never reprimand the student or engage in public displays of anger or frustration.

Self-esteem issues

- Capitalize on the student's strengths and talents. Children and adolescents with OCD usually have average to above average intelligence levels and frequently are extremely talented in art, poetry, creative writing, music, and a multitude of other areas. It even may be helpful to provide opportunities for students with OCD to demonstrate their talents. Such opportunities may help the student with OCD realize that he or she is not defined by OCD. They also will help peers see the student in a different light. Importantly, Giordano (n.d.) emphasizes that student talents not be misused as a "carrot" that is given and taken away in a behavior plan. An activity the student loves or one in which he or she excels should not be considered something to be taken away as a punishment or allowed only as a privilege to be earned.

- Be open to assigning the student with OCD to a teacher(s) who is/are more empathic to the needs of the student struggling with OCD. A particular teacher can "make or break" a student's school experience.

- Be a good role model with regard to appreciating diversity, including individual differences associated with various disabilities. If school personnel treat students who have OCD with respect and understanding rather than anger and punishment (which can be difficult, given the challenges these students sometimes present), they will provide peers a positive model. Treating students who have OCD with respect and understanding also can boost their self-esteem.

Social interaction problems/social isolation

- Structure classroom activities to promote social interaction among students with OCD and their peers (e.g., cooperative learning groups, lab or group projects). It may be helpful to assign the student with OCD to work with a partner/group comprised of students who demonstrate empathy/respect for others. Or, student groups may be formed by having students count off by numbers or assigning students to groups on the basis of an area of interest. If students are always allowed to self-select groups, the student with OCD may well be left out, leaving the teacher to assign him or her a group – a humiliating experience, indeed.

- Avoid situations in which team captains choose team players; the student with OCD may be the last one chosen.

- Establish a "buddy system" in which the student with OCD joins one or two other students (students who exhibit understanding, empathy) during recess, lunch time, and other social periods. This may reduce anxiety and help relieve the isolation and loneliness students with severe OCD often feel.

Note: The reader is referred to Chapter 19 of this book for a more in-depth discussion of specific strategies for supporting students with OCD who are struggling socially.

Some final thoughts about accommodations and support strategies for students with OCD

It cannot be emphasized strongly enough that an accommodation or support strategy may be extremely beneficial for one student but entirely unsuccessful with another. School personnel must be flexible and creative in terms of devising methods to help individual students with OCD function effectively at school.

Support strategies are critical not only because many students with OCD could not function at school without them but also for another very important reason: they may help the student stay in school. Professionals generally agree it is best to keep a student with OCD in school as long as possible — Chansky, 2000. Frequent absences from school due to overwhelming OCD symptoms – either because students are permitted to leave school or because they stay home from school – may lead to school avoidance. Having in place a support strategy that provides students the opportunity to go to a safe place and/or talk with a designated person when periods of emotional turmoil arise at school, for example, may greatly reduce stress. After even a short break of this nature, the student may be able to regroup and return to class. Such school-based support may preclude a student's need or desire to avoid being in school.

Finally, as indicated in the section on family stress in Chapter 9, siblings of children and adolescents with OCD frequently experience emotional distress. They may be teased because of their brother's or sister's bizarre behavior and may themselves become the target of peer ridicule. Embarrassed by their siblings, they may be reticent to invite friends to their home. They also may feel neglected by parents, whose energies and emotions frequently are tied up with the child who has OCD. In addition, they secretly may worry that they, too, will "catch" this illness. Therefore, when a child has OCD, it is important to address the needs of siblings, as well.

The humiliation and discomfort siblings sometimes experience due to their brother's or sister's OCD may be particularly pronounced when they attend the same school. As a result, the sibling may want to distance him or herself from the child with OCD. In these cases, the sibling's teacher may need to make certain accommodations. If a sibling is reticent to pass his sister's classroom while walking down the hall with his teacher and classmates, for example, the teacher may consider taking an alternate route to their destination.

Ch 19

SPECIAL ISSUES RELATED TO THE SCHOOL-BASED TREATMENT OF OCD

In addition to knowing about the accommodations and support strategies listed in Chapter 18, school personnel must be aware of a number of other issues related to the school-based treatment of OCD. Each of these topics merits its own book; indeed, multiple texts have been written on a number of the issues. For the purposes of this chapter, however, a brief discussion of each topic will be provided as it relates to students with OCD. A number of different resources are provided throughout the chapter for the reader interested in additional information.

Peer education

In some cases, students with OCD experience few, if any, symptoms at school. In other cases, students try to keep their symptoms concealed during the school day. If OCD symptoms are absent or inconspicuous at school, there may be no need or benefit to educating classmates about the student's OCD. In many situations, however, the student is performing rituals that are obvious to peers, and appear odd, if not bizarre. And when students are viewed as "different," they can become easy targets for peer ridicule and even bullying. Under these circumstances, it may be beneficial to educate peers about OCD.

Research and anecdotal records have indicated that providing education about various disabilities to significant individuals in the lives of children and adolescents – including peers – may greatly alleviate stress for young people who have these disabilities. The author once spoke with a school social worker who recounted an incident in which an elementary-school student was teased due to symptoms of Tourette Syndrome. Because the student was struggling socially, a decision was made to educate his peers about TS. Once his classmates understood the disorder, they made dramatically fewer negative remarks about him. As a result, the student became far less anxious in the school setting, and his symptoms greatly improved.

It is critical to note that a student's OCD should *never* be divulged to classmates without the permission of the child and his or her parents. Many young people do not want personal information shared with others, and parents sometimes fear repercussions from an open discussion of the disorder (e.g., they are concerned about the stigma and labeling frequently associated with mental illness). In some cases, older students may choose to do a class presentation on OCD or have an open discussion with their peers about the disorder. The decision to speak frankly with classmates *always* rests with the student, however, and should be supported by parents.

One option for educating peers is to have school personnel provide general information regarding a number of different disorders, such as asthma, epilepsy, AD/HD, learning disabilities, and OCD, within the context of the health curriculum (i.e., without focusing on a specific student). The more students are exposed to information about different conditions or disabilities, the greater likelihood that the students either have (themselves) or know someone with one of the disorders. Thus, the students' capacity to relate to others, as well as empathy and an acceptance of others' differences, may be engendered — *Chansky, 2000*.

Most websites dedicated to a particular disorder contain a wealth of information that can be shared with students (websites of a number of reputable organizations are included in Appendix A). Some of these websites have information and materials designed specifically for classroom use. A number of organizations even provide specific curricula on disability awareness training free of charge, (e.g., Easter Seals; *www.easterseals.com*). Other approaches to peer education include using educational curricula designed for disability awareness (e.g., Kids on the Block; *www.kotb.com*), having assemblies or guest speakers, showing documentaries and other films, and providing appropriate books and other print (e.g., newspapers) on the topic. When choosing an approach for providing peer education, the age and maturity level of the students will be important considerations. Appendix B contains a number of books pertaining to children and adolescents with OCD, and Appendix C includes a list of several videos about young people with this disorder.

Social difficulties

As previously noted, research has indicated that up to 80% of adults report that their OCD began during childhood. There is a high risk, therefore, that OCD will interfere with normal child development, including social functioning. Children and adolescents with OCD frequently are withdrawn and isolated from peers and may have few, if any, friendships. Moreover, OCD usually co-exists with one or more disorders (e.g., AD/HD, learning disabilities, nonverbal learning disabilities, Tourette Syndrome), each of which may bring to bear its own set of difficulties related to social functioning (see Chapter 8 for a discussion of comorbidity). Several specific strategies for addressing some of these social difficulties were listed in Chapter 18. The importance of this topic, however, begs additional attention.

According to Friend & Bursuck (2006), school personnel must consider a number of factors with regard to building relationships among students with and without disabilities. The first is providing ample opportunities for these groups to interact through activities such as structured in-class group assignments, service learning projects, peer buddies, and extracurricular activities. In addition to providing opportunities for interaction, school personnel must cultivate social relationships and friendships by incorporating into their instruction informal friendship-building strategies such as teaching social skills via role-playing. Other strategies, such as the Circle of Friends activity — *Demchak, n.d.*, also may be implemented. The Circle of Friends is a process in which students without disabilities discuss the importance of relationships and friendships in their own lives (circles) and generate ways in which they might become part of the circle of friends of peers who have disabilities (see *www.unr.edu/educ/ndsip*). In addition, it is extremely important that school personnel seek input from parents – who may provide a wealth of information – regarding suggestions for including their child in social activities.

Other components suggested by Friend & Bursuck (2006) as important in building positive relationships among students with and without disabilities include:

1. providing education to students about individuals with disabilities;

2. using peer tutoring programs such as Peer-Assisted Learning Strategies (see *kc.vanderbilt.edu/pals*) and Classwide Peer Tutoring (see *www.specialconnections.ku.edu*); and

3. implementing cooperative learning approaches such as Jigsaw Classroom (see *www.jigsaw.org*) and Numbered Heads Together (see *www.kaganonline.com*).

In addition, it is imperative that school personnel serve as positive role models for interacting with students who have disabilities.

The aforementioned strategies may go a long way toward fostering social relationships between students with OCD and their peers. In some cases, however, more direct and specific approaches are necessary. Developed by Rick Lavoie, the "social autopsy" is one such approach. The social autopsy is a process in which an adult assists a child who has difficulty with social interactions by:

1. analyzing, together with the child, errors he or she has made in given social situations, and

2. developing alternative strategies.

This procedure can be extremely effective in terms of helping the student see the cause and effect relationship between his or her social behavior and the reactions of other individuals (see *www.ldonline.org/lavoie* for a more in-depth discussion of social autopsies.)

There also are a number of commercial programs available for providing instruction in social skills, including *Think Aloud: Increasing Social and Cognitive Skills-A Problem-Solving Program for Children, Classroom Program, Grades 1-2* — Camp & Bash, 1985; the *Skillstreaming* series for early childhood — McGinnis & Goldstein, 2003, elementary — McGinnis & Goldstein, 1997, and adolescents — Goldstein & McGinnis, 1997 (see *www.skillstreaming.com*); and Carol Gray's Social Stories™ (see *www.thegraycenter.org*). The website of the National Association of School Psychologists also has an excellent fact sheet on social skills containing a wealth of information on various types of social skills, identifying social skills deficits, and social skills interventions, including a number of empirically-supported, commercially-published social skills training programs. This fact sheet can be accessed at: *www.nasponline.org/resources/factsheets/socialskills_fs.aspx*.

"Rage attacks"/meltdowns: A rare but serious OCD-related behavior

Research indicates that children and adolescents with Tourette Syndrome sometimes experience sudden, explosive outbursts of behavior, frequently referred to as "rage attacks." These outbursts are episodes of severe, impulsive verbal and/or physical aggression that occur in response to what seems to be trivial provocation or frustration — Budman et al., 2008. Rage attacks, which also have been called "storms" or "meltdowns," usually do not occur when Tourette Syndrome is the sole diagnosis. AD/HD and OCD, alone or in combination, frequently co-occur with TS in individuals who experience explosive outbursts. Moreover, explosive outbursts have been found to increase with the number of comorbid conditions — *Budman, Bruun, Park, Lesser, & Olson, 2000*. This information is important for school personnel, who should be alert to the potential for rage attacks when a student has comorbid TS, OCD, AD/HD, and/or other disorders (e.g., depression, bipolar disorder).

When young people with TS have OCD, rage attacks frequently are triggered when a ritual is interrupted or when unexpected events occur during a rigid obsessive-compulsive thought pattern — *Palumbo & Kurlan, 2007*. When a ritual is disrupted and cannot be completed, the individual may become overwhelmed that something terrible will happen. Rage and anger may be directed at the person or situation responsible for the disruption. For example, the child who feels compelled to tap his desk 20 times to prevent his mother from dying may become panicked and respond with rage to the teacher who interrupts his ritual. The teacher, who has observed no external trigger for this outburst, may view it as totally irrational.

Unlike tantrums, which represent goal-directed behavior – getting an individual(s) to do something you want – rage attacks do not stop, even if the child is given what he or she wants. Once a storm starts, it seems to take over control. Packer and Pruitt (2010) note "these episodes do not appear to be voluntary behaviors that would be modifiable by applying consequences after they occur" (p. 130).

Steven, a sophomore in high school, was sitting as his desk during history period. The teacher had just finished a lecture about weapons used during the Civil War and had given the class a worksheet to complete. But Steven wasn't doing his work. He couldn't stop thinking about a bayonet his grandfather had inherited from a relative who was a soldier in the Civil War. The bayonet was mounted in a glass case in his grandfather's study. A wicked-looking weapon, the bayonet was capable of inflicting horrific damage upon the human body.

Steven started to wonder whether he might be capable of using that bayonet to hurt someone. He could easily smash the glass case that contained it, grab it, and plunge the spear into someone's flesh. Dear God! What if his grandfather happened to be right there in the study?

An image of Steven stabbing his grandfather with the bayonet flashed across his mind. His anxiety skyrocketed; he had to do something to ensure that he would never hurt his grandfather. So he started praying, "Lord, please don't let me ever hurt Grandpa." He had to repeat this phrase an even number of times until it felt "just right." On the third repetition, the voice of his History teacher boomed, "Steven, you'd better get to work this instant!" Steven's ritual was interrupted; he became panicked and exploded in rage. His face reddened, and he started pounding his desk. He screamed at the teacher, telling him how much he hated him. The teacher, oblivious to what Steven was experiencing, was shocked by his outburst...

Rage attacks, most of which do not occur in school — *Dornbush & Pruitt, 2008* should be addressed within the context of clinical treatment (e.g., cognitive therapy, medication). Educators must be aware of how to manage rage attacks, however, when they do occur at school. First, it is very important that school personnel learn to be attentive to any signs of agitation or anxiety that precede the rages/meltdowns, such as a rapid increase in movement (e.g., child becomes increasingly fidgety or talkative). Or a student may exhibit a sudden and unusual reaction or overreaction to environmental stimuli such as touch and noise. It may be extremely helpful to solicit input from the parents of a child who experiences rage attacks regarding triggers or warning signs of rage. Helping the student learn to identify signs of an impending rage attack (e.g., feeling anxious, panicked, shaky) also may be beneficial. Once precursors to rage attacks are identified, the environment should be altered to reduce or eliminate them.

If a rage attack cannot be prevented and does occur, it is of utmost importance that school personnel not react with punishment, anger, or hostility; such responses can escalate the rage attack. Indeed, providing any additional sensory input likely will exacerbate symptoms. In essence, the rage attack must be allowed to run its course. To avoid any physical injury, it is best for school personnel and classmates to keep a distance from the student. In some cases, it may be necessary to remove other students and school personnel from the place where the rage attack is occurring rather than remove the student — *Packer & Pruitt, 2010.*

When a rage attack has subsided, the student may feel very guilty and remorseful for exhibiting inappropriate behaviors. In some cases, the student may not even remember what happened during the incident.

Nonetheless, it is very important that the student take responsibility for his or her actions and make amends, as necessary (e.g., apologizing to a peer or an adult for improper behavior).

It may be extremely beneficial to conduct a functional behavioral assessment on students who experience rage attacks to determine what, if any, environmental factors trigger them. A positive behavior intervention plan then could be developed to prevent or reduce the occurrence of these triggers (see section on functional behavioral assessment and positive behavior interventions and supports in Chapter 22). If rage attacks occur only at home, students may be suppressing explosive outbursts at school. In these cases, school personnel may work with the parents to determine if there are any school-related factors that should be addressed to decrease stress in the school environment
— *Packer & Pruitt, 2010.*

Teasing/bullying

Anecdotal records in the literature have suggested that students with OCD may be at higher risk for bullying than "normal" students for several reasons. First, when rituals are performed overtly, students with OCD look different, if not "strange." Second, because children and adolescents with OCD often have a limited network of friends, they may not have the physical and emotional support necessary to fend off bullying. Third, students with OCD usually have coexisting conditions, some of which may increase the risk of being teased and bullied (e.g., Tourette Syndrome often is characterized by noticeable motor and verbal tics).

The results of the first systematic study of peer victimization among children with OCD — *Storch, Ledley, et al., 2006* support anecdotal reports of bullying. Specifically, the results indicated that peer victimization is significantly higher among youth with OCD, with more than a quarter being victimized on a regular basis. Moreover, young people with OCD were significantly more likely to be targeted than youth with diabetes, whose behavior sometimes is viewed as different from their peers (e.g., taking insulin injections, being unable to eat certain foods such as candy). The findings also suggested that more severe OCD symptoms led to increased victimization, which, in turn, contributed to the presence of depression, externalizing behaviors, and, to some extent, loneliness among these children.

Although teachers may believe they almost always intervene in bullying incidents, studies involving actual observations of bullying have suggested very low rates of teacher intervention — *Heinrichs, 2003*. One explanation for this may be that many bullying episodes are verbal, brief, and frequently take place during times of little teacher supervision. Indeed, bullying can be very subtle and may not be obvious to school personnel. Moreover, students frequently do not report being bullied for a variety of reasons, including fears of:

1. being embarrassed because they don't defend themselves, and

2. repercussions from the "bully" if they report the incident.

Unfortunately, students may believe that school personnel are indifferent to bullying or simply can't do anything about it when they don't intervene. Research has indicated that when a teacher is present during a bullying incident and does nothing about it, it is even more harmful to the students being bullied, because it connotes acceptance of bullying — *Heinrichs, 2003*. It cannot be denied that some children and adolescents with OCD exhibit behaviors that annoy or even upset their peers, such as touching them or constantly asking them for reassurance. Nonetheless, it is the responsibility of adults in the educational environment to enforce codes of conduct whenever teasing and bullying are observed. It also is incumbent upon school personnel to provide positive school-based behavioral interventions and supports to help students with OCD who exhibit behavioral difficulties in the school context.

It is beyond the scope of this text to provide an in-depth discussion of strategies and systems for managing teasing and bullying in the school context; a huge body of literature on this topic exists. However, a few points deserve mention. First, it is vital that school personnel become knowledgeable about OCD and come to understand it as a "no-fault" disorder with a neurobiological basis. When school personnel treat students who have OCD with respect and understanding rather than anger and punishment, they provide students a positive model for social interactions with all individuals. In addition, school personnel should work to create a stable and non-threatening environment free from ridicule and stigma at both the classroom- and school-wide level.

Second, because children (and people, in general) tend to ridicule that which they do not understand, it is important to prevent or defuse teasing and bullying by educating students about OCD and other disorders. Understanding can foster empathy and compassion; ignorance can breed contempt (see previous section on peer education).

Third, because bullying frequently occurs in settings in which there is little adult supervision, it is important to evaluate how well various areas are monitored (e.g., gymnasium, playground, cafeteria, school bus) and provide added adult supervision, as necessary. Also, it is essential that students with OCD (and other students with disabilities) be watched closely, because they are at higher risk for being teased and bullied than students without disabilities.

Fourth, it is extremely important to work with students who are the "bullies." School personnel first should try to understand the needs and motivation behind the behavior of these students (e.g., looking for attention, trying to feel important) and then provide appropriate interventions to help them change their behavior. Something as simple as "catching the 'bully' being good," i.e., providing positive feedback to students prone to bullying for even small, helpful gestures, can be beneficial.

Finally, it is crucial to foster a sense of responsibility among bystanders – students who are witnesses to bullying incidents. Bystanders must be taught strategies such as telling the bully to stop, distracting the bully, providing support to the victim, and – very importantly – informing a school staff member about an episode of bullying — *Shore, 2009*. It is essential that bystanders also understand that:

1. laughing at or going along with the bully essentially contributes to the bullying, and

2. doing nothing conveys to the bully that it is okay to hurt other students.

A number of different anti-bullying programs are available today. School personnel interested in implementing a formal anti-bullying program must carefully review these programs to determine which one is the best match for their school with respect to the students' ages, the cultural/ethnic make-up of the school, etc. Below is a sample of several anti-bullying programs:

The Olweus Bullying Prevention Program — *www.olweus.org*

The "Bully-Proofing" Series: Early childhood, elementary, middle and high school — *www.sopriswest.com/Default.aspx*

The Bully Buster program — www.researchpress.com

Bully-Proofing Your School: A Comprehensive Approach for Elementary Schools (54BULLY) — Available at *www.amazon.com*

PATHS® (Providing Alternative THinking Strategies) — *www.channing-bete.com*

Medication at school

Treatment provided by outside professionals for children and adolescents with OCD varies. In some cases, young people receive exposure and response prevention therapy only, while others receive a combination of E/RP and medication. Still other students are treated with medication only, even though OCD experts do not support this as the first line of treatment for young people (see Chapter 12 on medications). Whenever students take medication(s) for OCD and/or comorbid disorders, school personnel have important responsibilities.

Students with OCD sometimes take their medications at home. Even when this is the case, it is important that school staff be aware of all drugs the child is taking. School professionals also should be informed of any changes in medication taken at home (e.g., increased or decreased dosage, change of medication, discontinuation of medication), so they can monitor students at school. Indeed, because school personnel interact with students for extended periods of time on a consistent basis, they are uniquely positioned to observe and report behavioral changes that potentially could be related to medication.

School districts are required to provide medication at school, including medication for OCD, as appropriate. When medication is taken at school, it should be done in compliance with all federal, state, and district regulations. School policies for administering medication must address issues such as:

1. the administration of short-term, over-the-counter, parent-recommended medications, long-term prescription medications, and emergency and urgent medications;

2. the security and storage of medication; and

3. protocols to prevent medication error. School personnel must be familiar with their school's policies; parents should have a copy of district regulations, as well.

The interested reader may find *Guidelines for the Administration of Medication in School*, the policy statement of The American Academy of Pediatrics, at *aappolicy.aappublications.org*.

Like all drugs, OCD medications have potential side effects. These effects may be particularly prominent during the initial stages of taking a medication for the first time or when there is a change in medications. Feedback from school personnel regarding student behavior is extremely important not only during these periods but also throughout treatment to help physicians determine if medication adjustments are necessary.

Anafranil, a serotonin reuptake inhibitor sometimes used to treat OCD, has been associated with side effects such as dry mouth, tremor, dizziness, sedation, constipation, and sweating. Although selective serotonin reuptake inhibitors (e.g., Prozac, Luvox, Paxil, Zoloft) usually are associated with fewer side effects than Anafranil, they, too, have known side effects, including agitation, insomnia, fatigue, diarrhea, and nausea. Side effects may lessen with time, but some children and adolescents experience difficulties throughout treatment. Side effects associated with drugs may lead to disruptive behavior or interfere with concentration, impeding a student's ability to learn. It may be very helpful for school personnel to request that the prescribing physician provide a list of possible side effects for the drug(s) a student is taking for OCD and any comorbid disorders.

School staff play a very important role in monitoring and documenting the school functioning of students on medication, which may include conducting observations of student behavior. When such observations are made, the time, setting, and ongoing activity should be documented to assist in determining if any patterns of behavior are noted (e.g., student has difficulty staying awake during the first period of the day). In some cases, physicians may provide school personnel with checklists or other tools for documenting student behavior. Or the health care provider may ask a teacher to keep track of three or four symptoms (e.g., trips to the bathroom, requests for reassurance, etc.) when medication dosage or side effects are an issue — Chansky, 2000. Some side effects are minor and barely perceptible; parents should be contacted immediately, however, if any side effects raise a concern.

Another important role school personnel play with regard to medication is providing accommodations and supports, as necessary, to assist the student who experiences side effects. A teacher may need to temporarily reduce the work load of the student who is fatigued due to an increase in medication dosage, for example. Or the student who is having difficulty with dry mouth may be allowed to carry a bottle of water at all times.

One potential side effect of antidepressants to which school personnel must pay careful attention is a phenomenon known as behavioral activation. Behavioral activation encompasses a variety of symptoms, including agitation, aggression, irritability, impulsivity, hyperactivity, increased depression or anxiety, and, among a small fraction of youth, an increased risk for suicidality, or suicidal thinking and behavior. Multiple studies have indicated that the benefits of using SSRIs to treat children and adolescents with OCD generally outweigh the risks. Whenever a student is taking an antidepressant, however, the prescribing physician should closely monitor its effects. In addition, school personnel must be vigilant with regard to any signs of suicidal or other troubling behaviors and report them to parents *immediately.*

Finally, in addition to monitoring adverse side effects, school personnel should note any positive behavioral changes observed when a student is on medication and share these observations with the parents and therapist, as appropriate. For instance, the student may be experiencing less difficulty concentrating in class, is carrying out tasks that previously could not be performed (e.g., student can walk through a particular doorway without repeating the behavior multiple times), or seems happier.

Communication systems

One factor crucial to the success of interventions for children and adolescents with OCD is effective collaboration among all parties involved in treatment: school professionals, parents, the student, outside professionals, and other individuals, as appropriate. One of the keys to successful collaboration is effective communication. Effective communication facilitates the creation of realistic and meaningful interventions for the student with OCD. Moreover, an exchange of information among treatment partners throughout the intervention is vital to determining its efficacy and making appropriate adjustments.

It is important that individuals participating in the treatment process develop a practical system for communicating with one another. Although information may be exchanged in person, via telephone, or e-mail, newer technologies such as texting have greatly improved the ease of communication. Communication can occur as frequently as necessary: biweekly, weekly, or even on a daily basis. A parent-teacher log, in which parents and teachers share written information/feedback about a student, can be used each school day.

Families typically are very eager to learn about any progress the student has made as a result of treatment (e.g., cognitive-behavioral therapy and/or medication, school-based interventions). What appears to be an inconsequential gain to the outside observer may, in fact, be monumental to the child and his or her family: a student who has been unable to touch the classroom door knob without first covering his or her hand with a glove or paper towel now is able to touch the door knob without a covering. In these instances, it is critical for school personnel not only to relay this information to parents but also to communicate directly with students, commending them for their hard work and successes. Of note is that school personnel should always praise effort – even in the absence of success.

Transitioning back to school after an extended absence

Fortunately, children and adolescents with OCD usually can be treated successfully on an outpatient basis. There are instances, however, in which OCD is so severe that hospitalization is warranted, and the student is removed from school temporarily. In other cases, OCD symptoms are so severe that although not hospitalized, a student cannot function at school and is homebound for a period of time. In any case, school personnel must be prepared to ease the transition back to school for students who have been absent for a considerable length of time.

It is very important that a transition plan consider the psychological, medical, and academic requirements of the returning student. From a psychological standpoint, one need only step into the shoes of a student who has been out of school for some time to understand the apprehension, fear, and embarrassment potentially associated with going back to school. In-school counseling (e.g., supportive and reflective listening, relaxation techniques) may benefit returning students. Medical needs may involve managing the side effects of medications such as fatigue, grogginess, or irritability. In these cases, it is important that all school personnel with whom the student has contact be informed of potential side effects and how they may interfere with the student's ability to function. Furthermore, academic accommodations such as a reduced schoolwork load or extended time on assignments may be necessary in the short term. Schools commonly develop written transition plans to address the needs of students returning to school after hospitalization.

It usually is preferable to make re-entry into school a gradual process to ensure successful reintegration and foster self-esteem. Gradual re-entry may involve the student's attending one class a day (e.g., a class the student likes) for a period of time and gradually adding other classes until he or she is able to attend for partial and then full days. There are a number of different ways to structure the transition back to school. In all cases, however, parents should be involved to ensure the smoothest reintegration possible. In addition, it is important that parents have a contact person at school in the event that problems arise. Effective planning prior to the student's return and sensitivity to his or her needs will go a long way toward easing the transition.

Assistive Technology

Chapter 18 was devoted to accommodations and support strategies that may help students with OCD access the general education curriculum. The following section provides a more in-depth discussion of another crucial component related to supporting students with disabilities: assistive technology (AT).

IDEA 1997 and the subsequent Individuals with Disabilities Education Act of 2004 mandate that students with disabilities have access to assistive technology devices and/or services. They also state that assistive technology must be considered for all students eligible for special education services. The federal definition of an assistive technology device is "any item, piece of equipment or product system, whether acquired commercially or off the shelf, modified, or customized, that is used to increase, maintain, or improve functional capabilities of a child with a disability" (IDEA 2004, 20 U.S.C. – 1401(1)(A)). An assistive technology service is "any service that directly assists a child with a disability in the selection, acquisition, or use of an assistive technology device" (IDEA 2004, 20 U.S.C. – 1401(2)). Assistive technology is used by individuals with disabilities to allow them to perform tasks that otherwise might be difficult if not impossible. AT can create new opportunities, break down barriers, and level the playing field for students with OCD and other disabilities.

Currently, there is no empirical research related specifically to the use of assistive technology with students who have OCD. Because these students frequently experience difficulty with reading, writing, and organization, however, a list of various assistive technologies addressing problems in these areas is provided. As is the case with any accommodation or support strategy for students with OCD, one type of assistive technology may be extremely effective for one student but ineffective with another. The word processor, for instance, has been a tremendous assist for many students who experience writing rituals. Other students with paper-and-pencil writing rituals, however, have been known to get "stuck" on the computer.

The following information is adapted from the work of Ms. Kristin Stanberry, a writer and editor whose expertise includes learning disabilities and AD/HD, and Dr. Marshall Raskind, a learning disability researcher. Dr. Raskind has conducted extensive research both in the fields of learning disabilities and assistive technology. Their work appears on LD Online (*www.ldonline.org*), a well-known website on learning disabilities and AD/HD, and GreatSchools (*www.greatschools. org*), a website for parents that addresses health, development, and a multitude of academic issues. It must be noted that inclusion of a specific AT in the following list does not suggest an endorsement, and the list is not exhaustive.

Difficulties with reading

Audio books and electronic publications: user listens to recorded books/other text materials via audiocassettes, CDs, Daisy readers, computers, and MP3 players. Available through the National Library Service for the Blind and Physically Handicapped, Recording for the

Blind and Dyslexic, Audible.com, Project Gutenberg, Kindle, Bookshare

Optical character recognition: user scans printed material into a computer/handheld unit; text is read aloud by means of a speech synthesis/screen reading system. Examples: Kurzweil 3000, Read and Write Gold, Wynn software, Quicktionary 2 (a pen-like, hand-held scanner that can scan a word or line of text; immediate word-by-word translation is provided)

Paper-based computer pen: user takes notes while recording a speaker (e.g., teacher). User later can listen to any part of the recording by touching the pen to the corresponding section of notes. Has many other features, as well. Example: Pulse Smartpen by Livescribe

Speech synthesizers/screen readers: display and read aloud text (typed, scanned, Internet print) on a computer screen. Examples: AspireReader, Read:Outloud, Write:OutLoud, Kurzweil 3000, Read and Write Gold, Wynn software

Variable speed control (VSC) tape recorders: user may listen to prerecorded text or tape a speaker (e.g., teacher) and listen to it later. Playback rate may be sped up or slowed down without voice distortion. Available through MaxiAids.com, Independentliving.com

Difficulties with writing/expressive writing

Text expanders: in conjunction with a word processor, user develops, stores, and reuses abbreviations for commonly-used words and phrases. Saves the writer keystrokes and promotes correct spelling of words and phrases that have been coded. Examples: TypeIt4Me (available through Shareware), ActiveWords

Alternative keyboards: standard keyboard customized by adding graphics to keys, grouping keys by color/location, etc. Example: Intellikeys, Big Keys

Portable word processors: keyboard devices that are lightweight and easy to transport. Examples: AlphaSmart, Neo, Fusion, Quickpad, Netbook

Graphic organizers and outlining programs: user organizes unstructured information into appropriate categories and order. Examples: Inspiration, Kidspiration, Draft:Builder

Paper-based computer pen: user takes notes while recording a speaker (e.g., teacher). User later can listen to any part of the recording by touching the pen to the corresponding section of notes. Has many other features, as well. Example: Pulse Smartpen by Livescribe

Speech recognition software programs: in conjunction with word processor, user speaks into a microphone and spoken words appear on computer screen as text. Examples: Dragon Naturally Speaking, Microsoft Windows (XP, Vista, Windows 7), Speech Recognition, SpeakQ, Macspeech Dictate, Voxforge

Talking spell-checkers/Electronic dictionaries: Talking devices display chosen words on the computer screen as they are "read aloud." Assists user with correct spelling while writing and proofreading. Examples: Franklin Electronic Dictionaries/Spell correctors, WordWeb Pro

Word prediction software programs: help with word processing by predicting the word the user intends to type; user selects appropriate word. Assists with correct spelling, grammar, and word choices with fewer keystrokes. Examples: Co:Writer, WordQ, IntelliTalk, Read and Write Gold, Kurzweil 3000, Wynn Software

Difficulties with organization/memory

Free-form Database software: in conjunction with word processor, helps user develop and store electronic notes by writing down information on any topic quickly. User later can retrieve information by typing any part of the original note. Examples: AskSam, Microsoft Office OneNote (Kurzweil also has sticky notes feature)

Information/Data Managers: help user plan, organize, store and retrieve information (e.g., calendar, contact data) in electronic form. Examples: Franklin (hand-held organizers), Palm, Pocket PC, iPod/ iPhone, Droid

Alarm Reminders: user can program alarms built within cell phones, handheld devices, or specialized watches to remind them of important appointments or assignments. Examples: cell phones with alarm features, productivity apps for iPhone/iPod Touch/iPad/Droid, alarm watches with or without vibration

Paper-based computer pen: user takes notes while recording a speaker (e.g., teacher). User later can listen to any part of the recording by touching the pen to the corresponding section of notes. Has many other features, as well. Example: Pulse Smartpen by Livescribe

Grading practices

When OCD has little to no impact on school performance (e.g., symptoms are very mild, child experiences symptoms at home but not at school), students with OCD should be graded in the same manner as their classmates without disabilities. Unfortunately, symptoms of OCD frequently interfere with attention and concentration, impair academic performance, and severely affect grades – even though children and adolescents with OCD typically have average to above average intelligence levels. The literature abounds with examples of "A" students whose grades plummeted after the onset of OCD. Therefore, it is extremely important for school personnel to determine whether changes in grading (i.e., on individual assignments and/or report cards) are warranted for these students, and if so, what kinds of changes should be implemented. Numerous books and articles have been devoted to the topic of grading students with disabilities. A few important considerations on this subject, however, are provided.

First, it is essential that school personnel carefully establish which kinds of assignments and expectations (e.g., tests, quizzes, homework assignments, oral reports), sometimes referred to as grading "elements," will be used to determine report card grades — Munk, 2009. It also is critical that educators communicate to students and parents which elements will and will not be counted toward a report card grade. For example, the trend in general education is to count only academic work for report card grades and to provide separate feedback on behaviors such as effort and the ability to engage in cooperative work. When parents and students are informed that effort, for example, is an element that will not be included in determining a report card grade, later misunderstandings may be avoided.

Second, when certain predetermined grading elements present challenges for students due to OCD symptoms (e.g., writing rituals render handwriting the answers to essay questions extremely difficult), it is important to provide accommodations that will minimize the "interaction" between the task and the student's disability — *Munk, 2009*. If writing the answers to essay questions is problematic, the student may be allowed to use a word processor (i.e., if using this tool precludes writing rituals). In a similar vein, a student with OCD whose reading rituals interfere with the ability to complete reading assignments may use a Kurzweil reader that reads printed material aloud via speech synthesis (see previous section on assistive technology).

Third, school staff should avoid certain practices when grading students with OCD. One such practice involves assigning zeroes for late or missing work — *Guskey & Bailey, 2001*. Zeroes not only have a severe overall impact on grades but also have the effect of punishing students for their OCD symptoms. It is far preferable to provide students with opportunities to earn full or partial credit for late work. Another tactic school personnel should avoid is threatening students with low or failing grades (on an assignment or report card) in an attempt to improve OCD symptoms. Telling a student that he will receive a failing grade on a worksheet if he doesn't stop erasing and reerasing his writing, for example, is an ineffective strategy for reducing OCD behavior. Indeed, such threats may create additional stress for the student and exacerbate symptoms.

Ch:20

LAWS PERTAINING TO EDUCATIONAL SERVICES
FOR STUDENTS WITH OCD

Chapter 18 provides a detailed listing of accommodations and support strategies school personnel may use to facilitate school functioning for students with OCD. When a student requires only minimal assistance, an accommodation that is extremely easy to implement and costs nothing (e.g., moving a student's seat) sometimes is provided for the student without going through any formal procedures. Many parents prefer having even simple accommodations documented in writing, however (see section below on 504 plans).

When students with OCD experience difficulties at school, two federal laws typically come into play: Section 504 of the Rehabilitation Act of 1973 — *Section 504; 29 U.S.C. § 794* and The Individuals with Disabilities Education Improvement Act of 2004 — *20 U.S.C. § 1400 et seq*. Both laws protect the rights of children and adolescents to a free, appropriate public education in the least restrictive environment (described in next section). Although most school personnel are familiar with Section 504 and IDEA, a discussion of these laws as they pertain to students with OCD is provided. It is important to note that each child's situation is different, and the information below does not substitute for the advice of a licensed attorney qualified in disability law.

Section 504 of the Rehabilitation Act of 1973

Many students with OCD – frequently those with milder cases – are served under Section 504. Section 504 is a civil rights law that states "No otherwise qualified individual with a disability in the United States... shall, solely by reason of her or his disability, be excluded from the participation in, be denied the benefits of, or be subjected to discrimination under any program or activity receiving Federal financial assistance..." — *29 U.S.C. § 794(a)*. Thus, all qualified children with disabilities within the jurisdiction of a school district are entitled to a free, appropriate education.

As defined in Section 504, a person who qualifies as having a disability is "any person who:

1. has a physical or mental impairment which substantially limits one or more of such person's major life activities;

2. has a record of such an impairment; or

3. is regarded as having such an impairment" — *29 U.S.C. § 705(20)(B)*.

Physical disabilities listed in Section 504 include (but are not limited to) physiological disorders or conditions that affect one or more body systems such as the neurological, musculoskeletal, respiratory, and cardiovascular systems. Mental impairments include mental retardation, organic brain syndrome, emotional or mental illness, and specific learning disabilities. Although not expressly listed, OCD does qualify as a disability under Section 504. When a diagnosis of OCD has been made, formal documentation of the diagnosis is required by school officials. Even without a formal diagnosis, however, a student's school performance may be such that he or she is regarded as having an impairment.

In addition to qualifying as a disability under Section 504, a student's OCD must substantially limit one or more "major life activities." Major life activities include not only basics such as walking, speaking, and breathing but also learning and behavior in school. To determine whether a student's OCD affects learning and/or behavior, a team of school staff members must evaluate information from a variety of different sources (a single source is considered insufficient), including teacher reports, information from parents, the student's grades, school-administered tests (e.g., state assessment tests), observations of the student, and other pertinent information. A Section 504 evaluation does not necessarily require formal testing to ascertain whether the disability is substantially limiting, although this depends upon the disability and the extent to which its impact is apparent.

Once it has been established that a student with OCD qualifies for services under Section 504, a program must be designed to meet his or her individual needs *to the same extent that the needs of students without disabilities are met.* In other words, Section 504 essentially levels the playing field for students with OCD. Interventions in the form of accommodations and modifications are documented in what commonly is referred to as a "504 plan." These interventions usually are implemented in the general education classroom. To meet the unique needs of students with OCD, however, an "appropriate" education under Section 504 also may include regular or special education and related aids and services.

As previously indicated, many parents prefer having even simple accommodations documented in writing under Section 504, rather than an informal verbal agreement with a teacher or other school staff member. Circumstances change (e.g., a teacher may leave), and a 504 plan documents, in writing, decisions that have been made regarding a student's services. Having a 504 plan in place also can be important because OCD symptoms tend to wax and wane; accommodations and supports may be needed during periods of heightened OCD symptoms but not at other times. Equally important, if a student is seeking eligibility for accommodations for college entrance exams, during the college years, or later in life, the presence of a history of prior formal recognition of the disability is important documentation of the disability and need for accommodations. Conversely, informal accommodations are less useful as documentation later on. Moreover, Section 504 plans may contain important procedures for managing learning, behavior, or medical problems that sometimes occur when a student has OCD. For example, procedures for managing a student who has an OCD-related outburst or dispensing emergency medications may be documented in a 504 plan.

Two provisions of Section 504 regarding the participation of students with disabilities are noteworthy. First, students with OCD must be educated in the least restrictive environment appropriate. In other words, to the greatest extent possible, students with disabilities must be educated in settings with students who do not have disabilities. Thus, students with OCD must be placed in the regular education environment unless it is demonstrated that their needs cannot be met satisfactorily in that setting, even with the use of supplementary aids and services. Second, students cannot be excluded from participation in nonacademic services and extracurricular activities because of OCD.

An additional provision of Section 504 pertains to procedural safeguards. Under 504, parents or legal guardians have the right to receive notice upon the identification, evaluation, and/or placement of their child. They also have the right to review pertinent school records (a right also guaranteed by the Family Educational Rights and Privacy Act, or FERPA), to request an impartial hearing challenging a district's actions related to identifying, evaluating, or placing a student, and to a review procedure if they disagree with the hearing decision.

The Individuals with Disabilities Education Act

Many students with OCD, particularly those with more severe cases, receive services under the Individuals with Disabilities Education Act of 2004, the federal law governing special education and related services. To be eligible for special education services under IDEA, a student must be between the ages of 3 and 21 (or as defined by state law) and meet the definition of either a preschool child with a disability or one or more of 13 disability categories listed in IDEA, e.g., emotional disturbance, other health impaired. Moreover, the disability(ies) must have an adverse effect on the student's learning, social and emotional functioning, life skills, and/or behavior at school.

A comprehensive evaluation is required to assess the student in all areas related to the suspected disability (written parental consent must be obtained prior to the assessment). After the evaluation is complete, a multidisciplinary team that includes parents, teachers, and others, as set forth by IDEA, convenes. If the team determines the student has a disability that adversely affects his or her education, an individualized education program, or IEP, is developed.

The IEP is an extremely detailed written document outlining all special education and related services the student should receive. It essentially serves as a blueprint for how the child is to be educated. After the IEP is written, the team must make a decision regarding the student's placement, or the location of his or her education. The student's placement should be driven by the student's IEP goals and not by what is available or most convenient for the school district. A very important requirement of IDEA, like Section 504, is that students with disabilities be educated, to the greatest extent possible, with peers who do not have disabilities, using accommodations and supports, if needed. If a student cannot be placed in the least restrictive environment (i.e., the general education classroom) for any part of the school day, an explanation must be provided in the IEP.

IDEA 2004 also specifies procedures for monitoring special education services, including annual reviews of a student's progress toward his or her IEP goals and a three-year reevaluation of the special education services provided to the student. IEP reviews may be conducted more frequently, however, if there is a lack of progress toward goals, reevaluation information is collected, or parents request a review or have additional information that affects the IEP.

IDEA 2004 also provides numerous safeguards for protecting the rights of children with disabilities and their parents, including the right to participate in all meetings, review all educational records, and obtain an independent educational evaluation. Moreover, parents have the right to written notice when a school proposes to change or refuses to change the identification, evaluation, or placement of a student. IDEA also outlines specific procedures regarding disagreements between school district personnel and parents. Prior to holding a due process hearing – a court-like review process available to parents and school districts to resolve special education disputes – districts first must offer more informal means for parents and school officials to resolve conflicts, including mediation and dispute resolution.

Parental consent is another issue addressed specifically in IDEA 2004. As previously noted, parental consent must be obtained prior to conducting an initial evaluation to determine a child's eligibility for special education and related services. Parental consent also must be obtained for reevaluations. If the parent does not provide consent for either an initial evaluation or reevaluation, the district may – but is not required to – pursue the evaluation using mediation or due process procedures. The district does not violate its obligations under IDEA, however, if it declines to pursue the evaluation.

Parental consent also is required prior to the provision of *initial* special education and related services to the student. If the parent refuses consent for services, however, the district may *not* use mediation or due process procedures to obtain those services. The district is neither in violation of IDEA nor required to convene an IEP meeting or develop an IEP for the student. Similarly, if, at any time *subsequent* to the provision of initial special education and related services the parent revokes consent for the continued provision of services (in writing), the district cannot continue to provide special education and related services for the student (after giving the parent written, prior notice regarding the cessation of the services) and may not pursue mediation or due process to obtain these services. Once again, the district has neither violated IDEA nor is required to convene an IEP meeting or develop an IEP for the student.

A separate chapter is devoted to each of two particularly noteworthy facets of IDEA as they relate to students with OCD. Specifically, Chapter 21 addresses the current controversy surrounding the appropriate IDEA category for students with OCD and presents Response to Intervention (RTI) as an alternative to the traditional IDEA classification system.

Chapter 22 provides a discussion of OCD-related behavior, functional behavioral assessment, and behavior intervention plans for students with OCD.

Summary of Section 504 vs. IDEA for students with OCD

In many cases, Section 504 is the appropriate vehicle for providing needed accommodations and interventions for students with OCD. Section 504 provides a quicker and more flexible means for supporting these students in the school setting. Section 504 also may be preferred over IDEA by parents and students who fear potential stigma associated with special education and related services. However, the requirements for a free, appropriate, public education are more detailed under IDEA than in Section 504. IDEA also includes more rights and safeguards for students with OCD and their parents than Section 504. Therefore, if a student with OCD is struggling with academic, social, and/or behavioral problems, it may be preferable to seek special education and related services for the student under IDEA. Of note is that if a student is eligible for services under IDEA, he or she still is protected under Section 504. Furthermore, if a student does not qualify for services under IDEA, he or she may qualify under Section 504.

Exploratory research on Section 504/IDEA services for students with OCD

Note: The information in this section was adapted from an article entitled "Current educational practices in classifying and serving students with obsessive-compulsive disorder" — Adams, Smith, Bolt, & Nolten, 2007 that appeared in The California School Psychologist, volume 12, pp. 93-105.

Exploratory research in which a random sample of school psychologists in the state of Illinois were surveyed yielded some interesting – though preliminary – findings regarding educational services students with OCD receive — Adams, Smith, Bolt & Nolten, 2007. Of the 94 students identified as having a primary diagnosis of OCD, school psychologists reported that 12 (12.8%) received services under Section 504, 70 (74.5%) were served under IDEA, and the remaining 12 students (12.8%) received no services. Acknowledging the role of OCD severity level, some respondents reported that when OCD symptoms were mild or well controlled by medication, no services or modifications were considered necessary. Given the large majority of students with OCD served under IDEA, however, the typical impact of OCD on educational performance was such that special education and related services were warranted.

The study also examined the types of educational settings in which students with a primary diagnosis of OCD served under IDEA were placed. As is evident in Table 1, placements for students with OCD represent almost the full continuum of IDEA services. Of the 70 students served under IDEA, 47 (67.1%) were reported as receiving their instruction in less restrictive environments. More specifically, 10.0% were placed in full-time regular classrooms only, 11.4% received instruction in the regular classroom and part-time special classes, and a sizeable percentage (45.7%) received instruction in the regular classroom with part-time resource assistance.

Approximately 29% of the students served under IDEA were educated in more restrictive settings. Of these students, 4.3%, 7.2%, and 5.7% were placed in LD, ED, and E/BD self-contained classrooms, respectively. An additional 11.4% received instruction in special day schools, and no students were placed in residential settings. Because there was only one residential school in the state of Illinois known to treat students with OCD at the time the survey was administered, this finding was not unexpected. As indicated in Table 1, 4.3% of students were reported as being served in placements designated as "Other."

The results of this study indicate that the large majority of students with a primary diagnosis of OCD were served under IDEA; most of these students received instruction in regular classrooms, alone or in combination with resource services or part-time special classes. Thus, it appears that the IDEA provision of the least restrictive environment was a guiding principle in decisions related to educational placements for students with OCD.

It must be emphasized that as the first of its kind to be conducted, this study was exploratory in nature. Additional research, including research at the national level, is necessary to confirm or refute the findings of this investigation.

Table 1
··········

Frequency Distribution of Responses: Reported Educational Placements
for Students with a Primary Diagnosis of OCD Served under IDEA

Placement	Frequency	Percent
FT regular classroom	7	10.0
Reg. class & PT resource room	32	45.7
Reg. class & PT special class	8	11.4
(Total)	(47)	(67.1)
FT self-contained LD	3	4.3
FT self-contained ED	5	7.2
FT self-contained BD	0	0.0
FT self-contained E/BD	4	5.7
FT self-contained OHI	0	0.0
Special day school	8	11.4
Residential setting	0	0.0
(Total)	(20)	(28.6)
Other	3	4.3
Grand total	**70**	**100.0**

Note. FT = Full time, PT = Part time, E/BD=Emotional/Behavioral Disorder, LD = Learning Disability, OHI
= Other Health Impaired

From: Adams, G. B., & Smith, T. S., & Bolt, S. E., & Nolten, P. (2007). Current educational practices in
classifying and serving students with obsessive-compulsive disorder. The California School Psychologist,
12, 93-105.

ch:21

CATEGORIZING STUDENTS WITH OCD UNDER IDEA

Note: The information in this chapter was adapted from an article entitled "Current educational practices in classifying and serving students with obsessive-compulsive disorder" — *Adams, Smith, Bolt, & Nolten, 2007* that appeared in *The California School Psychologist*, volume 12, pp. 93-105.

The current controversy

Students with OCD who have been served under IDEA frequently have been classified under the IDEA category "Emotional Disturbance" (ED). Parents of children with OCD and other concerned individuals, including mental health professionals and educational experts in the field of OCD, however, increasingly have expressed serious reservations about the ED classification and associated label. A number of these individuals have advocated that children and adolescents with OCD be identified under the IDEA "Other Health Impaired" (OHI) category — *Adams, 2004; Chansky, 2000; Dornbush & Pruitt, 1995,* for a number of reasons.

First, many individuals are troubled by the stigma sometimes associated with the ED label and the connotations it may invoke. Particularly in cases where the media describe perpetrators of criminal and/or violent behavior as "emotionally disturbed," parents of children with OCD may have serious and legitimate concerns when the same label is applied to their child.

Second, OCD has a documented neurobiological basis (see Chapter 7 on the causes of OCD), as do AD/HD and Tourette Syndrome, conditions currently listed under the IDEA "Other Health Impaired" category. Indeed, during the reauthorization of IDEA in 1997, many individuals and organizations (e.g., Children and Adults with Attention-Deficit/Hyperactivity Disorder, or CHADD) advocated vigorously that AD/HD be included under the Other Health Impaired category. In the final regulations enforcing Part B of IDEA 2004, Tourette Syndrome was listed as a disability under OHI rather than ED.

Immediately after the release of the final regulations, the Tourette Syndrome Association (TSA) issued a public announcement entitled *Major Victory for Children with Tourette Syndrome: Individuals with Disabilities Education Act to Classify Tourette Syndrome as Other Health Impaired* (2006). In its announcement, the TSA stated that "many educators...erroneously see TS as a behavioral or conduct disorder because of the nature of its symptoms and therefore classify these children under the Emotionally Disturbed (ED) category" — *para. 9.*

Third, some individuals are apprehensive about the ED label for students with OCD because of its potential ramifications for educational placement. One psychiatrist known for his work in childhood OCD expressed concern regarding students with OCD classified under ED who are placed in self-contained classrooms for students with behavioral disorders. He noted that in some cases, the students with behavior disorders who exhibit externalizing, aggressive, acting out behaviors "… have a feeding frenzy at the expense of the kids with OCD. It can result in either withdrawal – sometimes out of school – or lashing back (often futility)" — *A. J. Allen, personal communication, September 30, 2002.*

Similarly, in its public announcement regarding the inclusion of TS under OHI in IDEA 2004, the Tourette Syndrome Association stated that classifying students with TS under the ED category "frequently results in students being placed in programs that are designed for students with emotional disorders where bullying and teasing generally increase, as does the punishment for their symptoms" — *2006, para. 9.* Although no data exist as to whether this phenomenon applies to students with OCD, the potential for its existence raises serious concerns.

Response to Intervention: An alternative to traditional IDEA classification of students with OCD

Although there is strong support in the field for classifying students with OCD as Other Health Impaired rather than Emotionally Disturbed, an alternative approach might better ensure that these students receive appropriate services. More specifically, the time currently spent evaluating students with OCD to meet IDEA requirements might be used more effectively to implement evaluation procedures to identify successful services and interventions for these students. Such procedures commonly are used for students with learning disabilities as a result of the response-to-intervention focus within IDEA 2004 and state law requirements. As of January 1, 2009, for example, all districts in the state of Illinois were required to have a district RTI plan; by the 2010-2011 academic year, RTI was to be part of Illinois districts' evaluation procedure for making determinations of a specific learning disability.

Educational services for students with social-emotional problems increasingly are being provided through a response-to-intervention framework within the school setting — *Pavri, 2009*. Indeed, Gresham (2005) supports RTI as an alternative method for identifying students as having an emotional disturbance, stating that the RTI method is in direct contrast to current practice, which is based on a "refer-test-place model in which students are not exposed to systematic, evidence-based interventions to ameliorate behavior problems" — *p. 341*.

Application of a three-tier RTI model might encourage school systems to conduct universal screening for emotional and behavioral difficulties. An expert panel formed by individuals at the Stanford Research Institute and the Office of Special Education Programs recently conducted a review of the literature to determine the optimal behavioral screen for the early detection and assessment of students at risk for behavior disorders — *Severson, Walker, Hope-Doolittle, Kratochwill, & Gresham, 2007*. The panel chose the Systematic Screening for Behavior Disorders (SSBD) — *Walker & Severson, 1992* for a number of reasons, including its:

1. large, national normative samples;

2. multiple gating procedures (i.e., a series of assessment and decision steps are used to narrow a large population of students down to a small population of students who are most at risk for behavioral difficulties);

3. acceptability of the SSBD within the field of behavior disorders; and

4. ability to distinguish between students with externalizing vs. internalizing problems.

Although the SSBD was recommended by the panel of experts, other approaches may be used to facilitate behavioral screening and assessment of students. Two such approaches include teacher evaluation and rating of all students on common behavioral criteria (e.g., The Student Risk Screening Scale) and teacher nomination of problem students followed by Likert ratings of their behavioral characteristics and social skills (e.g., Child Behavior Checklist) — *Severson, et al., 2007*.

A three-tier RTI model also could address the implementation of intervention strategies that show promise for alleviating learning and behavior problems students with OCD frequently experience. With regard to prevention, techniques such as teaching all students strategies for coping with anxiety — *Merrell, 2001* and creating a positive and calm classroom environment with minimal sensory overload — *Lehr & Christenson, 2002* might be incorporated as part of a first-tier level of service provided to all students. Packer (2004) has developed an excellent checklist for teachers containing a multitude of suggestions for making the school environment student-friendly. Included in this checklist are suggestions for classroom environment and layout, transitions, organizational skills, prosocial skills, materials and presentations, and managing time. This checklist is available at *www.schoolbehavior.com/Files/TeacherChecklist.pdf*.

At the second tier, students with OCD whose symptoms interfere with learning and/or behavior might be brought to the attention of a school mental health professional. This individual could collaborate with families and professionals outside the school to implement empirically-based interventions such as cognitive-behavioral therapy — *Freeman et al., 2007*, and/or medication — *Franklin, March, & Garcia, 2006*. Clinical professionals would play the major role in implementing these interventions for OCD. Educational professionals, however, are instrumental in supporting and monitoring the effects of CBT (see Chapter 11) and medication interventions (see Chapter 12). School personnel actually may be involved in the implementation of CBT under the auspices of a clinician (see Chapter 23).

Within the school setting, interventions applied in small group settings that are not exceedingly time and personnel intensive may assist students with OCD. Involvement in social skills training groups, group counseling, or mentoring programs, as appropriate, may be very beneficial to students with OCD. Inservices and workshops to train school personnel about OCD and other anxiety disorders also could prove extremely valuable at the second tier.

Students with OCD who do not respond to Tier II interventions may require individualized, resource-intensive, and comprehensive interventions associated with Tier III. One-to-one counseling or programs such as The Coping Cat (for children aged 7-13 years) — *Kendall & Hedtke, 2006* or the C.A.T. Project Workbook for the Cognitive-Behavioral Treatment of Adolescents (for youth 14-17 years) — *Kendall, Choudhury, Hudson, & Webb, 2002* may be used initially with these students. Coping Cat and the

C.A.T. project are cognitive-behavioral therapy interventions that help young people recognize and analyze anxious feelings and develop strategies to cope with anxiety-provoking situations.

If these strategies prove ineffective or are highly resource intensive (e.g., additional funding is needed to ensure that the student receives ongoing services to facilitate appropriate progress), an evaluation might be conducted to determine whether the student qualifies for special education services. The evaluation process might be part of a third tier of support provided to students with substantial needs. This evaluation may involve the implementation of intervention strategies that are very resource intensive (e.g., frequent therapy sessions, comprehensive behavioral intervention plan) to identify the conditions under which the student is successful. If it is determined that the student requires such intervention strategies in order to make sufficient progress, they eventually may be provided on an ongoing basis using funding available through special education. Monitoring of progress over time would be essential to verify the efficacy of these interventions.

Within the three-tier RTI model described above, interventions that are effective for a given individual are identified via the evaluation process, placing the focus on instructional needs rather than disability categorization. Instead of having to fit into a particular disability category, a student may receive special education services based on the conditions under which he or she was found to be successful.

Although the RTI service delivery model for students with or at-risk for OCD may be ideal for some school systems, traditional categorical service delivery models may continue in many locations. To ensure that students with OCD receive appropriate services, the potential consequences of categorical diagnoses must be considered carefully. For example, an appropriate categorization would preclude the placement of children and adolescents with OCD into classrooms with other students whose behavior might aggravate the emotional and behavioral difficulties of the student with OCD. More specifically, a student with OCD might need substantial structure to avoid being overwhelmed by his or her thoughts and corresponding rituals. Such structure initially might be considered as being most easily facilitated in a self-contained setting. However, other students in that type of setting may engage in behaviors (e.g., teasing, bullying) that have the potential to exacerbate the student's obsessions and compulsions. At the same time, care should be taken to place students with OCD in a setting that optimizes access to services that address their needs. Within the evaluation process, consideration should be given to the students' specific educational needs and how those can best be met within the existing categorical service delivery system.

Ch:22

IDEA, DISCIPLINE, AND OCD BEHAVIOR

Functional behavioral assessment and positive behavior interventions and supports

The Individuals with Disabilities Act of 1997 — *IDEA '97; 20 U.S.C. § 1401 et seq.* — the predecessor to IDEA 2004 – instituted a number of new concepts, two of which were crucial to students experiencing behavioral difficulties:

1. positive behavior support, and

2. functional behavioral assessment.

One instance in which IDEA '97 refers to these concepts pertains to suspending a student with a disability. Specifically, IDEA '97 states that within 10 school days of a decision to change the placement of a student with a disability due to a violation of a code of student conduct, school officials must hold a manifestation determination meeting to decide whether the behavioral offense was related to a student's disability or poor implementation of the IEP — *20 U.S.C. § 615(k)(4)(A)(ii)*. If it is determined that the behavior was related to the disability or poor implementation of the IEP, a functional behavioral assessment, or FBA, must be conducted (if one has not been conducted previously) — *20 U.S.C. § 615(k)(1)(B)(i)*.

The purpose of an FBA is to determine *why* a student engages in challenging behaviors by examining variables in the current environment that trigger those behaviors (antecedents) and/or support them (consequences). The underlying assumption of functional behavioral assessment is that challenging behavior occurs because it produces an outcome or serves a function (e.g., student obtains something positive, escapes or avoids something aversive, obtains sensory input).

After a student's behavior is assessed, the results of the FBA are used to design and implement a positive behavior intervention plan (PBIP) that addresses the function of the behavior. If a behavior plan already was in place, it must be reviewed and modified, as necessary, to address the behavior of concern (i.e., violation of student code of conduct) — *20 U.S.C. § 615(k)(1)(B)(ii)*.

IDEA '97 also includes another instance in which a functional behavioral assessment and corresponding behavior intervention plan are required. According to IDEA '97, whenever a child's behavior impedes his or her own learning or that of others, school personnel need to consider using positive behavior interventions, supports, and other strategies to address that behavior — 20 U.S.C. § 614(d)(3)(B)(i). Thus, when a student's problem behavior does not respond to standard, effective practices that are used with all students, or when school personnel cannot provide data to explain why the inappropriate behavior is occurring, IDEA '97 requires that a functional behavioral assessment be conducted and a corresponding behavior intervention plan developed. Of note is that FBAs and PBIPs are appropriate not only for students with disabilities but also for students with behavioral problems who do not have disabilities, or students not already receiving special education services under IDEA. A more in-depth discussion of functional behavioral assessment and positive behavior intervention plans for students with OCD is provided later. Background information regarding OCD-related behavior first must be presented, however, to establish a rationale for the significance of FBAs and PBIPs with this population of students.

Traditional perspectives of challenging behavior

A model proposed by Dr. Terry Illes, a school psychologist and expert on attention-deficit/hyperactivity disorder in children and adolescents, may provide insight into how educators sometimes view the behavior of students with OCD. Illes has closely examined the issue of why some teachers resist implementing classroom accommodations and interventions for students with AD/HD. According to Illes, there are a number of possible reasons for this resistance, including lack of time, energy, supplies and other resources, poor parent support, and misinformation about AD/HD. He believes, however, that a more compelling explanation may be found in the way teachers often perceive students with behavioral difficulties – the assumptions and inferences used to interpret their behavior.

In order to increase awareness of how teachers' attitudes about behavioral difficulties may shape their responses to students with problem behaviors, Illes (2001) developed the Academic and Behavioral Models of Disability. One of the basic tenets of this model is that teachers sometimes use one set of assumptions to understand children with academic problems and a different set for students with behavioral difficulties.

According to the Academic Model, teachers frequently respond to students with learning difficulties in a characteristic fashion. They observe that a student has an academic problem, and because research has suggested that learning problems have an underlying neurological basis, teachers assume they are involuntary. Because neurological symptoms are beyond the control of the student, the teacher reacts with empathy and believes the student would prefer to be as academically proficient as his or her peers. Thus, the focus is on skill building, and the responsibility for change lies within the educational system, rather than the student. In addition, change is gradual, and positive consequences are implemented to facilitate progress.

According to the Behavioral Model, the teacher observes that a student has a behavioral problem – a need for attention, for example – which is assumed to be linked to student motivation. If the behavior is triggered by motivation, it is assumed to be voluntary or deliberate; the teacher reacts with frustration, disappointment, or anger, because it was the student's intent to misbehave. In other words, teachers assume that the student is choosing to engage in challenging behavior and that he or she just as easily could choose to engage in appropriate behavior. As a result, the teacher believes the problem behavior must be eliminated. The focus is on getting the student to stop his or her behavior rather than on teaching new skills. The change must be achieved rapidly, and therefore, punishment or other negative consequences are used. The responsibility for change lies within the student, rather than the educational system, so there is no need to make accommodations for the child with AD/HD. The undergirding principle of Illes' model is that learning problems have a neurological basis, but behavior does not.

Illes (2001) posits that teachers frequently have a Behavioral Model mindset when it comes to students with AD/HD, a disorder which, like learning disabilities such as reading disorders, has a neurological basis. Illes' model logically may be extended to students who have OCD, which also is a neurobiological disorder. Many behaviors exhibited by these students are a function of the OCD: the student who "refuses" to do a writing assignment because she has to erase and reerase all of her letters until they are "perfect." And yet school personnel sometimes view such behavior as a problem that must be eliminated with swift and negative consequences. Thus, the student who refuses to do an assignment because writing rituals make it almost impossible for her to write may lose all recess privileges until she has completed the task.

According to Illes (2001), school personnel who use the Behavioral Model to interpret many of the challenging behaviors exhibited by students are doing so not out of hostility or indifference. It is, rather, an approach that seems to come naturally to interpret human behavior. Educating school personnel about OCD, particularly with regard to its neurobiological basis, may help counteract the flawed assumptions inherent in the Behavioral Model.

Illes' model also raises another very important point. If behavior is directed by motivation, as suggested by the Behavioral Model, then the application of traditional behavior modification principles (e.g., positive and negative consequences) to alter motivation is likely to resolve the difficulty. In other words, reducing or eliminating obsessions or compulsions should be a simple matter of finding the appropriate reward or punishment. Obsessions and compulsions are a function of the OCD, however, and may not respond to positive and negative consequences. Examples of typical classroom consequences include:

1. giving a student ten minutes of free time for completing his morning work (positive reinforcement);

2. taking away recess for a week because of an incident on the playground (negative punishment);

3. yelling at a student because she was talking out in class (positive punishment); and

4. telling a student he will have to do his classwork at home if he doesn't finish it in school (negative reinforcement).

Indeed, such traditional behavior modification principles not only may be ineffective, but in some cases, actually may worsen the behavioral difficulties of children and adolescents with OCD. (The reader is referred to *Behavior Management: A Practical Approach for Educators* by Walker, Shea, Bauer, 2007, 9th edition, for a thorough review of the principles of behavior management.)

A parallel may be drawn to a student who has asthma. One would never consider trying to control a student's asthma attack by applying traditional consequences. It would be ludicrous to tell a student that he will receive a candy bar if he stops his asthma attack or lose recess for a week if he doesn't stop wheezing. It is understood that an asthma attack is not within the student's control – that it is not a willful behavior that can be stopped simply by altering motivation. And yet, when students with OCD are consequated for behavior that occurs in the throes of an "OCD attack," the same principle is being applied. Applying positive or negative consequences to alter the motivation of a student who is extremely anxious because he is "stuck" in a checking ritual at his locker not only may be ineffective but very possibly could increase his anxiety and exacerbate symptoms.

According to Packer (2002), there are a number of pitfalls related to using certain facets of traditional behavior modification for behavior that is related to a student's neurobiological disorder. One is that behavior modification plans usually do not consider whether the student can suppress a behavior consistently, even if he or she is highly motivated to do so. It is true that students sometimes can control/suppress their symptoms (e.g., rituals, tics) for a period of time (although symptom suppression may result in high levels of anxiety or stress). If the student cannot suppress them continuously, however, applying positive or negative contingencies is likely to increase stress, make symptoms worse, and even create new behavioral problems.

Packer (2002) indicates that another pitfall of behavior modification for students with neurobehavioral problems is that these children – like all children – are motivated to earn rewards and avoid punishment. If an attempt is made to alter a truly involuntary symptom, however, these students may try to modify their behavior, but potentially at great cost to the student. For instance, the student who expends a great amount of time and energy trying to suppress a tic to avoid punishment or earn a reward may experience high levels of stress and fatigue and have difficulty concentrating on school-related tasks.

Given the concerns related to the use of positive and negative consequences with students who have OCD, Packer and Pruitt (2010) recommend taking certain precautions when using them. First, school personnel should consider consequences only after they first have discussed with the parents and student whether such techniques would be likely to help or hurt. Second, school staff must monitor a student's behavior carefully if they are used to ensure that symptoms are not getting worse.

It is important to note that despite the caveats associated with positive and negative consequences, *positive reinforcement* may be effective for students with OCD in certain situations. Rewards may be effective, for example, when used within the context of positive behavioral intervention plans to:

1. teach a student to use and maintain a behavior that replaces an inappropriate/interfering behavior (e.g., teaching a student to use hand sanitizer at her desk in lieu of constantly going to the school bathroom to wash her hands), and

2. reinforce students for making progress on their intervention plans or even for exerting effort (see next section).

Rewards also may be used in some cases to increase current levels of a desirable behavior that is incompatible, or competes, with a challenging OCD behavior. Thus, consequences are not applied to modify the OCD behavior directly; rather, rewards are used to reinforce or strengthen acceptable, alternative behaviors already in the student's behavioral repertoire. Chapter 24 contains a hypothetical case example of how positive reinforcement might be implemented successfully with a student who has OCD to increase on-task behavior. As previously indicated, however, student behavior always should be monitored closely when consequences – even positive reinforcement – are used with students who have OCD.

Functional behavioral assessment and positive behavior intervention plans for students with OCD

When a student's behavior is interfering with his or her own learning or the learning of others, it must be addressed, whether or not it is a symptom of OCD. That is a given. The key is how to address it *appropriately*. The IDEA '97 requirement that schools incorporate functional behavioral assessment and positive behavior intervention plans to address the problem behaviors of students with disabilities was crucial for students with OCD. Instead of focusing on positive and negative consequences as a first-line intervention to "fix" problematic behavior (i.e., the responsibility for change lies within the *child*), FBAs and PBIPs place emphasis upon first determining why students with disabilities engage in certain behaviors. A plan then can be developed to address why the behavior is occurring and to provide the necessary behavioral supports and interventions that will lead to acceptable behavior (the responsibility for change lies within the *educational system*). With this approach, school personnel can be *proactive* by identifying and modifying factors (whenever possible) that may contribute to problematic behavior before it occurs, rather than *reactive* by applying consequences after the problematic behavior occurs.

Because environmental and contextual factors frequently trigger or increase the frequency of OCD-related behaviors, an FBA may provide school personnel important information for designing accommodations, supports, and behavioral interventions to address or prevent challenging behaviors. It is beyond the scope of this book to address all aspects of FBAs and PBIPs thoroughly. It is highly recommended that individuals doing FBAs and PBIPs for students with OCD obtain a copy of *A Workbook for Conducting a Functional Behavioral Assessment and Writing a Positive Behavior Intervention Plan for a Student with Tourette Syndrome — Conners & Giordano, 2005*, available for a nominal fee at www. tsa-usa.org. This workbook is designed specifically for students with neurobiological disorders such as Tourette Syndrome, OCD, AD/HD, and learning disabilities. An overview of this process is provided below.

In their workbook on FBAs and FBIPs for students with Tourette Syndrome and other neurobiological disorders, Conners and Giordano (2005) recommend that at the middle or high school level, a team of at least 3-5 school staff who work closely with the student (e.g., teacher, paraprofessional) complete an FBA worksheet (included in workbook). On this worksheet, the informant provides information regarding the behavior(s) impeding the target student's learning, the frequency of the behavior, where it does and does not occur, and when it occurs most frequently. Such information should be gathered from as many different sources as possible (e.g., evaluations, data collection, observations, student work samples). Information regarding possible reasons for the behavior also must be provided on the worksheet. Conners and Giordano recommend that at the elementary level, at least 2-5 individuals who work closely with the student complete this worksheet.

Key members of the child's educational team then complete another worksheet (included in workbook) summarizing the information collected from the completed FBA worksheets. The team must analyze this information and draw conclusions as to why the behavior may be occurring. Conners and Giordano (2005) state that involving the parents and the student can be extremely beneficial, because they frequently are well-informed about the disorder. Indeed, many experts consider parent and child input a critical component *throughout* the FBA process.

It is important to note that in functional behavioral assessment, hypotheses regarding why the behavior occurs, or the function of the behavior, traditionally relate to a student's:

1. obtaining something positive;

2. avoiding/escaping something negative; or

3. sensory stimulation.

And FBAs for children and adolescents with neurobiological disorders may reveal that a student is avoiding something: a student with OCD may avoid completing a worksheet because it will trigger writing rituals; a student with Tourette Syndrome may avoid completing a test because test-related anxiety will exacerbate his tics. For students with neurobiological disorders, however, a critical factor must be considered during the process of developing a hypothesis: the reason for the behavior frequently is directly related to *symptoms of the disorder* (e.g., interfering obsessions/rituals, interfering tics, anxiety in testing situations, attentional difficulties, etc.).

Once the team members have analyzed the summarized results and drawn conclusions as to possible reasons for the interfering behavior, they must decide upon changes or supports that are necessary to decrease the likelihood of the interfering behavior(s) and positive interventions that may be implemented to help the student maintain appropriate behavior. These interventions are then written into a positive behavior intervention plan (included in workbook) that is shared with all school staff who work with the student. PBIPs may involve modifying the environment, teaching more acceptable replacement behaviors, adjusting the curriculum or instructional strategy, or changing the antecedents or consequences to a student's behavior. Following is a table containing several examples of strategies that may be incorporated into a PBIP for students with OCD.

Intervention: Modify the environment

Current Situation	Intervention
The student has emotional outbursts in class due to overwhelming anxiety related to obsessions	Seat the student close to the door so he or she can exit the classroom (using a pre-arranged pass) and go to a safe place when anxiety builds
When a student sees or is in the presence of a pair of scissors, it triggers harm-related obsessions and checking rituals	Place classroom scissors (including teacher's scissors) out of the student's line of sight

Intervention: Teach a more acceptable replacement behavior

Current Situation	Intervention
The student has a ritual that involves touching peers, which they find annoying	Teach the student to touch the underside of his desk instead of touching people (student might also stretch fingers or engage in another version of the ritual that doesn't disrupt classmates)
The student leaves the classroom frequently throughout the school day to wash his/her hands	Allow the student to have a small bottle of hand sanitizer at his/her desk to use in place of going to the bathroom to engage in hand washing

Part V | School-Based Treatment of OCD

203

Intervention: Adjust the curriculum

Current Situation	Intervention
The student has writing rituals that involve writing and rewriting words. Student becomes frustrated because he/she cannot complete written assignments	Allow the student to write responses only to items the teacher has marked with an asterisk instead of all items
The student experiences severe reading rituals (must count how many letters are in each sentence) that make it virtually impossible for him/her to read	Allow the student to scan reading material and use the Kurzweil reader to read it to him/her out loud through headphones

Intervention: Change the antecedents/consequences

Current Situation	Intervention
The student experiences contamination obsessions while walking through crowded hallways during passing times (e.g., student fears that others' breath will cause him/her to become ill). The student holds his/her breath in response to these obsessions	Allow the student to leave the classroom 5 minutes before the passing bell rings to avoid crowds in the hallway (change antecedent)
When student arrives late to class, teacher makes negative comments about student's being tardy	When student arrives late, teacher ignores student's entrance and actively engages other students (change consequence)

Conners and Giordano (2005) emphasize the complexity and misunderstanding of neurobiological disorders. As a result, they strongly recommend that someone who knows about – or is willing to become knowledgeable about – the disorder be a member of the team throughout the FBA/PBIP process.

As noted earlier in this chapter, the application of positive and negative consequences may be ineffective in modifying symptoms and behaviors related to OCD. And when consequences are used, they should be applied cautiously. Positive reinforcement may play an important role, however, during the implementation of PBIPs. It may be helpful, for instance, when teaching a student to use (and maintain) an acceptable replacement behavior, e.g., providing positive reinforcement to the student who learns to touch the underside of his desk rather than ritualistically touching classmates. In addition, school personnel may reward students for making progress on their intervention plans. Even when students are not successful in reaching a particular goal, it is extremely important to positively reinforce effort.

In sum, students with OCD may benefit greatly from functional behavioral assessments that result in the development of positive and proactive supports and interventions. Conners (2008) very aptly has summarized the FBA/PBIP process in what she refers to as the Platinum Rule: "What can we do FOR the child PRIOR to the behavior instead of What do we do TO the child AFTER the behavior has occurred."

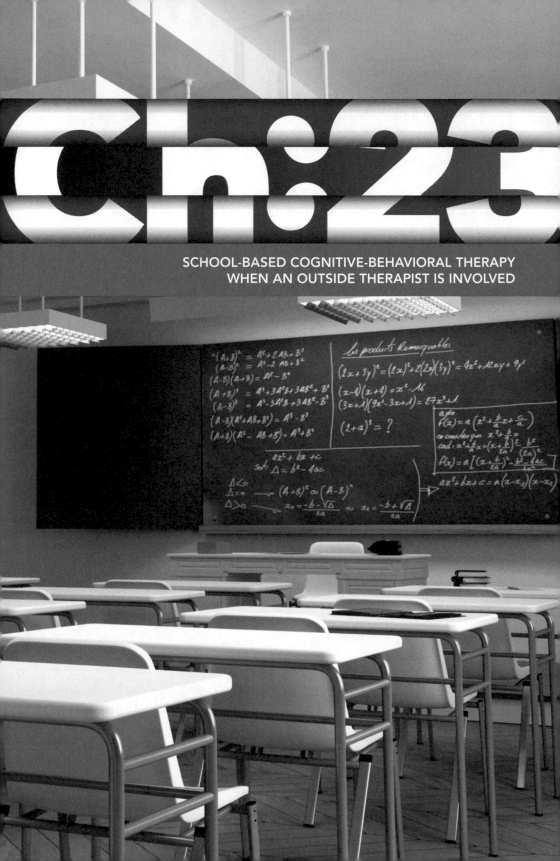

Ch:23

SCHOOL-BASED COGNITIVE-BEHAVIORAL THERAPY WHEN AN OUTSIDE THERAPIST IS INVOLVED

Many students with OCD are under the care of a physician and/or other mental health therapists. When a child is receiving cognitive-behavioral therapy, the best possible scenario is that the CBT therapist is in close contact with school personnel. Under these circumstances, it may be possible for school professionals to participate in cognitive-behavioral therapy interventions at school *in association with the therapist*. It is of utmost importance that school personnel work in conjunction with and under the supervision of the clinician to ensure that school-based interventions are implemented consistently and have the same end goals as clinical interventions. It is not appropriate for a teacher, however well-intentioned, to take the lead in implementing CBT. Inconsistent interventions could prove very confusing to the student and actually worsen his or her OCD symptoms.

Wagner guidelines

In her book *What to do When your Child has Obsessive-Compulsive Disorder* (2006), Dr. Aureen Pinto Wagner, a noted child psychologist who has worked extensively in the field of pediatric OCD, states that when a child is involved in cognitive-behavioral therapy, the therapist, in conjunction with the child, must decide upon CBT treatment goals and the pace of treatment. When some of those goals involve difficulties in the school setting, school-based interventions may be beneficial. The success of these interventions depends upon systematic planning, coordination, and execution. Wagner further states that a number of issues must be carefully understood, agreed upon, and communicated among school personnel, parents, the outside therapist, and the student before *any* CBT interventions are implemented in school. Only when each of these questions has been carefully addressed should school-based CBT interventions be put into practice. Following is a list of those questions.

- Who is responsible for implementing and monitoring each intervention?

- What are the precise parameters of each intervention?

- What specific roles are to be played by the child, parent, teacher, other school staff and community provider?

- What resources and services will be needed to put the plans into action?

- Do staff or parents need to be trained before proceeding?

- Has the child been prepared adequately for each intervention?

- Where and when will each intervention occur?

- What exactly will happen when the intervention is carried out?

- How will the child's response to each treatment be recorded?

- How will the plan be scrutinized?

- How will the need for modifications be determined?

- How will changes be incorporated and executed?

Reprinted with permission. Aureen P. Wagner, Ph.D. Copyright Lighthouse Press Inc.

Ledley/Pasupuleti model

Two researchers who have examined school issues as they relate to children with OCD, Dr. Deborah Ledley and Ms. Radhika Pasupuleti, have developed a clinician-teacher collaboration plan for the treatment of OCD symptoms in the school setting (2007). Described below, this plan includes five steps, each of which has distinct goals.

Step 1 of Collaborative Plan: Initial phone call between the clinician and teacher (approximately 30 minutes in length)

Goals of Step 1:

- Teacher informs the clinician how OCD manifests in school.

- Clinician inquires about ways the teacher might be maintaining OCD symptoms (e.g., providing unlimited reassurance) or reacting negatively toward the student (e.g., verbal reprimand).

- Clinician explains the nature of OCD to the teacher, describes exposure and response prevention, and suggests ways in which the teacher may be able to participate in the treatment plan.

- If the teacher agrees to be involved in the treatment plan, the teacher and clinician determine how both parties will communicate in the future (e.g., method of communication, mutually agreed-upon times for communicating).

Step 2 of Collaborative Plan: Clinician informs the teacher, via a telephone conversation (approximately 15 minutes in length), of the first classroom-based treatment assignment (previously agreed upon by the child and parents during a treatment session)

Goals of Step 2:

- To integrate exposure into the classroom. Example: Student A, who fears inhaling fumes from the teacher's marker, will be moved one row closer to the teacher (teacher may need to move other students' seats).

- To establish ritual prevention rules in the classroom. Example: Student A will be asked to refrain from holding her breath and hiding her face in her shirt to avoid fumes. If the teacher observes the student doing rituals, the teacher will tap her on her arm with a marker as a "code" to remind her to try to stop ritualizing. The teacher will not reprimand the student for failing to do exposure or for doing rituals. It will primarily be the student's responsibility to report to the therapist how school-based E/RP is proceeding (progress will be discussed in therapy).

- To implement (as appropriate) a predetermined reward system to encourage exposure and ritual prevention. The teacher may play an important role in implementing the reward system (e.g., keeping track of daily progress; providing stickers for achieving daily objectives), but the parents/family should dispense the actual reinforcer (e.g., parents take student out to favorite restaurant for meeting daily objectives for the week).

- To determine the time frame for the next contact between the clinician and teacher after the first assignment has been carried out.

209

Step 3 of Collaborative Plan: Next contact between the clinician and teacher

Goals of Step 3:

- To discuss the effectiveness of the first treatment assignment:

    – Was the student able to engage in E/RP in the classroom?

    – Was the teacher able to implement the process without undue interference in the classroom?

    – Was the reward system effective, if one was implemented?

    – To determine if the first classroom-based E/RP assignment should be continued or a new assignment given (using input from patient and parents as well as teacher). Example: Should student A repeat the same exposure or move up another row closer to the teacher?

Step 4 of Collaborative Plan: Step 3 is repeated for each assignment throughout treatment. Progress each week informs the treatment plan for the following week. The treatment plan thus is a collaborative effort among the student, parents, clinician, and teacher.

- Example: Student A was instructed to move up a row each time she was able to spend a few days in a row without doing rituals and experienced minimal anxiety.

Step 5 of Collaborative Plan: Final phone call at the completion of treatment (all classroom-based E/RP goals have been accomplished)

Goals of Step 5:

- To review the student's progress from the clinician's and teacher's perspectives.

- To discuss how the teacher can aid in relapse prevention. A plan is developed that will be implemented if symptoms begin to re-emerge in the classroom. If the teacher observes symptoms, he or she should contact the parents, who can communicate with the clinician.

- To encourage the teacher to contact the clinician with any future concerns or questions.

The reader is referred to Ledley and Pasupuleti (2007) for a more complete discussion of this model.

A review of Wagner's recommendations and the clinician-teacher treatment plan proposed by Ledley and Pasupuleti highlight the importance of collaborative efforts in school-based CBT interventions. These interventions require time, effort, patience, effective communication, and a commitment on the part of school personnel. In reality, school professionals frequently are overwhelmed trying to meet the needs of all their students, completing paperwork, attending meetings, and tending to a myriad of other tasks. Therefore, clinicians should attempt to make reasonable time requests of school personnel and to design E/RP exercises that can be implemented without undue classroom intrusion. On the other hand, it is important for school staff to participate in CBT interventions to the greatest extent possible; treatment of school-related difficulties may be critical to the student's recovery.

Ch:24

SCHOOL-BASED INTERVENTIONS WHEN AN
OUTSIDE THERAPIST IS NOT INVOLVED

Some students exhibit distinct symptoms of OCD but have not been evaluated by a clinician; a formal diagnosis of OCD therefore is absent. Many students who have been diagnosed receive medication but not cognitive-behavioral therapy. In other instances, children are receiving CBT, but the clinician basically is inaccessible or unavailable to school personnel. When assistance from a physician or clinician is absent, conjoint behavioral consultation (CBC) may be an appropriate and effective model for using home-school collaboration and shared problem solving to remediate difficulties exhibited by younger students with OCD. Although no studies, to date, have examined the implementation of CBC specifically with children who have OCD, it has been applied to the treatment of childhood anxiety in the school setting — *Auster, Feeney-Kettler, & Kratochwill, 2006*. The reader is strongly encouraged to refer to *Conjoint Behavioral Consultation: Promoting Family-School Connections and Interventions* by Sheridan and Kratochwill (2007) for a detailed discussion of CBC. A general overview, however, is provided below.

Conjoint behavioral consultation

In traditional school-based behavioral consultation, the consultant (a school mental health professional), works in tandem with a consultee (usually a teacher) to remediate students' learning and behavioral problems. This model excludes a critical element in the collaborative relationship: the parents. Parents play an essential role not only because behavioral problems frequently are evident in both the home and school settings but also because the success of interventions and students' classroom performance is enhanced by strong home-school alliances — *Wilkinson, 2006*.

In CBC, the collaborative partnership includes all parties who share responsibility for the child, i.e., parents, teachers, and other caregivers and service providers, as appropriate. These parties collaborate in the problem-solving process with the assistance of a consultant – a school mental health professional. CBC originally was used to address problems that occurred in *both* the home and school contexts. It can be used for difficulties that occur in only one of the two settings, however, because both the school and home interact to affect a student's functioning. In the CBC model, parents and teachers are not expected to implement a comprehensive cognitive-behavioral therapy program that would require extensive education and training. Rather, they use (or are taught to use) various intervention strategies or skills that can be implemented realistically within the home and/or school environment.

Numerous studies have provided empirical support for the efficacy and acceptability of CBC as a tool for providing interventions to students with a wide range of learning and behavioral difficulties. It is important to note, however, that the majority of these studies have been conducted with elementary- or preschool-aged children — *Sheridan & Kratochwill, 2007*. Moreover, research indicates that when students leave elementary-school settings and enter secondary-school systems, parental involvement decreases. Therefore, conjoint behavioral consultation may be preferable for implementation at the elementary, rather than middle- or high-school, level. Older children and teens with OCD may be better served by a more traditional behavioral consultation method, which includes the same stages as CBC (see below), but involves only a school mental health professional (e.g., school psychologist) and a teacher — *Adams, Waas, March, & Smith, 1994*.

It must be emphasized, however, that the choice of consultation method depends upon the student and his or her family situation. Although parents tend to be less involved at the high school-level, their involvement may be extremely beneficial, for example, for a middle-school student with OCD who is transitioning to high school, where he or she will encounter a new set of staff members and a novel environment. On the other hand, consultation involving only a school mental health professional and the teacher may be preferable for a different student at the elementary level.

The conjoint behavioral consultation process consists of four interrelated and dynamic stages:

1. conjoint needs (problem) identification;

2. conjoint needs (problem) analysis;

3. plan implementation; and

4. conjoint plan evaluation — *Sheridan & Kratochwill, 2007*.

Structured interviews are implemented in the first, second, and fourth phases. These stages and corresponding interviews serve as guides to structuring this problem-solving process but do not rigidly dictate interactions among team members. Conjoint behavioral consultation usually is initiated by a referral made by a student's teacher or other school professional due to academic, social, or behavioral concerns.

Stage I of CBC is the *conjoint needs identification* stage, during which the consultant (school mental health professional) conducts an interview with the consultees (e.g., parents and teacher) to identify concerns (as well as strengths) regarding the child's functioning. Although the student may exhibit difficulties in many areas, it is important to prioritize and select one target concern to address in CBC. During this stage, the team operationally defines the target behavior and decides which observational recording systems are most appropriate for collecting baseline (i.e., pre-intervention) data. Information regarding contextual, environmental, and cross-setting factors that may contribute to the child's behavioral difficulties (e.g., time of day, subject matter) also is vital. Therefore, data pertaining to when the behavior occurred, e.g., time, setting, and ongoing activity should be recorded, as well as events occurring directly prior to the target behavior (antecedents) and after the behavior (consequences), as appropriate. It may be necessary for the consultant to train the teacher in the chosen data collection system.

Several weeks after the initial meeting, the second stage of CBC, the *conjoint needs analysis*, takes place. During this meeting, the consultant, teacher, and parents evaluate baseline data and jointly determine goals based upon the data. The team also determines the impact of any contextual factors (e.g., time of day, patterns of events occurring in the environment before and/or after the target behavior). Furthermore, the team develops hypotheses or reasons as to why the behavior is occurring.

During the conjoint needs analysis stage, the team discusses possible intervention strategies for the target behavior. The consultant may suggest a certain evidence-based intervention, but consultees shape it to fit both the home and school environments. Specific guidelines for implementation of the intervention also are developed. If a positive reinforcement system is incorporated into the intervention, the consultees may involve the student in the selection of incentives that will be used at school and home. In addition, the team must decide how data will be collected throughout the intervention.

The third stage of CBC is *plan implementation*. During this stage, the consultant provides the teacher with intervention training, if necessary. The teacher discusses the chosen intervention with the student and gives positive and negative examples of the target behavior, as appropriate. Or the teacher may model, rehearse, and role-play positive behavior with the student. When the student understands and is comfortable with the components of the intervention, the treatment plan is carried out and data on the target behavior are collected on a daily basis. If daily goals are established, the teacher will need to meet with the student each day to determine if the goal was met. If the goal is achieved, the student may receive/choose a preferred reinforcer. It is important that parents be informed of the student's progress; they may play an important role by providing reinforcers at home, as well.

Although no formal interview is conducted during this stage, the consultant has several important responsibilities. First, he or she must monitor the implementation of the intervention across settings to ensure that the plan is conducted as developed and intended. If the consultant determines that the consultees require additional information or skills, he or she can provide any necessary training. In addition, the consultant should assess the student's immediate response to the intervention and, if necessary, modify it to be more responsive to the student's needs.

The final stage of CBC is *conjoint plan evaluation*. During this phase, the consultant and consultees meet to evaluate the effectiveness of the intervention and determine if treatment goals have been met. In addition, the team must decide whether current services should be kept in place, modified, or terminated. During this meeting, issues related to maintenance and generalization of treatment effects also must be addressed (e.g., team may set up maintenance interviews for several weeks after the final plan evaluation to evaluate the student's ongoing progress and promote continued collaboration between the home and school). In addition, the parents and teacher may be asked to provide feedback on their opinions of the acceptability and effectiveness of the conjoint behavioral consultation process.

Hypothetical case of CBC with a student who has OCD

To illustrate how conjoint behavioral consultation might work with a student whose OCD symptoms have negatively affected school functioning, the following hypothetical case example is provided.

Richard was an eight year-old third grader (fully included in the general education classroom) referred to the school psychologist by his teacher due to serious academic concerns and some behavioral concerns. He had been diagnosed with OCD approximately six weeks prior to the referral. Although Richard was seeing a mental health clinician, he was not receiving exposure and response prevention therapy or medication. Because the clinician was largely unavailable to school personnel, the school psychologist decided to engage in conjoint behavioral consultation as a vehicle for supporting Richard.

Scenario 1

Stage 1: Conjoint needs identification

During the conjoint needs identification stage, the school psychologist conducted an interview with Richard's parents and classroom teacher, Mrs. Z. In addition to explaining the consultation process, the psychologist solicited information from the consultees regarding Richard's difficulties as well as his strengths. Mrs. Z was extremely concerned about Richard's trips to the restroom, which lasted for considerable periods of time. According to her anecdotal records, the bathroom trips occurred predominantly during reading instruction, which took place the first 90 minutes of each school day. Richard was an above-average reader, so his difficulties were not related to a skill deficit in reading.

Mrs. Z also noted that because Richard appeared somewhat anxious when he made requests to use the bathroom, she did not restrict him from using it. The school psychologist remarked that for some students with OCD, having unlimited access to go to the restroom actually reduces their anxiety and decreases their need to use it. This was not the case, however, for Richard.

In addition, Mrs. Z indicated that Richard didn't like working in groups, because he thought his classmates would touch him, causing him to be "dirty." Moreover, Richard avoided using the blackboard because he

*didn't like using chalk. The teacher stated that although Richard had a
very pleasant demeanor and was very good in reading, he was able to
complete very few of his reading assignments, and his grades had been
slipping for some time.*

*Richard's parents stated that they were extremely worried about his
contamination fears. He avoided objects and people he thought were
contaminated and spent a great deal of time in the bathroom at home
washing his hands. In fact, his hands were dry and chapped; on
occasion, they cracked and bled. Moreover, the time he spent in the
bathroom prevented him from engaging in other leisure activities at
home (e.g., playing with siblings). Richard's parents agreed with the
teacher that he was good in reading and had a very pleasant demeanor,
overall. They had witnessed some "moodiness" of late, however.*

*Although Richard exhibited several school-based difficulties related
to OCD, the team's major concern was that his bathroom trips were
negatively affecting his on-task behavior during reading instruction.
Although these trips were relatively infrequent, they appeared to occur
for fairly extended periods of time. As a result, the time he spent
productively engaged in classroom activities was greatly reduced.
Richard was missing important academic information during reading
instruction. Because he was unable to complete many of his reading
assignments, he also was receiving very poor grades.*

*The conjoint behavioral consultation team decided to target Richard's
on-task behavior. Because on-task behavior tends to be durational in
nature and does not always have a clear beginning and ending point
(i.e., it is not easily counted), momentary time sampling, or MTS, was
selected as the observational recording system for this behavior. As its
name implies, momentary time sampling provides a sampling, or
estimate, of the actual amount of time a behavior occurs.*

*With MTS, a given observation period is subdivided into equal intervals
of time (e.g., 3 minutes). At the exact end of each time interval, the
observer looks at the specified student to determine if he or she is
engaging in the target behavior at that moment – not before or after. If
the behavior is occurring, a mark (e.g., "X") is written on the record
sheet for that interval. If the behavior does not occur, a different mark
(e.g., "O") is placed on the record sheet for the interval. To determine
the percent of intervals the target behavior occurred, the number of*

intervals the behavior occurred is divided by the total number of observation intervals. If a behavior occurred 15 out of 20 intervals, for example, it occurred 75% of the intervals.

In Richard's case, the teacher would observe and record data during reading instruction, the period during which he experienced most difficulty with on-task behavior. The team decided that the 90-minute reading instruction period would be divided into 5-minute time intervals, for a total of 18 intervals. Five-minute intervals were chosen because the team believed they would provide a good estimate of the actual amount of time Richard was on task. The teacher would record whether or not he was on task at the end of each of the 18 intervals.

> Note: With MTS recording, the observer is not required to observe the student continuously and is free to engage in normal activities between intervals. Therefore, it is a technique that many teachers implement while they teach. If the task becomes too cumbersome for the teacher, however, another school staff member (e.g., paraprofessional) may be trained to collect data. Technology also may be instrumental in facilitating teachers' capacity to collect data in the classroom.

Richard's school recently had purchased two iPhones as well as the ABC Data Pro application (app), version 1.29 – available through iTunes – for the purpose of recording student behavior. With these devices, the observer can be prompted to observe the target student(s) at designated intervals and record the results electronically, rather than with paper and pencil.

Because Mrs. Z already was very familiar and comfortable with technology and had an iPhone of her own, the team decided to use ABC Data Pro to implement MTS recording with Richard. Mrs. Z had not used this app previously; the school psychologist therefore would train her how to use it.

The ABC Data Pro app would be programmed so the iPhone would vibrate at the end of 5-minute intervals. At the end of each interval, Mrs. Z would observe Richard and touch a pre-labeled button to record whether he was or was not on task. Mrs. Z also would make a brief note of the ongoing activities in which Richard was involved during reading instruction (e.g., 9:30: small group reading; 10 a.m.: independent seatwork). This would help the team discern potential patterns regarding the impact of the class activity on Richard's on-task behavior.

Using the school's other iPhone and ABC Pro Data app, the school psychologist would collect some data on the on-task behavior of several other randomly-chosen students in Mrs. Z's classroom during reading instruction to provide social comparison data. Such social comparison data would be considered representative of a "typical" peer's on-task behavior in the same setting.

Stage 2: Conjoint needs analysis

*After baseline data were collected, the psychologist conducted a conjoint needs analysis interview with Richard's teacher and parents. The team reviewed the data and found that on average, Richard was on task 50% of the intervals during reading instruction. No pattern was detected with regard to the impact of the ongoing activity on his behavior. Social comparison data collected by the school psychologist indicated that other students were on task an average of 85% of the intervals during reading instruction. Therefore, the team's **ideal** goal for Richard was that he increase his on-task behavior to 85% of the intervals, the level at which typical peers were performing. The team further decided, however, that if Richard were unable to eliminate bathroom trips entirely (and it is true, indeed, that individuals with OCD frequently are able to reduce, but not eradicate, OCD symptoms), a goal of 75-80% of the intervals on task would still represent a profound improvement over baseline. In addition, the team hypothesized that Richard's contamination fears were responsible for the bathroom trips (i.e., he was carrying out washing rituals), which greatly reduced his levels of on-task behavior.*

As the team was discussing intervention options, Richard's mother mentioned that he loved anything related to soccer: soccer cards, posters, magazines, movies, etc. This comment prompted the school psychologist to think about the possibility of incorporating soccer reinforcers into Richard's intervention. Because she was familiar with the potential concerns related to using positive reinforcement with students with OCD (see Chapter 22), the psychologist asked Richard's parents what they thought about his earning soccer items for very gradual increases in on-task behavior. Aware of his passion for anything soccer-related, his parents said they believed Richard would respond favorably to this approach.

After additional discussion, the team decided Richard's intervention would involve a positive reinforcement program in which he would be rewarded for increasingly higher levels of on-task behavior. To confirm the appropriateness of this plan, the teacher would solicit Richard's feedback prior to its implementation. If Richard were responsive to this plan, his behavior would be closely monitored throughout the intervention to ensure that his symptoms were not worsening as a result of this approach.

Because Richard exhibited some anxiety when making requests to use the bathroom, his on-task behavior would be increased slowly. Each criterion therefore would be increased by one additional interval of on-task behavior. In other words, Richard was on task an average of 50%, or 9 out of 18 intervals, during baseline. The first criterion would be set at 55% (approximately 10 out of 18) of the intervals on task. When he achieved this criterion for three consecutive school days, the next criterion would be set at 61% (approximately 11 out of 18 intervals) for three consecutive school days. Criteria would be increased in this manner until Richard achieved the final goal of being on task 85% of the intervals (or 75-80%, depending upon how Richard responded) during reading instruction.

For each day he met criterion, Richard would receive an in-class reinforcer (e.g., a card with a soccer player). Furthermore, because daily home-school communication was built into the plan, his parents would provide a reinforcer at home when he met criterion at school. The team also discussed that it was important to be non-punitive and praise Richard for effort when he didn't meet a criterion. Finally, it was decided that the teacher would continue to use MTS recording during the intervention phase.

Stage 3: Plan implementation

During stage 3, plan implementation, Mrs. Z discussed with Richard the team's concerns about his missing classroom time during reading while he was in the bathroom. Richard stated that he, too, was very concerned about his inability to complete his assignments and its serious effect on his grades. In addition, he reported that didn't like "feeling lost" when he returned to class, i.e., he frequently didn't know

what activity the rest of the class was on when he came back from
the bathroom, and it took some time to figure out what he needed
to work on.

When Mrs. Z asked Richard what he liked or was interested in, he
immediately mentioned soccer. The teacher asked him if he thought
earning soccer rewards for working – very slowly – to increase the time
he spent working in class during reading would be helpful. Richard said
that it might be "kinda hard to do." But he said he "really liked the idea
of getting some cool soccer stuff" and wanted to get better grades in
reading, as well.

In addition to explaining and discussing the intervention, the teacher
talked with Richard about instances in which it is appropriate to wash
one's hands, e.g., after using the toilet, before eating. At the end of the
discussion, the teacher was confident that Richard understood and was
comfortable with all components of the intervention.

During the implementation of the plan, the teacher observed and
recorded data on Richard's on-task behavior. At the end of each day,
she briefly met with him to determine whether he had met his daily
criterion and provided reinforcers as appropriate. Reinforcers were
provided according to the predetermined schedule at home, as well.

During the intervention, the school psychologist monitored the
teacher's data collection system and visited Richard's classroom
occasionally to ensure the intervention was going according to plans.
Because Richard responded positively to the intervention, both initially
and throughout the program, the team decided that no program
modifications were necessary.

Stage 4: Conjoint plan evaluation

During the final stage of CBC, conjoint plan evaluation, the school
psychologist met once again with Richard's teacher and parents. They
carefully reviewed the data collected by the teacher and determined
that Richard had, indeed, met the ideal goal of being on task 85% of
the intervals during reading instruction for one entire school week. In
fact, Richard actually proceeded ahead of schedule: he was able to
move to the next, higher criterion after an average of two days at each
level, rather than three. The team decided that data collection would
continue as the reinforcement program was faded gradually.

The school psychologist also asked the parents and teacher to provide feedback on their perspectives regarding the acceptability and effectiveness of CBC. Overall, the parents and teacher were very satisfied. The assessment and intervention phases were relatively easy for the teacher to implement, and the parents were pleased that they had an important role in a program that had such a positive effect on Richard's behavior. Because he was completing more assignments and earning better grades, he seemed happier and had more self-confidence. His parents also reported that he was spending less time in the bathroom at home, as well, and was involved in more activities (e.g., playing games with siblings).

The conjoint behavioral consultation process does not always proceed in a smooth fashion. Indeed, CBC team members should be aware that roadblocks can and do occur at any stage of the process. Therefore, another hypothetical scenario follows providing an example of difficulties encountered with Richard during Stage 3 (plan implementation) and how they were resolved.

Scenario 2

For the first two weeks of the implementation of the intervention, Richard made good progress and reached the first two criteria by the middle of the second week. By the end of the third week, however, Richard hit a plateau. The school psychologist reviewed the intervention plan with Mrs. Z and his parents to be certain it was being implemented appropriately. The psychologist also observed the teacher to ensure that data were being collected properly. Overall, it appeared the plan was being implemented with fidelity.

The team members decided to speak with Richard to solicit his input with regard to problems that might be occurring. In their respective discussions, Mrs. Z and Richard's parents learned that although he initially liked the soccer reinforcers (e.g., cards, pictures), he had earned so many of them that he was "kinda getting tired of them." He indicated that he would prefer to earn a variety of rewards.

Based upon Richard's feedback, the team decided to use a menu of reinforcers, wherein he could choose a reinforcer from a number of different options listed on a sheet each day he met his objective. In addition, the team decided that Mrs. Z would give Richard 1 point for each day he met his objective. When he met his objective for 3 consecutive days, he could use his 3 points to "buy" an item from the class Treasure Chest, a large box containing a variety of small toys.

Richard's parents also agreed to allow him to choose from a reinforcer menu at home each day he met his objective. Once the new reinforcement plan was implemented, Richard began to make progress again, gradually increasing his on-task behavior until he met his ideal goal of being on task 85% of the intervals during reading instruction.

An important note about CBC for students with OCD

It has been emphasized throughout this text that OCD is an extremely heterogeneous disorder. Students may share the same diagnosis – OCD – yet exhibit entirely different symptoms and corresponding difficulties at school. Therefore, a "one size fits all" approach to working with these students is inappropriate. In the hypothetical case example provided above, Richard's time on-task behavior was increased successfully using positive reinforcement within the context of conjoint behavioral consultation, even when roadblocks were encountered (see Scenario 2 above). Targeting this behavior within the context of CBC might be inappropriate, however, for another child with OCD. A different student may have experienced an increase in levels of anxiety and an exacerbation of symptoms when positive reinforcement was implemented to increase on-task behavior. It is incumbent upon school personnel to devise interventions that fit the needs of individual students.

Anxiety management strategies and cognitive techniques

Anxiety management strategies and cognitive techniques – which may be implemented within the context of conjoint behavioral consultation or independently – can be extremely helpful in supporting students with OCD. Situations often arise in which the student is overwhelmed by OCD symptoms and needs help managing feelings of anxiety and frustration. Individuals already trained in anxiety management and cognitive strategies (e.g., school mental health professionals) may implement them directly with students. Or school mental health professionals may train teachers and other school staff members to use them. These techniques can benefit not only students with OCD but also students with other anxiety disorders or those experiencing high levels of stress.

Following is a brief overview of several anxiety-management techniques and cognitive strategies. The majority of the information is adapted from the work of March and Mulle (1998) and March (2007).

Anxiety management: Deep breathing. Deep breathing involves diaphragmatic breathing (breathing using the diaphragm as opposed to the chest). The student first must be instructed in how to use the diaphragm to breathe (e.g., student puts a pillow on stomach and watches how diaphragmatic breathing causes pillow to rise, whereas breathing from the chest does not). *Directions to the student:* Take a deep breath through the nose, inhaling as much air as possible. Hold your breath for a count of 3, then exhale slowly while saying "Relax" to yourself. Practice this skill.

Anxiety management: Relaxation. Relaxation techniques frequently involve deep muscle relaxation, in which large muscle groups systematically are tensed and relaxed. *Directions to the student:* Choose a comfortable position, either sitting or lying down, and take several deep breaths, using diaphragmatic breathing (as above). Tense your neck muscles by shrugging your shoulders and counting to 5 or 10. Slowly relax your neck muscles while counting back from 10 or 5 to 1. Continue with a head roll (drop your head so chin is on the chest, roll head to one side, drop head to back, to other side, then slowly to the front; repeat once or twice). Follow with arm tensing: lift your arms with palms up to a count of 5 or 10, then lower them, counting back to 1. Continue the same steps, tensing and relaxing your hands, stomach, legs, and feet. You may repeat the exercise, working from feet back to head. End with diaphragmatic breathing.

"Short form" of anxiety reduction. The short form of anxiety reduction may help a student keep from "getting lost" in OCD. *Directions to the student:* Take a deep breath (using diaphragmatic breathing) and let it out slowly to anchor yourself in your body. Look around and see what's happening. Now that you know where you are, let your body relax. Take a deep breath and accept that OCD is present, but try not to think about it over and over again; try to resist OCD the best you can.

Anxiety management: Visualization and guided imagery. Visualization and guided imagery help a child relax by imagining a place he or she enjoys and feels relaxed and peaceful. *Directions to the student:* Imagine a favorite place (this need not be a calm or relaxing place – can even be funny or silly; use whatever imagery helps with relaxation) and describe the details of what is imagined, including sights, sounds, smells, tastes, textures, etc. Note: If the student has difficulty with visualization, the instructor may use imagery scripts to guide the experience. Music may be used in place of visual imagery for children whose sensory preference is auditory rather than visual. The goal is that the imagery produce a positive affect that promotes relaxation. Imagery frequently is used at the end of deep muscle relaxation exercises.

Other anxiety-reduction techniques. In addition to the aforementioned anxiety management training activities, school personnel may help students reduce stress by providing opportunities to exercise (e.g., walk, run, play, exercise to music, shoot baskets), have fun, e.g., watch a humorous movie, read a funny comic book, tell jokes (laughter triggers the release of endorphins, the body's natural feel-good chemicals that can reduce tension and pain), and listen to music. Schools increasingly are promoting the use of yoga and meditation techniques to help students manage stress.

Cognitive strategies. As indicated in Chapter 7, cognitive factors may play a role in the genesis and maintenance of OCD. Individuals with OCD frequently experience faulty or dysfunctional beliefs such as the overestimation of risk or threat and an inflated sense of responsibility. Although OCD tends to be a very secretive disorder, some students are willing to discuss their OCD symptoms with school personnel. In these cases, school staff may be able to implement certain cognitive techniques to help the student. Three techniques, in particular, may be helpful: constructive self-talk, cognitive restructuring, and cultivating detachment.

Cognitive strategies: Constructive self-talk. Many children and adolescents are critical of themselves for having OCD, especially when their symptoms create problems at home or school. As a result, they may engage in punitive self-talk, e.g., "I'm so stupid for doing these things over and over again," or "What's wrong with me? Why can't I just stop this?" When negative self-talk is identified, it can be corrected by teaching the child to replace negative comments with positive but realistic statements emphasizing his or her ability to cope. Constructive self-talk may be extremely helpful both on a more general level, e.g., "This isn't really me; it's the OCD," as well as in situations in which the student is working to reduce specific symptoms. During the conjoint behavioral consultation process, for example, the team may determine that a student is making negative statements such as "This is never going to work. I'll never be able to stop doing these stupid things." The student could be taught to replace negative self-talk with a statement such as "This is probably going to be hard, but I really think I can do it."

Students also may punish themselves with negative self-talk when they are unable to achieve a specific goal. In these situations, the student may be taught to replace statements such as "I knew I wouldn't be able to do this. This is impossible to change!" with constructive self-talk: "It's OK if I couldn't do this today. I'm doing my best, and I'm going to give it another try tomorrow." Importantly, if a student is unable to meet a particular goal, the current intervention should be evaluated to determine if a standard is set too high, the process is moving too quickly, or the intervention is inappropriate for the student.

A second type of constructive self-talk may be used when students have been taught to externalize OCD and see it as an illness separate from who they really are. Children receiving cognitive-behavioral therapy for OCD are asked to provide a nasty nickname for OCD – e.g., "Germy," or "Killer," or just to call it by its name, "OCD" – to help with the externalization process. This type of self-talk involves the student having conversations with and "talking back" to the OCD. The child essentially refuses to give in to OCD and talks back to it using positive and forceful statements: "I will NOT get sick from germs and die if I don't go to the bathroom." When such specific statements are too difficult for the child to make (i.e., the statement itself has the potential to trigger OCD symptoms), more general statements may be appropriate: "Get away from me, OCD; I'm the boss," or "You won't get me this time, OCD."

Cognitive strategies: Cognitive restructuring. Another technique for helping students with OCD is cognitive restructuring. This technique may be used when the overestimation of risk or threat occurs. Cognitive restructuring involves helping the child analyze his or her estimation of the occurrence of a catastrophe or dangerous event. For instance, a child may feel that if he doesn't tell his mom to drive carefully, the chances or probability of her having an automobile accident are 100%.

Moreover, he, alone, is 100% responsible for this catastrophe. With cognitive restructuring, the child would be asked to provide an estimate of the *realistic* chances or probability of the catastrophe's occurrence (e.g., perhaps 1%). Comparing this estimate (1%) with the risk estimate provided by OCD (100%) should provide evidence that the OCD estimate completely lacks credibility. For some children, especially younger children, estimation or probability arguments may be difficult to understand and therefore should not be used.

Cognitive restructuring also may be used with a sense of overresponsibility. Even when very small risks are involved, some children and adolescents fear they are still responsible for a catastrophe, e.g., "If mom does have a car accident, it's all my fault." In these cases, it may be helpful to draw a pie chart to indicate factors that could contribute to the mother's having a car accident as well as a realistic estimate of the percent of responsibility each factor might carry. For example, the pie chart might indicate the following: a 25% chance of another driver hitting mom's car; a 25% chance that mom will run a red light; a 25% chance that mom will hit an animal; a 20% chance that bad weather (e.g., rain, snow, ice) will occur; a 4% chance the brakes on the car will fail; and a 1% chance that failing to tell mom to be careful before she drove will cause her to have an accident. Once again, when the realistic estimate of 1% is compared to the previous estimate of 100%, the student may come to realize OCD's lack of credibility. Self-talk is an effective complement to cognitive restructuring: "I'm smarter than you are, OCD; there's almost NO chance Mom will have a car accident if I don't tell her to drive carefully," or "I'm not buying it, OCD; what you're saying just isn't true!"

Cognitive strategies: Cultivating detachment. Another cognitive strategy that may help students with OCD is cultivating detachment. Cognitive detachment involves asking the student to view OCD as a cloud in the sky, wind blowing, rain falling, or birds flying – something that comes and goes in its own time, whether or not rituals are done. March and Mulle (1998) suggest that the child use four simple steps and corresponding self-statements when obsessions arise:

1. recognize the obsessions as OCD: "Oh, it's you again, OCD;"

2. attribute OCD to its neurobiological basis: "My brain is just acting up again;"

3. recognize the content of the obsession as meaningless: "It's no big deal that my brain is acting up – it's not important," and

4. recognize that the meaningless symptoms will pass on their own: "I think I'll just go and do something fun while the OCD goes away."

A final note about anxiety management and cognitive techniques. As previously indicated, individuals who are trained in the use of anxiety management and cognitive techniques (e.g., school mental health professionals) can either implement them directly with students or instruct teachers and other school staff members how to use them. Individuals interested in implementing these techniques are encouraged to consult the work of March and Mulle (1998) and March (2007). It is important to note, however, that these techniques likely would be most successful for students with mild to moderate cases of OCD. When students are very ill with OCD, it is best that a trained clinician be involved.

Ch:25

SOME FINAL THOUGHTS ABOUT STUDENTS WITH OCD

In doing the research for this book, the author reviewed hundreds upon hundreds of pages of information pertaining to children and adolescents with neurobiological disorders, in general, and OCD, specifically. In an Education Paper published by the Tourette Syndrome Association, Ms. Susan Conners, an expert on TS and an individual who, herself, has TS, wrote about "Learning Problems and the Student with TS" (2003). Ms. Conners closes her article with words describing the experience of students with TS – words this author found more poignant than any words in any other text. Importantly, they apply equally well to students with OCD. Following is Ms. Conners' message; with her permission, "OCD" or "obsessive-compulsive disorder" has been substituted in place of "TS" or "Tourette Syndrome." It is, perhaps, the most powerful message school personnel can receive regarding children and adolescents with obsessive-compulsive disorder...

"Many diseases kill children in this country and around the world every day. Obsessive-compulsive disorder is not a fatal disease, but children die slowly each day from OCD. Their spirit is killed; their potential is killed; their self-esteem is killed. OCD is not responsible. Ignorance is. These children luckily do not appear disabled, although it might be better if they did. They bear the outward appearance of a child with a behavior problem: a defiant child, a stubborn child, a bizarre child, an emotionally disturbed child, a spoiled child. They are disciplined for things they cannot control and receive low grades on things they cannot accomplish. They are teased and imitated by other students and yes, sometimes by teachers. Their spirit dies a slow and painful death. Only when the impact of this disorder on educational performance is understood by all concerned can the greatest amount of learning take place."

OCD

International OCD Foundation (IOCDF)
P.O. Box 961029
Boston, MA 02196
617.973.5801
www.ocfoundation.org

OCD Chicago
2300 Lincoln Park West
Chicago, IL 60614
773.880.1635
www.ocdchicago.org (has a very
extensive section for school personnel)

**The Awareness Foundation for
OCD & Related Disorders**
P.O. Box 1795
Soquel, CA 95073
www.afocd.org

Obsessive Compulsive Anonymous
P.O. Box 215
New Hyde Park, NY 11040
516.739.0662
www.obsessivecompulsiveanonymous.org

General Mental Health/ Multiple Disorders

National Alliance on Mental Illness
3803 N. Fairfax Dr., Suite 100
Arlington, VA 22203
703.524.7600
www.nami.org

Madison Institute of Medicine
6515 Grand Teton Plaza, Suite 100
Madison, WI 53719
608.827.2470
www.miminc.org

**National Institute of Mental Health
Science Writing, Press, and
Dissemination Branch**
6001 Executive Blvd., Room 8184, MSC 9663
Bethesda, MD 20892
866.615.6464
www.nimh.nih.gov

Freedom from Fear
308 Seaview Ave.
Staten Island, NY 10305
718.351.1717 (ext. 19)
www.freedomfromfear.org

Mental Health America
2000 N. Beauregard St. 6th Floor
Alexandria, VA 22311
800.969.6642
www.mentalhealthamerica.net

**Substance Abuse and Mental
Health Services Administration**
1 Choke Cherry Rd.
Rockville, MD 20847
877.SAMHSA7 (877.726.4727)
www.samhsa.gov

**National Institute of Child
Health and Human Development
(National Institutes of Health)**
P.O. Box 3006
Rockville, MD 20847
800.370.2943
www.nichd.nih.gov

Healthy Minds. Healthy Lives. (Online
site; American Psychiatric Association)
www.healthyminds.org

Tourette Syndrome

Tourette Syndrome Association
42-40 Bell Blvd., Suite 205
Bayside, NY 11361
718.224.2999
www.tsa-usa.org

Body Dysmorphic Disorder

BDDCentral
12819 E. Summit Dr.
Scottsdale, AZ 85259
www.bddcentral.com

Eating Disorders

National Eating Disorders Association
603 Stewart Street, Suite 803
Seattle, WA 98101
206.382.3587
www.nationaleatingdisorders.org

Anxiety Disorders

**Anxiety Disorders
Association of America**
8730 Georgia Avenue
Silver Spring, MD 20910
240.485.1001
www.adaa.org

Attention-Deficit/Hyperactivity Disorder

**Children and Adults with Attention-
Deficit/Hyperactivity Disorder**
8181 Professional Place, Suite 150
Landover, MD 20785
301.306.7070
www.chadd.org

**Affiliated National Resource
Center on AD/HD:**
www.help4adhd.org

Trichotillomania

Trichotillomania Learning Center
(Note: includes information on
skin picking and nail biting)
207 McPherson St., Suite H
Santa Cruz, CA 95060
831.457.1004
www.trich.org

Asperger's Syndrome

**National Institute of Neurological
Disorders and Stroke (National
Institutes of Health)**
NIH Neurological Institute
P.O. Box 5801
Bethesda, MD 20824
800.352.9424
www.ninds.nih.gov/disorders/
asperger/asperger.htm

OASIS@MAAP (Online site)
www.aspergersyndrome.org

Depression/Bipolar Disorder

Depression and Bipolar Support Alliance
730 N. Franklin Street, Suite 501
Chicago, Illinois 60654
800.826.3632
www.dbsalliance.org

**National Institute of Mental Health:
Depression Science Writing, Press,
and Dissemination Branch**
6001 Executive Blvd., Room 8184, MSC 9663
Bethesda, MD 20892
866.615.6464
www.nimh.nih.gov/health/publications/
depression/complete-index.shtml

Disruptive Behavior Disorders

**Mental Health Association
of Westchester**
(Note: includes information on oppositional
defiant disorder and conduct disorder)
2269 Saw Mill River Road, Building 1A
Elmsford, NY 10523
914.345.5900
www.mhawestchester.org/
diagnosechild/cbehavior.asp

Obsessive-Compulsive
Personality Disorder

**US National Library of Medicine
(National Institutes of Health)**
Reference and Web Services
National Library of Medicine
8600 Rockville Pike
Bethesda, MD 20894
www.nlm.nih.gov

Autism

Autism Society
4340 East-West Hwy, Suite 350
Bethesda, Maryland 20814
800.3AUTISM (800.328.8476)
www.autism-society.org

TEACCH Autism Program
Division TEACCH, CB 7180, UNC-CH
Chapel Hill, NC 27599-7180
Phone: 919.966.2174
www.teacch.com

Yale Child Study Center
230 South Frontage Rd.
New Haven, CT 06520
203.785.3420
www.childstudycenter.yale.edu/autism

Resources for School Personnel

**National Association of
School Psychologists**
4340 East West Highway, Suite 402
Bethesda, MD 20814
866.331.NASP
www.nasponline.org

Council for Exceptional Children
2900 Crystal Dr., Suite 1000
Arlington, VA 22202
800.232.7733
www.cec.sped.org

**Council for Children with Behavioral
Disorders** (Online site)
www.ccbd.net

**Center for Effective
Collaboration and Practice***
(Online site; supports children with
or at risk of developing serious
emotional disturbance)
www.cecp.air.org/center.asp

*Link within CECP that pertains to
functional behavioral assessments
and positive behavioral intervention
plans and supports:
www.cecp.air.org/fba/
problembehavior/introduction.htm

SchoolBehavior.com
(Online site; created by Dr. Leslie
Packer for educators of students
with neurobehavioral problems)
www.schoolbehavior.com

Resources for School
Personnel and Parents

**School Psychiatry Program & MADI
Resource Center** (OCD + other disorders)
Massachusetts General Hospital
MADI Resource Center
50 Staniford Street, Suite 580
Boston, MA 02114
617.726.2725 (for children & adolescents)
www2.massgeneral.org/schoolpsychiatry

**National Dissemination Center for
Children with Disabilities (NICHCY)**
1825 Connecticut Ave NW, Suite 700
Washington, DC 20009
800.695.0285
www.nichcy.org

WorryWiseKids (Online
site; OCD + Anxiety)
www.worrywisekids.org

Tourette Syndrome "Plus"
(Online site; addresses difficulties
in children and adolescents with
Tourette Syndrome and many other
associated disorders, e.g., AD/
HD, OCD, bipolar disorder)
www.tourettesyndrome.net

LDOnline*
WETA Public Television
2775 S. Quincy St.
Arlington, VA 22206
Fax: 703-998-2060
www.ldonline.org

*Resources created by Rick Lavoie,
primarily on social competence;
includes "social autopsy"
www.ldonline.org/lavoie

**Resources on Educational Laws
Pertaining to Students with Disabilities
Wrightslaw ***
(Online site; special education
law, education law, and advocacy
for children with disabilities)
www.wrightslaw.com

Directory of best school websites chosen by Wrightslaw:
www.fetaweb.com/best.htm

KidsSource (Online site)
Overview of ADA, IDEA, and Section 504
www.kidsource.com/kidsource/
content3/ada.idea.html

Information and Technical Assistance on the Americans with Disabilities Act (ADA) (Online site)
www.ada.gov

Section 504 of the Rehabilitation Act of 1973 (Online site)
www.hhs.gov/ocr/civilrights/
resources/factsheets/504.pdf

Resources for Parents

American Academy of Child and Adolescent Psychiatry: Facts for Families
(Online site)
www.aacap.org/cs/root/facts_
for_families/facts_for_families

KidsHealth (Online site)
www.kidshealth.org

Parents' Online Support Groups

Yahoo Health Groups: The OCD and Parenting List
(Online List serv for parents)
www.health.groups.yahoo.com/
group/ocdandparenting

Yahoo Health Groups: Parents of Teens and Young Adults
(Online support group for parents of middle school, high school, and college-age students)
www.health.groups.yahoo.
com/group/OCD-POTAYA

Children's/Teens online support groups

Yahoo Health Groups: OCDKidsloop
(Online support group for children under 16; moderated by parents)
www.health.groups.yahoo.
com/group/ocdkidsloop

Note: Please refer to the International OCD Foundation website at www. ocfoundation.org for a number of other online support groups (e.g., various comorbidities, special groups)

Note: Please refer to the International OCD Foundation website at www.ocfoundation.org for books on adult OCD, including general and self-help books, books for therapists, personal memoirs, and books on disorders related to OCD.

Technical Books on OCD in Children and Adolescents

Handbook of Child and Adolescent Obsessive-Compulsive Disorder
2007, edited by Eric Storch, Gary Geffken, and Tanya Murphy

Cognitive Behavioral Treatment of Childhood OCD: It's Only a False Alarm, Therapist Guide
2007, John Piacentini, Audra Langley, and Tami Roblek

Treatment of OCD in Children and Adolescents: Professional Kit
(2nd edition) 2007, Aureen Pinto Wagner

OCD in Children and Adolescents: A Cognitive-Behavioral Treatment Manual
1998, John March and Karen Mulle

Self-Help

Talking Back to OCD: The Program That Helps Kids and Teens Say "No Way"—and Parents Say "Way to Go"
2007, John March with Christine Benton

Parents/Families

Freeing your Child from Obsessive-Compulsive Disorder: A Powerful, Practical Program for Parents of Children and Adolescents
2000, Tamar Chansky

Helping Your Child with OCD: A Workbook for Parents of Children with Obsessive-Compulsive Disorder
2003, Lee Fitzgibbons and Cherry Pedrick

Talking Back to OCD: The Program That Helps Kids and Teens Say "No Way"—and Parents Say "Way to Go"
2007, John March with Christine Benton

What to do When Your Child Has Obsessive-Compulsive Disorder: Strategies and Solutions
2006, Aureen Pinto Wagner

Obsessive-Compulsive Disorder: Help for Children and Adolescents
2000, Mitzi Waltz

Obsessive-Compulsive Disorder: New Help for the Family
2004, Herbert Gravitz

Children and Adolescents

You Do That Too? Adolescents and OCD
2000, Rena Benson and Jose Arturo

Repetitive Rhonda
2007, Jan Evans

Not As Crazy As I Seem
2004, George Harrar

No One is Perfect and YOU Are a Great Kid
2006, Kim Hix

What to do When Your Brain Gets Stuck: A Kid's Guide to Overcoming OCD
2007, Dawn Huebner

Blink, Blink, Clop, Clop: Why Do We Do Things We Can't Stop? An OCD Storybook
2001, E. Katia Moritz and Jennifer Jablonsky

Mr. Worry: A Story About OCD
2003, Holly Niner

A Thought is Just a Thought: A Story of Living with OCD
2004, Leslie Talley

Up and Down the Worry Hill: A Children's Book about Obsessive-Compulsive Disorder and its Treatment
2004, Aureen Pinto Wagner

Kissing Doorknobs
1999, Terry Spencer Hesser

Multiple Choice
2008, Janet Tashjian

Passing for Normal: A Memoir of Compulsion
2000, Amy Wilensky

Devil in the Details: Scenes from an Obsessive Girlhood
2006, Jennifer Traig

The Thought That Counts: A Firsthand Account of One Teenager's Experience with Obsessive-Compulsive Disorder
2008, Jared Kant with Martin Franklin and Linda Wasmer Andrews

Touch and Go Joe: An Adolescent's Experience of OCD
Joe Wells, 2006

Funny, You Don't Look Crazy: Life with Obsessive-Compulsive Disorder

Polly's Magic Games: A Child's View of Obsessive-Compulsive Disorder

Kids Like Me: Children's Stories about Obsessive-Compulsive Disorder
1994, 1994, and 1997, respectively, Constance Foster

School Personnel/Parents

Teaching Kids With Mental Health & Learning Disorders in the Regular Classroom: How to Recognize, Understand, and Help Challenged (and Challenging) Students Succeed
2007, Myles Cooley

Challenging Kids, Challenged Teachers: Teaching Students with Tourette's, Bipolar Disorder, Executive Dysfunction, OCD, ADHD, and More
2010, Leslie Packer and Sheryl Pruitt

Find a Way or Make a Way: Checklists of Helpful Accommodations for Students with ADHD, Executive Dysfunctions, Mood Disorders, Tourette's Syndrome, OCD and Other Neurological Challenges
2009, Leslie Packer

Teaching the Tiger: A Handbook for Individuals Involved in the Education of Students with Attention Deficit Disorders, Tourette Syndrome or Obsessive-Compulsive Disorder
1995, Marilyn Dornbush and Sheryl Pruitt

Tigers, Too: Executive Functions/Speed of Processing/Memory
2009, Marilyn Dornbush and Sheryl Pruitt

Worried no More: Help and Hope for Anxious Children
2005, Aureen Pinto Wagner

Multimedia Kit (for school personnel and parents)

OCD in the Classroom: A Multi-Media Program for Parents, Teachers, and School Personnel
Marlene Targ Brill and Gail Adams
Available at www.ocfoundation.org/booksales.aspx

The Touching Tree: A Story of a Child with OCD
Awareness Films, in association with the International OCD Foundation (IOCDF). This is a film about Terry, an elementary-aged boy with OCD, who exhibits unusual behaviors at school. A compassionate teacher learns that Terry has obsessive-compulsive disorder and guides him to treatment, which changes both their lives. Available through IOCDF at www.ocfoundation.org

How to Recognize and Respond to OCD in School-Age Children
International OCD Foundation. This is an educator awareness and training module designed for teaching professionals and parents of school-age children with OCD. It contains two videos and four helpful booklets. Available through IOCDF at www.ocfoundation.org

Hope and Solutions for OCD
The Awareness Foundation for OCD & Related Disorders (AFOCD). This four-part series features: (1) Dr. A.J. Allen (What OCD is and How to Treat It; (2) Mr. James Callner (Recovery from OCD); (3) Dr. Gail Adams (OCD and the Schools); and (4) Dr. Herbert Gravitz (OCD and the Family). All four speakers are available on one DVD. Available through AFOCD at www.afocd.org

Step on a Crack
Arlene Lorre. This video features six individuals discussing how OCD has affected their lives and how they have come to cope with it. Available at www.fanlight.com

In the Shoes of Christopher
Awareness Films, The Awareness Foundation for OCD & Related Disorders. This is a film about a middle school bully and a boy with OCD. A creative and empathic teacher devises a series of challenges that literally puts the bully "in the shoes" of a person with OCD. This challenge changes the bully's life forever; intolerance is transformed to compassion. Available from through AFOCD at www.afocd.org

Sharing the Hope: A Parental Guide for Managing Obsessive Compulsive Behavior
Solvay Pharmaceuticals. This video provides information for parents of children and teens with OCD. It features the story of three families, each coming to grips with the diagnosis of OCD and the subsequent impact of effective treatment. Available at www.amazon.com

The Risk
Awareness Films, The Awareness Foundation for OCD & Related Disorders. This 20-minute dramatic film educates viewers about OCD symptoms and its impact on the family. It emphasizes what is crucial for those affected with OCD: the willingness to take the risk to seek help. This film is an excellent tool for understanding the trauma of OCD and how to take "The Risk" to start recovery. Available through AFOCD at www.afocd.org

Appendix | C: Films on Childhood OCD

239

Part A Instructions: Please circle YES or NO for the following questions, based on your experiences with the above-named student *over the past week.*

Has this student displayed a tendency to have upsetting thoughts or perform certain acts over and over again, such as:

Yes / No 1. Erasing and re-writing notes, worksheet answers, test responses, or essays even when there is nothing wrong with them?

Yes / No 2. "Getting stuck" and unnecessarily re-reading the same sentence or paragraph?

Yes / No 3. Needing to touch, tap, or rub certain objects or people repeatedly?

Yes / No 4. Excessive/ritualized washing or restroom trips (e.g., repetitive handwashing)?

Yes / No 5. Counting, arranging, or "evening up" behaviors (e.g., making sure the left and right side are balanced)?

Yes / No 6. Collecting useless items or inspecting garbage before it is thrown out (e.g., saving old school papers that are no longer needed)?

Yes / No 7. Checking his/her backpack, desk, or assignment book repeatedly?

Yes / No 8. Making excessive lists (e.g., "to do" lists)?

Yes / No 9. Needing to "confess" or repeatedly asking for reassurance that s/he did something correctly?

Yes / No 10. Avoiding certain colors (e.g., "red" means blood), numbers (e.g., "13" is unlucky), or names?

Yes / No 11. Refraining from stepping on lines in the tile, cracks on the pavement, etc.?

Yes / No 12. Seeming overly concerned with contamination (e.g., avoids touching or being near objects that might be "dirty" or have "germs")?

Yes / No 13. Focusing excessive energy or concern on keeping objects in perfect order or arranged exactly?

Yes / No 14. Worrying that s/he may cause or may have caused something bad to happen?

Yes / No 15. Other (please specify) _____

_____

Part B Instructions: Please rate how much the symptoms you endorsed on the first page have caused this student problems *over the past week. If the question does not apply,* please mark "None at all."

	None at All	Just a Little	Quite a Bit	Very Much
1. Being prepared for classes (e.g., having supplies and assignments ready when needed)	___	___	___	___
2. Getting to classes on time during the day	___	___	___	___
3. Staying in class (e.g., not going to school office) during the school day	___	___	___	___
4. Remaining at school for the entire day	___	___	___	___
5. Paying attention in class/concentrating on his or her work	___	___	___	___
6. Giving oral reports or reading aloud	___	___	___	___
7. Writing in class/taking notes	___	___	___	___
8. Taking tests or exams	___	___	___	___
9. Turning in homework	___	___	___	___
10. Earning good grades	___	___	___	___
11. Participating in physical activities	___	___	___	___
12. Doing fun things during free time or recess	___	___	___	___
13. Eating lunch with other students	___	___	___	___
14. Going to school outings or field trips	___	___	___	___
15. Other (please specify):	___	___	___	___

Used with permission of Lisa J. Merlo, Ph.D., Department of Psychiatry Addiction Medicine and Child & Adolescent Psychiatry, University of Florida, Gainesville, FL.

Appendix | D: The Florida Obsessive-Compulsive Student Inventory

241

Achenbach, T. M., & Rescorla, L. A. (2001). *Manual for the ASEBA School-Age Forms & Profiles.* Burlington, VT: University of Vermont, Research Center for Children, Youth, & Families.

Adams, G. B. (2004). Identifying, assessing, and treating obsessive-compulsive disorder in school-aged children: The role of school personnel. *TEACHING Exceptional Children, 37*(2), 46-53.

Adams, G. B., & Burke, R. W. (1999). Children and adolescents with obsessive-compulsive disorder: A primer for teachers. *Childhood Education, 76*(1), 2-7.

Adams, G. B., Smith, T. S., Bolt, S. E., & Nolten, P. (2007). Current educational practices in classifying and serving students with obsessive-compulsive disorder. *The California School Psychologist, 12,* 93-105.

Adams, G. B., Waas, G. A., March, J. S., & Smith, M C. (1994). Obsessive-compulsive disorder in children and adolescents: The role of the school psychologist in identification, assessment, and treatment. *School Psychology Quarterly, 9*(4), 274-294.

American Academy of Child and Adolescent Psychiatry. (in press). Practice parameters for the assessment and treatment of children and adolescents with obsessive–compulsive disorder. *Journal of the American Academy of Child and Adolescent Psychiatry.*

American Psychiatric Association. (2000). *Diagnostic and statistical manual of mental disorders* (4th ed., text revision.). Washington, DC: Author.

Auster, E. R., Feeney-Kettler, K. A., & Kratochwill, T. R. (2006). Conjoint behavioral consultation: Application to the school-based treatment of anxiety disorders. *Education and Treatment of Children, 29*(2), 243-256.

Björgvinsson, T., Hart, J., & Heffelfinger, S. (2007). Obsessive-compulsive disorder: Update on assessment and treatment. *Journal of Psychiatric Practice, 13*(6), 362-372.

Bloch, M. H., Craiglow, B. G., Landeros-Weisenberger, A., Dombrowski, P. A., Panza, K. E., Petersen, B. S., & Leckman, J. F. (2009). Predictors of early adult outcomes in pediatric-onset obsessive-compulsive disorder. *Pediatrics, 124*(4), 1085-1093.

Budman, C. L., Bruun, R. D., Park, K. S., Lesser, M., & Olson, M. (2000). Explosive outbursts in children with Tourette's Disorder. *Journal of the American Academy of Child and Adolescent Psychiatry, 39*(10), 1270-1276.

Budman, C., Coffey, B. J., Shechter, R., Schrock, M., Wieland, N., Spirgel, A., & Simon, E. (2008). Aripiprazole in children and adolescents with Tourette disorder with and without explosive outbursts. *Journal of Child and Adolescent Psychopharmacology, 18*(5), 509-515.

Burke, R. W., & Adams, G. B. (1999). Teaching students with neurobiological disorders. *The Educational Forum, 63*(4), 371-379.

Calvocoressi, L., Mazure, C. M., Kasl, S. V., Skolnick, J., Fisk, D., Vegso, S. J.,...Price, L. H. (1999). Family accommodation of obsessive-compulsive symptoms: Instrument development and assessment of family behavior. *Journal of Nervous and Mental Disorders, 187*(10), 636-642.

Camp, B. W., & Bash, M. A. (1985). *Think aloud: Increasing social and cognitive skills—A problem-solving program for children, classroom program grades 1-2.* Champaign, IL: Research Press.

Chansky, T. E. (2000). *Freeing your child from obsessive-compulsive disorder.* New York: Crown Publishers.

Choate-Summers, M. L., Freeman, J. B., Garcia, A. M., Coyne, L., Przeworski, A., & Leonard, H. L. (2008). Clinical considerations when tailoring cognitive behavioral treatment for young children with obsessive compulsive disorder. *Education and Treatment of Children, 31*(3), 395-416.

Conners, S. (2003). *Learning problems and the student with TS.* Retrieved from Tourette Syndrome Association website: www.tsa-usa.org/educ_advoc/educ_ed_strat_main.htm

Conners, S. (2008, April). *Functional behavioral assessments and positive behavior intervention plans.* Paper presented at the 2008 Tourette Syndrome Association National Conference, Alexandria, VA. Retrieved from www.tsa-usa.org/educ_advoc/images/Conf0833FBAConners.pdf

Conners, S. & Giordano, K. (2005). *A workbook for conducting a functional behavioral assessment and writing a positive behavior intervention for a student with Tourette Syndrome.* Retrieved from Tourette Syndrome Association website: www.tsa-usa.org/educ_advoc/educ_ed_strat_main.htm

Council for Exceptional Children. (2008). Improving executive function skills—An innovative strategy that may enhance learning for all children. *CEC Today.* Retrieved from Council for Exceptional Children website: www.cec.sped.org/AM/Template.cfm?Section=CEC_Today1&TEMPLATE=/CM/ContentDisplay.cfm&CONTENTID=14463

Council of Chief State School Officers. (2005). *Accommodations manual: How to select, administer, and evaluate use of accommodations for instruction and assessment of students with disabilities* (2nd ed.). Washington, DC: Author.

Demchak, M. A. (n.d.). Tips for home or school: Circles of Friends. Retrieved from University of Nevada, Reno, website: www.unr.edu/educ/ndsip/tipsheets/circlesoffriends.pdf

Dornbush, M. P., & Pruitt, S. K. (1995). *Teaching the tiger: A handbook for individuals involved in the education of students with attention deficit disorders, Tourette Syndrome or obsessive-compulsive disorder.* Duarte, CA: Hope Press.

Dornbush, M. P., & Pruitt, S. K. (2008). *Tigers, too: Executive functions/speed of processing/memory.* Atlanta: Parkaire Press.

Findley, D. B., Leckman, J. F., Katsovich, L., Lin, H., Zhang, H., Grantz., H.,...King, R. A. (2003). Development of the Yale Children's Global Stress Index (YCGSI) and its application in children and adolescents with Tourette's syndrome and obsessive-compulsive disorder. *Journal of the American Academy of Child and Adolescent Psychiatry, 42*(4) 450-457.

Flament, M. F., Geller, D., Irak, M., & Blier, P. (2007). Specificities of treatment in pediatric obsessive-compulsive disorder. *CNS Spectrums, 12*(2, Suppl. 3), 43-58.

Foa, E. B., Coles, M., Huppert, J. D., Pasupuleti, R. V., Franklin, M. E., & March, J. S. (2010). Development and validation of a child version of the Obsessive Compulsive Inventory. *Behavior Therapy, 41*(1), 121-132.

Franklin, M. E., March, J. S., & Garcia, A. (2006). Treating obsessive-compulsive disorder in children and adolescents. In M. Antony, C. Purdon, & L. Summerfeldt (Eds.) *Psychological treatment of obsessive-compulsive disorders: Fundamentals and beyond* (pp. 253-266). Washington, DC: American Psychological Association.

Freeman, J. B., Choate-Summers, M. L., Moore, P. S., Garcia, A. M., Sapyta, J. J., Leonard, H. L., & Franklin, M. E. (2007). Cognitive-behavioral treatment for young children with obsessive compulsive disorder. *Biological Psychiatry, 61*(3), 337-343.

Freeman, J. B., Garcia, A. M., Coyne, L., Ale, C., Przeworski, A., Himle, M.,…Leonard, H. L. (2008). Early childhood OCD: Preliminary findings from a family-based cognitive-behavioral approach. *Journal of the American Academy of Child and Adolescent Psychiatry, 47*(5), 593-602.

Friend, M., & Bursuck, W. D. (2006). *Including students with special needs: A practical guide for classroom teachers.* Boston: Allyn & Bacon.

Geller, D. A., Wieland, N., Carey, K., Vivas, F., Petty, C. R., Johnson, J.,…Biederman, J. (2008). Perinatal factors affecting expression of obsessive compulsive disorder in children and adolescents. *Journal of Child and Adolescent Psychopharmacology, 18*(4), 373-379.

Gilbert, A. R., & Maalouf, F. T. (2008). Pediatric obsessive compulsive disorder: Management priorities in primary care. *Current Opinions in Pediatrics, 20*(5), 544-550.

Giordano, K. J. (n.d.). *TS is more than tics.* Retrieved from Tourette Syndrome Association website: www.tsa-usa.org/educ_advoc/morethantics.htm

Goldstein, A. P., & McGinnis, E. (1997). *Skillstreaming the adolescent: New strategies and perspectives for teaching prosocial skills.* Champaign, IL: Research Press.

Grados, M. A., Labuda, M. C., Riddle, M. A., & Walkup, J. T. (1997). Obsessive-compulsive disorder in children and adolescents. *International Review of Psychiatry, 9*(1), 83-97.

Grados, M. A., Vasa, R. A., Riddle, M. A., Slomine, B. S., Salorio, C., Christensen, J., & Gerring, J. (2008). New onset obsessive-compulsive symptoms in children and adolescents with severe traumatic brain injury. *Depression and Anxiety, 25*(5), 398-407.

Grados, M., & Wilcox, H. C. (2007). Genetics of obsessive-compulsive disorder: A research update. *Expert Review of Neurotherapeutics, 7*(8), 967-980.

Gravitz, H. L. (2005). *Obsessive compulsive disorder: New help for the family* (2nd ed.). Santa Barbara, CA: Healing Visions Press.

Gresham, F. M. (2005). Response to intervention: An alternative means of identifying students as emotionally disturbed. *Education and Treatment of Children, 28*(4), 328-344.

Guskey, T. R., & Bailey, J. M. (2001). *Developing grading and reporting systems for student learning.* Thousand Oaks, CA: Corwin Press, Inc.

Heinrichs, R. R. (2003). A whole-school approach to bullying: Special considerations for children with exceptionalities. *Intervention in School and Clinic, 38*(4), 195-204.

Horesh, N., Zimmerman, S., Steinberg, T., Yagan, H., & Apter, A. (2008). Is onset of Tourette syndrome influenced by life events? *Journal of Neural Transmission, 115*(5), 787-793.

Illes, T. (2001). Breaking down teacher resistance: A tale of two models. *The ADHD Report, 9*(3), 9-11.

Illes, T. (2008). *Meeting the homework challenge.* Retrieved from Children and Adults with Attention-Deficit Hyperactivity Disorder website: www.chadd.org/AM/Template. cfm?Section=Education&Template=/MembersOnly.cfm&NavMenuID=1056&Conte ntID=11525&DirectListComboInd=D

Individuals with Disabilities Education Act of 1997, 20 U.S.C. § 1401 *et seq.* (1997).

Individuals with Disabilities Education Improvement Act of 2004, 20 U.S.C. § 1400 *et seq.* (2004).

Ivarsson, T., & Melin, K. (2008). Autism spectrum traits in children and adolescents with obsessive-compulsive disorder (OCD). *Journal of Anxiety Disorders, 22*(6), 969-978.

Kant, J. D. (with Franklin, M., & Andrews, L. W.) (2008). *The thought that counts: A firsthand account of one teenager's experience with obsessive-compulsive disorder.* New York: Oxford University Press.

Kaufman J., Birmaher, B., Brent, D., Rao, U., Flynn, C., Moreci, P.,...Ryan, N. (1997). Schedule for Affective Disorders and Schizophrenia for School-Age Children-Present and Lifetime Version (K-SADS-PL): Initial reliability and validity data. *Journal of the American Academy of Child and Adolescent Psychiatry, 36*(7), 980-988.

Keeley, M. L., Storch, E. A., Dhungana, P., & Geffken, G. R. (2007). Pediatric obsessive-compulsive disorder: A guide to assessment and treatment. *Issues in Mental Health Nursing, 28*(6), 555-574.

Keeley, M. L., Storch, E. A., Merlo, L. J., & Geffken, G. R. (2008). Clinical predictors of response to cognitive-behavioral therapy for obsessive-compulsive disorder. *Clinical Psychology Review, 28*(1), 118-130.

Kendall, P. C., Choudhury, M., Hudson, J., & Webb, A. (2002). *The C.A.T. Project workbook for the cognitive behavioral treatment of anxious adolescents.* Ardmore, PA: Workbook Publishing, Inc.

Kendall, P. C., & Hedtke, K. A. (2006). *Coping cat workbook* (2nd ed.). Ardmore, PA: Workbook Publishing, Inc.

Lack, C. W., Storch, E. A., Keeley, M. L., Geffken, G. R., Ricketts, E. D., Murphy, T. K., & Goodman, W. K. (2009). Quality of life in children and adolescents with obsessive-compulsive disorder: Base rates, parent-child agreement, and clinical correlates. *Social Psychiatry and Psychiatric Epidemiology, 44*(11), 935-942.

Larson, M. J., Storch, E. A., & Murphy, T. K. (2007). Pediatric autoimmune neuropsychiatric disorders associated with streptococcal infections. In E. Storch, G. Geffken, & T. Murphy (Eds.), *Handbook of child and adolescent obsessive-compulsive disorder* (pp. 163-174). Mahwah, NJ: Lawrence Erlbaum Associates.

Ledley, D. R., & Pasupuleti, R. V. (2007). School issues in children with obsessive-compulsive disorder. In E. Storch, G. Geffken, & T. Murphy (Eds.), *Handbook of child and adolescent obsessive-compulsive disorder* (pp. 333-350). Mahwah, NJ: Lawrence Erlbaum Associates.

Lehmkuhl, H. D., Storch, E. A., Rahman, O., Freeman, J., Geffken, G. R., & Murphy, T. K. (2009). Just say no: Sequential parent management training and cognitive-behavioral therapy for a child with comorbid disruptive behavior and obsessive compulsive disorder. *Clinical Case Studies, 8*(1), 48-58.

245

Lehr, C. A., & Christenson, S. L. (2002). Best practices in promoting a positive school climate. In A. Thomas & J. Grimes (Eds.), *Best practices in school psychology IV* (pp. 929-948). Bethesda, MD: National Association of School Psychologists.

Lenane, M. (1989). Families and obsessive-compulsive disorder. In J. Rapoport (Ed.), *Obsessive-compulsive disorder in children and adolescents* (pp. 237-249). Washington, DC: American Psychiatric Press, Inc.

Lewin, A. B., Storch, E. A., Geffken, G. R., Goodman, W. K., & Murphy, T. K. (2006). A neuropsychiatric review of pediatric obsessive-compulsive disorder: Etiology and efficacious treatments. *Neuropsychiatric Disease and Treatment, 2*(1), 21-31.

Mansueto, C. S., & Keuler, D. J. (2005). Tic or compulsion? It's Tourettic OCD. *Behavior Modification, 29*(5), 784-799.

March, J. S. (with Benton, C. M.) (2007). *Talking back to OCD: The program that helps kids and teens say "No way"—and parents say "Way to go."* New York: Guilford Press.

March, J. S., & Mulle, K. (1998). *OCD in children and adolescents: A cognitive-behavioral treatment manual.* New York: Guilford Press.

Masi, G., Millepiedi, S., Mucci, M., Bertini, N., Pfanner, C., & Arcangeli, F. (2006). Comorbidity of obsessive-compulsive disorder and attention-deficit/hyperactivity disorder in referred children and adolescents. *Comprehensive Psychiatry, 47*(1), 42-47.

Masi, G., Millepiedi, S., Perugi, G., Pfanner, C., Berloffa, S., Pari, C.,...Akiskal, H. S. (2010). A naturalistic exploratory study of the impact of demographic, phenotypic, and comorbid features in pediatric obsessive-compulsive disorder. *Psychopathology, 43*(2), 69-78.

Mataix-Cols, D., Frost, R. O., Pertusa, A., Clark, L. A., Saxena, S. Leckman, J. F.,...Wilhelm, S. (2010). Hoarding disorder: A new diagnosis for DSM-V? *Depression and Anxiety, 27*(6), 556-572.

Matsunaga, H., Maebayashi, K., Hayashida, K., Okino, K., Matsui, T., Iketani, T.,...Stein, D. J. (2008). Symptom structure in Japanese patients with obsessive-compulsive disorder. *The American Journal of Psychiatry, 165*(2), 251-253.

McGinnis, E., & Goldstein, A. P. (1997). *Skillstreaming the elementary school child: New strategies and perspectives for teaching prosocial skills.* Champaign, IL: Research Press.

McGinnis, E., & Goldstein, A. P. (2003). *Skillstreaming in early childhood: New strategies and perspectives for teaching prosocial skills* (Rev. ed.). Champaign, IL: Research Press.

Merrell, K. (2001). *Helping students overcome depression and anxiety: A practical guide.* New York: Guilford Publications.

Merlo, L. J., & Storch, E. A. (2005). *Development and preliminary validation of the Florida Obsessive-Compulsive Student Inventory.* Unpublished manuscript.

Merlo, L. J., & Storch, E. A. (2006). Obsessive-compulsive disorder: Tools for recognizing its many expressions. *The Journal of Family Practice, 55*(3), 217-222.

Moore, P. S., Mariaskin, A., March, J. S., & Franklin, M. E. (2007). Obsessive-compulsive disorder in children and adolescents: Diagnosis, comorbidity, and developmental factors. In E. Storch, G. Geffken, & T. Murphy (Eds.), *Handbook of child and* adolescent obsessive-compulsive disorder (pp. 17-45). Mahwah, NJ: Lawrence Erlbaum Associates.

Munk, D. D. (2009, July). Grading students with disabilities: FAQs. CEC Today. Retrieved from www.cec.sped.org/AM/Template.cfm?Section=Home&CONTENTID=12679&TEMPLATE=/CM/ContentDisplay.cfm

National Eating Disorders Association. (2008). NEDA Educator Toolkit. Retrieved from National Eating Disorders Association website: www.nationaleatingdisorders.org/uploads/file/toolkits/NEDA-Toolkit-Educators_09-15-08.pdf

National Institute of Mental Health. (n. d.). PANDAS. Retrieved from intramural.nimh.nih.gov/pdn/web.htm

Obsessive Compulsive Cognitions Working Group. (1997). Cognitive assessment of obsessive-compulsive disorder. Behaviour Research and Therapy, 35(7), 667-681.

O'Leary, E. M., Barrett, P., & Fjermestad, K. W. (2009). Cognitive-behavioral family treatment for childhood obsessive-compulsive disorder: A 7-year follow-up study. Journal of Anxiety Disorders, 23(7), 973-978.

Packer, L. E. (2002). Pitfalls in school-based behavior modification plans. Retrieved from School Behavior website: www.tourettesyndrome.net/wp-content/uploads/pitfalls.pdf

Packer, L. E. (2004). Checklist for teachers: Creating a student-friendly environment. Retrieved from www.schoolbehavior.com/Files/TeacherChecklist.pdf

Packer, L. E., & Pruitt, S. K. (2010). Challenging kids, challenged teachers: Teaching students with Tourette's, bipolar disorder, executive dysfunction, OCD, ADHD, and more. Bethesda, MD: Woodbine House.

Paige, L. Z. (2007, September). Obsessive-compulsive disorder. Principal Leadership, 8(1),12-15.

Pallanti, S. (2008). Transcultural observations of obsessive-compulsive disorder. The American Journal of Psychiatry, 165(2), 169-170.

Palumbo, D., & Kurlan, R. (2007). Complex obsessive compulsive and impulsive symptoms in Tourette's Syndrome. Neuropsychiatric Disease and Treatment, 3(5), 687-693.

Pavri, S. (2010). Response to intervention in the social-emotional-behavioral domain: Perspectives from urban schools. TEACHING Exceptional Children Plus, (6)3 Article 4. Retrieved from: www.escholarship.bc.edu/education/tecplus/vol6/iss3/art4

Piacentini, J., Bergman, R. L., Keller, M., & McCracken, J. (2003). Functional impairment in children and adolescents with obsessive-compulsive disorder. Journal of Child and Adolescent Psychopharmacology, 13(Suppl. 1), S61-S69.

Piacentini, J., Peris, T. S., Bergman, R., L., Chang, S., & Jaffer, M. (2007). Functional impairment in childhood OCD: Development and psychometrics properties of the Child Obsessive-Compulsive Impact Scale-Revised (COIS-R). Journal of Clinical Child and Adolescent Psychology, 36(4), 645-653.

Prado, H. S., Rosario, M. C., Lee, J., Hounie, A. G., Shavitt, R. G., & Miguel, E. C. (2008). Sensory phenomena in obsessive-compulsive disorder and tic disorders: A review of the literature. CNS Spectrums, 13(5), 425-432.

Rachman, S. (1997). A cognitive theory of obsessions. Behaviour Research and Therapy, 35(9), 793-802.

Rapoport, J. L. (1991). *The boy who couldn't stop washing.* New York: Signet.

Ravindran, A. V., da Silva, T. L., Ravindran, L. N., Richter, M. A., & Rector, N. A. (2009). Obsessive-compulsive spectrum disorders: A review of the evidence-based treatments. *Canadian Journal of Psychiatry, 54*(5), 331-343.

Robertson, M. M., & Cavanna, A. E. (2007). The disaster was my fault! *Neurocase, 13*(5), 446-451.

Savage, C. R., & Rauch, S. L. (2000). Cognitive deficits in obsessive-compulsive disorder. *The American Journal of Psychiatry, 157*(7), 1182.

Scahill, L., Riddle, M. A., McSwiggin-Hardin, M., Ort, S. I., King, R. A., Goodman, W. K.,... Leckman, J. F. (1997). Children's Yale-Brown Obsessive Compulsive Scale: Reliability and Validity. *Journal of the American Academy of Child and Adolescent Psychiatry, 36*(6), 844-852.

Section 504 of the Rehabilitation Act of 1973, 29 U.S.C. § 794 et seq. (1973).

Severson, H. H., Walker, H. M., Hope-Doolittle, J., Kratochwill, T. R., & Gresham, F. M. (2007). Proactive, early screening to detect behaviorally at-risk students: Issues, approaches, emerging innovations, and professional practices. *Journal of School Psychology, 45*(2), 193-223.

Shafran, R., Frampton, I., Heyman, I., Reynolds, M., Teachman, B., & Rachman, S. (2003). The preliminary development of a new self-report measure for OCD in young people. *Journal of Adolescence, 26*(1) 137-142.

Shalev, I., Sulkowski, M. L., Geffken, G. R., Rickets, E. J., Murphy, T. K., & Storch, E. A. (2009). Long-term durability of cognitive behavioral therapy gains for pediatric obsessive-compulsive disorder. *Journal of the American Academy of Child and Adolescent Psychiatry, 48*(7), 766-767.

Shapira, N. A., Liu, Y., He, A. G., Bradley, M. M., Lessig, M. C., James, G. A.,...Goodman, W. K. (2003). Brain activation by disgust-inducing pictures in obsessive-compulsive disorder. *Biological Psychiatry, 54*(7), 751-756.

Sheridan, S. M., & Kratochwill, T. R. (2007). *Conjoint behavioral consultation: Promoting family-school connections and interventions* (2nd ed.). New York: Springer Science + Business Media, LLC.

Shore, K. (2009). Preventing bullying: Nine ways to bully-proof your classroom. *The Education Digest: Essential Readings Condensed for Quick Review, 75*(4), 39-44.

Silverman, W. K., & Albano, A. M. (2004). Anxiety Disorders Interview Schedule (ADIS-IV) Child and Parent Interview Schedules. USA: Oxford University Press.

Stewart, S. E. (2008). Obsessive-compulsive disorder in children and adolescents. *OCD Newsletter, 22*(3), 5, 14.

Stewart, S. E., Geller, D. A., Jenike, M., Pauls, D., Shaw, D., Mullin, B., & Faraone, S. V. (2004). Long-term outcome of pediatric obsessive-compulsive disorder: A meta-analysis and qualitative review of the literature. *Acta Psychiatrica Scandinavica, 110*(1), 4-13.

Stewart, S. E., Rosario, M. C., Baer, L., Carter, A. S., Brown, T. A., Scharf, J. M.,...Pauls, D. L. (2008). Four-factor structure of obsessive-compulsive disorder symptoms in children, adolescents, and adults. *Journal of the American Academy of Child and Adolescent Psychiatry, 47*(7), 763-772.

Stewart, S. E., Rosario, M. C., Brown, T. A., Carter, A. S., Leckman, J. F., Sukhodolsky, D,... Pauls, D. L. (2007). Principal components analysis of obsessive-compulsive disorder symptoms in children and adolescents, *Biological Psychiatry, 61*(3), 285-291.

Storch, E. A., Geffken, G. R., Merlo, L. J., Mann, G., Duke, D., Munson, M.,...Goodman, W. K. (2007). Family-based cognitive-behavioral therapy for pediatric obsessive-compulsive disorder: Comparison of intensive and weekly approaches. *Journal of the American Academy of Child and Adolescent Psychiatry, 46*(4), 469-478.

Storch, E. A., Khanna, M., Merlo, L. J., Loew, B. A., Franklin, M., Reid, J. M.,...Murphy, T. K. (2009). Children's Florida Obsessive Compulsive Inventory: Psychometric properties and feasibility of a self-report measure of obsessive-compulsive symptoms in youth. *Child Psychiatry and Human Development, 40*(3), 467-483.

Storch, E. A., Lack, C. W., Merlo, L. J., Geffken, G. R., Jacob, M. L., Murphy, T. K., & Goodman, W. K. (2007). Clinical features of children and adolescents with obsessive-compulsive disorder and hoarding symptoms. *Comprehensive Psychiatry, 48*(4), 313-318.

Storch, E. A., Larson, M. J., Muroff, J., Caporino, N., Geller, D., Reid, J. M.,...Murphy, T. K. (2010). Predictors of functional impairment in pediatric obsessive-compulsive disorder. *Journal of Anxiety Disorders, 24*(2), 275-283.

Storch, E. A., Ledley, D. R., Lewin, A. B., Murphy, T. K., Johns, N. B., Goodman, W. K., & Geffken, G. R. (2006). Peer victimization in children with obsessive–compulsive disorder: Relations with symptoms of psychopathology. *Journal of Clinical Child and Adolescent Psychology, 35*(3), 446–455.

Storch, E. A., Lehmkuhl, H., Pence, S. L., Geffken, G. R., Ricketts, E., Storch. J. F., & Murphy, T. K. (2009). Parental experiences of having a child with obsessive-compulsive disorder: Associations with clinical characteristics and caregiver adjustment. *Journal of Child and Family Studies, 18*(3), 249-258.

Storch, E. A., Lehmkuhl, H. D., Ricketts, E., Geffken, G. R., Marien, W., & Murphy, T. K. (2010). An open trial of intensive family based cognitive-behavioral therapy in youth with obsessive-compulsive disorder who are medication partial responders or nonresponders. *Journal of the American Academy of Child and Adolescent Psychiatry, 39*(2), 260-268.

Storch, E. A., Merlo, L. J., Keeley, M. L., Grabill, K., Milsom, V. A., Geffken, G. R.,... Goodman, W. K. (2008). Somatic symptoms in children and adolescents with obsessive-compulsive disorder: Associations with clinical characteristics and cognitive-behavioral therapy response. *Behavioural and Cognitive Psychotherapy, 36*(3), 283-297.

Storch, E. A., Merlo, L. J., Larson, M. J., Geffken, G. R., Lehmkuhl, H. D., Jacob, M. L.,... Goodman, W. K. (2008). Impact of comorbidity on cognitive-behavioral therapy response in pediatric obsessive-compulsive disorder. *Journal of the American Academy of Child and Adolescent Psychiatry, 47*(5), 583-592.

Storch, E. A., Murphy, T. K., Bagner, D. M., Johns, N. B., Baumeister, A. L., Goodman, W. K., & Geffken, G. R. (2006). Reliability and validity of the Child Behavior Checklist Obsessive-Compulsive Scale. *Journal of Anxiety Disorders, 20*(4), 473-485.

Storch, E. A., Murphy, T. K., Geffken, G. R., Mann, G., Adkins, J., Merlo, L. J.,...Goodman, W. K. (2006). Cognitive-behavioral therapy for PANDAS-related obsessive-compulsive disorder: Findings from a preliminary waitlist controlled open trial. *Journal of the American Academy of Child and Adolescent Psychiatry, 45*(10), 1171-1178.

Storch, E. A., Murphy, T. K., Lack, C. W., Geffken, G. R., Jacob, M. L., & Goodman, W. K. (2008). Sleep-related problems in pediatric obsessive-compulsive disorder. *Journal of Anxiety Disorders, 22*(5), 877-885.

Sukhodolsky, D. G., Rosario-Campos, M. C., Scahill, L., Katsovich, L., Pauls, D. L., Peterson, B. S.,...Leckman, J. F. (2005). Adaptive, emotional, and family functioning of children with obsessive-compulsive disorder and comorbid attention deficit hyperactivity disorder. *American Journal of Psychiatry, 162*(6), 1125-1132.

Telzrow, C. F., & Bonar, A. M. (2002). Responding to students with nonverbal learning disabilities. *TEACHING Exceptional Children, 34*(6), 8-13.

The Pediatric OCD Treatment Study (POTS) Team. (2004). Cognitive-behavior therapy, sertraline, and their combination for children and adolescents with obsessive-compulsive disorder. *The Journal of the American Medical Association, 292*(16), 1969-1976.

Tourette Syndrome Association. (2006). *Major victory for children with Tourette Syndrome: Individuals with Disabilities Education Act to classify Tourette Syndrome as Other Health Impaired.* Retrieved from Tourette Syndrome Association website: www.tsa-usa.org/news/TOURETTEOHI0806.htm

Trifiletti, R. R., & Packard, A. M. (1999). Immune mechanisms in pediatric neuropsychiatric disorders. Tourette's syndrome, OCD, and PANDAS. *Child and Adolescent Psychiatric Clinics of North America, 8*(4), 767-775.

Valderhaug, R., & Ivarsson, T. (2005). Functional impairment in clinical samples of Norwegian and Swedish children and adolescents with obsessive-compulsive disorder. *European Child and Adolescent Psychiatry, 14*(3), 164-173.

van den Hout, M., & Kindt, M. (2003). Repeated checking causes memory distrust. *Behaviour Research and Therapy, (41)*3, 301-316.

Van Grootheest, D. S., Cath, D. C., Beekman, A. T., & Boomsma, D. I. (2005). Twin studies on obsessive-compulsive disorder: A review. *Twin Research and Human Genetics, 8*(5), 450-458.

Varni, J. W., Burwinkle, T. M., Seid, M., & Skarr, D. (2003). The PedsQL 4.0 as a pediatric population health measure: Feasibility, reliability, and validity. *Ambulatory Pediatrics, 3*(6), 329-341.

Volz, C., & Heyman, I. (2007). Case series: Transformation obsession in young people with obsessive-compulsive disorder (OCD). *Journal of the American Academy of Child and Adolescent Psychiatry, 46*(6), 766-772.

Wagner, A. P. (2007). *Treatment of OCD in children and adolescents: Professional's kit* (2nd ed.). Apex, NC: Lighthouse Press., Inc.

Wagner, A. P. (2006). *What to do when your child has obsessive-compulsive disorder: Strategies and solutions.* Apex, NC: Lighthouse Press, Inc.

Walitza, S., Zellman, H., Irblich, B., Lange, K. W., Tucha, O., Hemminger, U.,...Warnke, A. (2008). Children and adolescents with obsessive-compulsive disorder and comorbid attention-deficit/hyperactivity disorder: Preliminary results of a prospective follow-up study. *Journal of Neural Transmission, 115*(2), 187-190.

Walker, H. M. & Severson, H. (1992). *Systematic screening for behavior disorders (SSBD)* (2nd ed.). Longmont, CO: Sopris West.

Walker, J. E., Shea, T. M., & Bauer, A. M. (2007). *Behavior management: A practical approach for educators* (9th ed.). Old Tappan, N.J.: Pearson Education.

Watson, H. J., & Rees, C. S. (2008). Meta-analysis of randomized, controlled treatment trials for pediatric obsessive-compulsive disorder. *The Journal of Child Psychology and Psychiatry, 49*(5), 489-498.

Wilkinson, L. A. (2006). Conjoint behavioral consultation: An emerging and effective model for developing home-school partnerships. *The International Journal of Behavioral Consultation and Therapy, 2*(2), 224-238.

Williams, M., Powers, M., Yun, Y. G., & Foa, E. (2010). Minority participation in randomized controlled trials for obsessive-compulsive disorder. *Journal of Anxiety Disorders, 24*(2), 171-177.

World Health Organization. (2001). *The world health report 2001—Mental health: New understanding, new hope.* Retrieved from www.who.int/whr/2001/en/

Zandt, F., Prior, M., & Kyrios, M. (2009). Similarities and differences between children and adolescents with autism spectrum disorder and those with obsessive compulsive disorder: Executive functioning and repetitive behaviour. *Autism, 13*(1), 43-57.

S